Motty's Diary

MOTTY'S DIARY

A Year in the Life

John Motson

John Motson's views on football, television and life in general are his own and do not necessarily represent those of the BBC or his colleagues.

First published in Great Britain in 1996 by
Virgin Books
an imprint of Virgin Publishing Ltd
332 Ladbroke Grove
London W10 5AH

A catalogue record for this book is available from the British Library.

ISBN 1 85227 620 7

Typeset by TW Typesetting, Plymouth, Devon.

Printed and bound by Mackays of Chatham, Lordswood, Kent.

John Motson is donating the royalties he receives from the sale of *Motty's Diary* to NCH Action for Children.

To Annie, Frederick and the lads who helped me along the way, especially those who found time to read the manuscript.

CONTENTS

ILLUSTRATIONS

ACKNOWLEDGEMENTS

Grateful thanks are due to Mal Peachey for persuading me to sit down and write, and to Wendy Brown and Hannah MacDonald for not letting me stop.

FOREWORD BY DES LYNAM

John Motson does not play golf. If he ever decided to take up the game, I would imagine something like the following scenario: Three months of dedicated reading on the game. A month of video-tape viewing analysing the rudiments of the golf swing. Several weeks discussing the best possible clubs to buy, followed by enrolment at the David Leadbetter Golf Academy in Florida for three weeks' devotion to the basics of the game.

A year or so later, after three mornings a week spent on his local driving range, John would invite me to play – and although I have been playing the game for many years, he would beat me.

Ever since I have known him, and our friendship goes back well over 25 years, John has never, to my knowledge, done anything half-heartedly. He is the epitome of the man who says, 'If it's worth doing . . .'

Even at sheepskin coat wearing, Motty is the tops. He is also the undisputed champion of the 'Tidiest Briefcase In The World' title. You will never see the Lynam equivalent – with its unanswered letters, packets of chewing gum and fifteen-year-old address book held together with Sellotape – opened in the same building let alone the same room as Motson's pristine affair. I could not stand the shame of comparison.

But there I go, you see, falling into the trap that Rory Bremner and others have failed to avoid. While there are aspects of the Motsonian character that induce words like 'train' and 'spotting' to spring to mind, the fellow is actually a class act.

I know; I have had lunch with him and evenings out. Actually, in most cases they tend to be the same thing. The man is witty and funny and tells a yarn as well as anyone I know.

We share certain things. A love of football and racing and of course Angus Mackay. Angus was the man responsible for finding us and giving us both our real chance at the big wide world of broadcasting. John was already a very youthful but established member of BBC Radio's *Sports Report* team when I arrived at the end of 1969 to join him at the famous 'academy' of sports broadcasting that set up the careers of the likes of Eamonn Andrews, Brian Moore, Peter Jones and many others.

Motson was probably the youngest ever to pass muster under the fearsome Mackay examination. His work in front of the sound microphone with a script was, well . . . sound.

But when they sent him to a football match and stuck an outside broadcast mike into his hand, John came alive. It was like popping an Alka-Seltzer into a glass of still water. Now you had fizz. He was simply a natural. Television listened and liked what they heard and Motson was on his way to TV fame, seventeen Cup Finals and numerous other glories.

Commentating on football is easy. I know; I've done it.

Commentating on football well is the difficult bit. I know; I haven't done it.

For my money, Motty remains the best at his business. In the ensuing chapters you will learn a lot about his art. You will also find out a good deal about the man.

I hope to God he never takes up golf.

INTRODUCTION

Graham Taylor was quite emphatic. 'There is no way this man should still be here,' he said, venting out his exasperation to a group of gawping Watford players. 'He's been doing his job for too long and should have been replaced by now.'

His words were greeted by expressions of either astonishment or complete indifference. He wasn't talking about Gary Lineker, John Barnes, or for that matter, any of the lesser-known players in the room at the time. His target was a bewildered television commentator who probably *was* well past his sell-by date – me. The scene was Watford's training ground on a chilly Thursday afternoon back in the early eighties. The only thing the least bit glamorous about it were the floodlights at Wembley Stadium – you could just see them in the distance from the car park. There weren't too many 'legends' in the venue in Edgware that day though, I can assure you.

Quite what Taylor's purpose was in making me the scapegoat for his lecture in motivation, I never ascertained. Years later, in Poznan, Oslo, or some other place where we were marooned together, I meant to ask him, but never got round to it.

Maybe he had run out of ways to warn his players against complacency, and chose my profession, and my presence at the training ground, as an example of people desperately trying to hang on to their job. If I couldn't tell John Barnes from Luther Blissett after ten years and more, perhaps I shouldn't be there. That sort of stuff.

I took it as a backhanded compliment, because Taylor was breaking new ground there, in the area where I lived. Whatever was said later about his time with England and Wolves, the man brought a new dimension of decency and dignity to football in the community in those ten years at Watford.

Still, I didn't look too dignified as I crept, embarrassed, out of the Watford training ground. The only consolation I get from the incident is that, with hindsight, it helps me to answer at least the first of the three questions I get tired of facing: What do you do the rest of the week? How did you become a commentator? And why do you always wear a sheepskin coat?

The first question almost runs in the family, as it were, since it was also addressed to my father for most of his life. The Revd William Motson spent 40 dedicated years in the Methodist ministry, and people always thought he only worked on Sundays.

What with his pastoral work, hospital visiting, weddings, funerals, Sunday services and correspondence, I am still amazed he managed to find time to take his only son to football matches.

But he did, and like many other war babies (or in my case, a VE baby), the drug we took with our condensed milk and cod liver oil was called football – and a simple, pure ecstasy if a goal was scored.

Growing up amid post-war austerity in south-east London, we didn't have a television. And even if we had, there wasn't much football to be found on its single channel.

It was only the Coronation in 1953 that persuaded families to forsake the ration books and hand-me-down clothes for something new called hire purchase. And only then did they discover that the nine inch black and white box in the corner could bring sport into the living room.

It wasn't a bad year for a football fan. Not only was the Queen crowned amid great pomp and ceremony, not only did Edmund Hillary and Sherpa Tensing take a giant step for mankind on to the summit of Everest, but Stanley Matthews wrote his name all across Stan Mortensen's Cup Final, and a little fat fellow called Puskas turned England's Billy Wright inside out at Wembley.

We came home from school on a foggy afternoon in November to stare goggle-eyed at a half-time score of England 2, Hungary 4, and when it finished 3-6 it seemed as if the men with placards were right – the world really had come to an end.

It was only the beginning, of course, for football and television. Alf Ramsey, who slotted in an apologetic penalty for England's third goal that day, spent the next thirteen years working out how to put matters right. And he did, but only because he went to Ipswich in between.

We didn't all become Hidegkuti in the playground the following day, though. It would be nice to think everybody went out and started to practise skills, but they didn't then, any more than they do now. We had goalposts chalked up on the wall in the playground, we put coats down on the local recreation ground, but basically we just played. It was a way of passing the time and it sure beat collecting cigarette cards, playing five stones or getting out your John Bull printing set.

If you weren't good enough to get in the school team, then you got on the tram or the trolleybus and went to the Valley to watch Sam Bartram and Benny Fenton. Or you took solace in your scrapbooks, your programmes, or your 'Newfooty', which, believe it or not, was the forerunner of Subbuteo.

Perhaps it was trying to be Raymond Glendenning or Kenneth Wolstenholme that was my undoing. In those days there was no local radio, no media courses at college or university, and precious little regional television. Satellite was something you saw at the London Planetarium and the only cable we had heard of was a street name.

So a career in the communications industry (unless you wanted to be a telephone engineer) meant an apprenticeship on a local weekly newspaper; a job which gave a much earlier meaning to the epithet 'Four Weddings and a Funeral' – where I worked, that was what I had to cover just about every day.

Which helps to answer the second question. The only college course I took on the way to being a sports commentator consisted of a day release arrangement when I was serving my indentures on the *Barnet Press*, a privately owned newspaper on the north London/Hertfordshire border.

Fridays meant a trip on the tube from Finchley Central to Camden Town (if caught in a time warp now, you could be piped on by the New Vaudeville Band at the journey's beginning and met at the other end by Suggs busking). At the North-West London Polytechnic we studied essential law for journalists and an English course that revolved around *Catcher in the Rye* and Richard Hoggart's *Uses of Literacy*.

Quite how that led to BBC Television sport remains something of a grey area. But it was enlightened and brightened by the advent of colour television and local radio in the late sixties, the advanced technology opening up new opportunities.

A number of sports reporters who made the transition from the written to the spoken word have reason to be grateful for catching the eye, or ear, of a doyen figure called Angus Mackay. He was the innovator of *Sports Report* in 1948 and was for two generations the autocratic head of BBC Radio Sport. He was also the only man I ever saw who could frighten and fluster Desmond Lynam.

From unpromising beginnings in radio days, reading the racing results and learning that a two-second over-run meant one's career could end almost as quickly, a number of Mackay's products graduated into the Brave New World. A world he himself always treated with surly suspicion.

'Television!' he snarled at a tremulous interviewee who was asked where his ultimate ambition lay. 'Television, did you say? Don't you think if television was important, my assistant Mr Burrows and I would be in television ourselves?'

The interviewee was Alan Parry, who's probably got the best sense of humour of any modern commentator, but it was definitely on the back burner that day.

Which is almost where we came in, or at least a way of answering the third question. Parry went on to become a director of Wycombe Wanderers, and it was there that the sheepskin coat achieved its notoriety.

A snowstorm on the morning of an FA Cup tie meant a sudden postponement and a live report into *Grandstand*. The coat changed colour in the course of those 60 seconds and somebody had the bright idea of taking a photo of the huddled figure inside it.

Which is pretty much what it's like being a commentator. The prime qualification for the job is to absorb the jibes and the jokes, and, most of all, be able to poke fun at yourself. Over the course of one very important season for English football, I'm going to have a go.

AUGUST
1995

Friday 18th
Tomorrow sees the start of the football season, and for the first time in over 25 years this commentator will not be working. That might come as a huge relief to a lot of people, but no more so than to the man himself, who spent the day collecting a visa from the Egyptian embassy and having an injection in preparation for a Nile cruise. As far as the BBC and the *Match of the Day* audience is concerned, J. Motson is taking a 'sabbatical' – a three-month break to recharge the batteries and rest the voice after a quarter of a century of broadcasting. I think I may be suffering from commentator's cramp. To say so publicly would, of course, sound monumentally ungrateful. For a man lucky enough to be paid for his hobby throughout his entire working career, such a sentiment would come across as precious to the point of pathetic. And coming from a commentator who has managed to lose the World Cup Final and the FA Cup Final in the space of ten months (which takes a bit of doing), it would leave him open to accusations of sulking if not bitterness. Fortunately, the incumbent himself knows there is no connection. The brain has been screaming for a pause longer than the voice, and the idea was first planted nearly two years ago. Since the season which starts tomorrow is going to run until the end of next June, when the European Championship will be held in England, it seems as good a time as any to step out of the firing line. So we're calling it a sabbatical, if that's all right with everybody else.

Saturday 19th
So what did you do on the first real day of your holiday? Well, without wanting to sound comical, I went to see Wimbledon play. Old habits die hard, and since my late father first took me to football in nineteen-fifty-something, I have never missed the

opening day of the season, either as a spectator or a working journalist. There was a time, which my generation will remember with affection, when you were desperate for football to start again; when you put away the cricket bat that you had taken out the day after the Cup Final in early May, and lovingly spread dubbin on the football boots that had been in the cupboard for the summer months. Yes, in those days we had a three-month break from football *every* year, and most of us felt all the fresher and keener for it. Nobody needs telling that we are now at the other end of the spectrum – though you'd hardly call it a rainbow. Mind you, because so many football clubs are chasing a pot of gold, they have to play as many matches as possible to pay the wages. So they have to play for as *long* as they can, and start again as *soon* as they can. Very soon we shall be in danger of playing all the year round – with the iniquitous Inter-Toto Cup we nearly made it a twelve-month season in 1995. So as I drove to Selhurst Park to see Wimbledon play promoted Bolton, having deliberately chosen the Premiership match with the lowest profile, my fear that the game is losing its scarcity value was mitigated by the relief of only facing 38 Premiership games rather than 42. Let's hope the chairmen stick to it this time – not like four years ago when they went back to 22 clubs.

Sunday 20th
I enjoyed myself yesterday. It was a pleasant change to witness the opening of a new season without having to worry about the names of new players, the confusing squad numbers, the precarious climb up the ladder to the commentary position, and most of all, the nagging fear that you got something wrong. Whatever you think about Wimbledon's style, there is certainly nothing wrong with it off the field. Theirs is one of the most hospitable boardrooms in the game, and you are guaranteed a good time there. I once went out, or maybe fell out, of the old ground at Plough Lane with a flowerpot on my head.

Sam Hammam, the owner, has my commentary card from the 1988 Cup Final framed in his office. They came from the Southern League in 1977 to win the FA Cup eleven years later (also finishing seventh in the top division that season). Their fulfilment of the 'impossible dream' is what sustains and inspires non-League footballers every time they go out to play.

By a happy coincidence, I also bumped into Dennis Strudwick, the secretary/treasurer of the Southern (now Beazer Homes) League, who gave me the handbook for their 102nd season. Whether Hastings, Grantham or Paget Rangers can ever 'do a Wimbledon' in the modern era is open to debate, but it's the grass roots of football that makes the game what it is, and one or two high fliers in the upper echelons of the Premiership would do well to remember that. Come to think of it, that probably explains why I went to Wimbledon yesterday.

Monday 21st
Now I'm properly on holiday. Instead of attending meetings at the BBC to plan football coverage for the week ahead, the family and I have repaired to Suffolk for a few days at a small cottage we bought about twelve years ago. It has proved a valuable bolt-hole, but my connections with Ipswich Town, which go back to my schooldays at nearby Bury St Edmunds, are a happy reminder of how much football has enriched my life.

David Sheepshanks, who has just taken over as chairman from John Kerr at Ipswich, rang to ask why I wasn't working on Saturday. One week gone, and my absence is noted already. I'm not sure whether that's a good or a bad sign, but I accepted his invitation to lunch.

Tuesday 22nd
The restaurant at Portman Road is called the Centre Spot, and in the days when the brothers Johnny and Patrick Cobbold were alive some of their antics would put even Wimbledon into the shade. I was having lunch with Johnny one day, when Russell Osman, then the Ipswich centre half, rode into the restaurant and up to our table on a bicycle. Nobody batted an eyelid. That was Ipswich Town in the eighties. The Cobbold family brought professional football to Ipswich just before the war, but the brothers' father, Captain Ivan Cobbold, was killed by a stray bomb in the Guards Chapel in London. When Patrick died last season, the memorial service was held there. He and Johnny were lovable eccentrics. In the 1968/69 season, they appointed Bobby Robson as manager and left him to get on with it while they had a good time. So good, they spent nine years out of ten in Europe with the club, while never having to sign a cheque bigger than £250,000 for a player. Reminiscence is one thing. Reality is another. Ipswich could become one of

the victims of the mega-rich Super League, and David Sheep-shanks is charged with the task of turning a corner shop into a superstore in commercial terms.

Wednesday 23rd

I spent the morning on the beach at Aldeburgh with my wife Anne and my ten-year-old son Frederick, and in the afternoon we visited John Kerr and his family at their house on the beach at Thorpeness. On this part of the Suffolk coastline you feel transported back to a much earlier generation, when life was a lot less frantic and time stood still a bit more. John and I discussed the condition of Bobby Robson, who has had a serious operation for facial cancer – which has not yet been made public. Fortunately, the prognosis is good.

Thursday 24th

Brendan Foster rang to ask how my preparations are going for the Great North Run. The race is less than four weeks away and even for a fun runner like myself, mileage is important! He managed to tweak my conscience and I went out and did six miles. A poor time, though.

Friday 25th

People who query my accent are generally surprised that the Motson family hailed from Lincolnshire. Both my parents came from Boston, where I spent much of my childhood holidays, and today my only surviving uncle is 80 so there was a bit of a family reunion.

In the evening, I took the family on to Grantham where we spent the night at the Belton Woods Hotel. It's surprising how many hoteliers are football fans, and Roland Ayling is no exception. But he couldn't puzzle out why I'm on holiday in the first week of the season.

Saturday 26th

I could get used to this. The second Saturday of the season and I'm not missing commentating for a moment. Still in the mood for touching base with old friends, I called in at Peterborough where I have known the chief executive, Chris Turner, since he was a seventeen-year-old centre half under Noel Cantwell. Chris and his commercial manager, Michael Vincent, have opened a new restaurant in an attempt to attract local business sponsorship to the football club. That's the way the game is going now, even at Second and Third Division level. Peterborough also have a new stand going up, but even after admiring the glitzy all-seater stadiums in the Premiership, it's quite comforting to see supporters standing quite happily behind the goal on Endsleigh League grounds. Surely some small, controlled provision could have been made in the revamped grounds for those who still wish to stand? I was present at Hillsborough in 1989 and accept the full implications of the Taylor Report and all the benefits that have accrued, but now that safety and security measures are watertight, we don't want to lose the lively banter between rival supporters that was so much part of going to football. Unless we are careful, segregation will soon become sanitisation and we shall drift towards the American concept of polite applause and themed cheerleaders. Let's get back to some irreverent singing and chanting and remind ourselves that the game still belongs to the fans.

Sunday 27th
While we are on the subject of supporters, without whom there would be no game and most of whom wouldn't want to sit in executive boxes even if they could afford it, I have some sympathy when they complain about the distorted fixture list. This may sound rich coming from someone who earns his living from television, but matches used to kick off at three o'clock on a Saturday afternoon and finish at twenty to five. Now they are spread over an entire weekend like this one. When they start is dictated by television schedules, and when they finish is at the behest of a man in green (not the goalkeeper any more) whose interpretation of stoppage time is a secret beholden only unto himself. If we're really trying to move with the times, literally, why don't we put a clock on the top of the stand and stop and start it as the referee does his watch? Then we will all know how long the game is going to last. As for the fixtures, everybody accepts that television money is now essential to the game in order to pay the players' wages, but a friend of mine with a season ticket at a Premiership club saw fewer than half their home games on a Saturday afternoon last season. The others were all moved for one reason or another. I also wonder how many supporters with families, or a life outside football, can put aside sufficient time or money to watch all the matches now available to them. Read on. I fear it is going to get worse.

Monday 28th
Just to show how perverse the whole argument is, this is a day when the League clubs *could* and *should* have played. It's a Bank Holiday, it's good weather, and decent crowds would have been guaranteed. So where do we have to go to watch a game today? To the GM Vauxhall Conference in my case. The most senior fixture north of London was Stevenage v. Telford, but on the pretext that you learn something wherever you go, it proved to be an insight into how to crack the closed ranks of the Football League. Victor Green, the Stevenage chairman, has brought his club through the non-League pyramid to nudge the top of the Conference. The fact they have a player called Venables is beside the point. If they win the Conference, they will not be admitted to the Endsleigh League because, like Kidderminster before them, their ground will not pass the litmus test of an inspection this December – in other words, several months before you know whether you will win the Conference or not. So Victor is in a Catch 22 situation. Does he commit huge sums of money to seats and safety barriers in the hope that his club will earn the right to promotion, or does he hold fire for a year or two in case they don't? Either way, it seems as though the Endsleigh League, perhaps scarred by one or two previous experiences, are making it mighty hard for the 'wannabes' to achieve senior status. The irony is, within five years the lower sections of the Football League could be facing part-time football anyway.

Tuesday 29th
With the schools still on holiday, I am able to snatch a few more days on the beach with Frederick. We are now in Bournemouth, in a small hotel used by my old Sunday team when they go on tour. It's half a minute from the promenade at Boscombe and it beats a long trip to Middlesbrough, which is where I might have been going had I been working. In my absence, *Match of the Day* has gone midweek as the BBC, manfully and strategically, tries to retain a foothold in a sporting arena increasingly dominated by the financial resources of independent, sponsored, and satellite television. In that sense, it's going to be a tough year.

Wednesday 30th
Tonight I made the short trip from Bournemouth to Southampton, where they still kick off at 7.30 for midweek matches –

Hampshire people like to get to bed at a sensible time. Although I am in favour of fewer clubs in the Premiership, I remain a devoted admirer of the way a club like Southampton conduct their housekeeping in order to remain among the élite. Their main sponsor, who I found myself sitting next to, is a practising Methodist whose company is based in Sheffield. He's a long way from Southampton in distance, but close to them in spirit, which seems to me to hold the key to successful sponsorship. Southampton's short-term problem was handling Leeds and Tony Yeboah, which they managed pretty well, the result being 1-1. Their long-term problem is building a new stadium, but I would miss The Dell. The new grounds will never recreate the character of the ones they replace.

Thursday 31st
On the last day of the month, and two weeks into the season, I have the whole of September to look forward to before reporting back for duty at the beginning of October. It feels as though the holiday is only just starting.

SEPTEMBER
1995

Friday 1st

Two appointments today, both stemming from my well-publicised position on the substitutes' bench for the last two major Cup Finals. Neither decision elicited any complaint from me, publicly or privately, largely because I honestly found it quite difficult to be angry or upset. But the broadcasting business being what it is, everybody else had something to say about it in one way or the other. The nicest letter I received came from a journalist and playwright called Martin Trew, who I had never met but turned out to be a good friend of Paul Hayward, the *Daily Telegraph* sports writer who had also been very supportive. So the three of us had lunch together, and I was delighted to hear from Paul that the *Telegraph*, where I also have a few other friends, had appointed Giles Smith from the *Independent* as their new sports television critic. A good signing, as they say.

Next, I had afternoon tea with a bright young journalist called Anthony Clavane, of the *East Anglian Daily Times*. He feels he grew up listening to my voice, which both dates and embarrasses me – but he will go on to better things.

Saturday 2nd

Any intentions I had of keeping out of the way have now been firmly rebuffed. Dennis Signy, the well-connected freelance football journalist, has asked me to be the celebrity reporter for the *Sunday Express* at the Barnet v. Lincoln match. It's a popular series where old affiliations are revived for a day, and the reporter later receives a framed memento of his printed words, an effort usually owing as much to Dennis as to the figure concerned. Bearing in mind I started my career as a junior reporter on the *Barnet Press* – hence the local connection – I should really have phoned the copy through myself, but talking to Dennis about a 30-year association with Barnet is much easier.

The day started badly for my team when Lincoln's Darren Huckerby snatched an early goal, but then Barnet's Dougie Freedman took over and scored twice in a 3-1 win. In the course of the match, Freedman totalled seventeen strikes at goal and in my search for a decent line for my report, I ventured the view that he's worth £1 million at current values.

A cracking advertisement for the Endsleigh League as a breeding ground.

Sunday 3rd

Today was the 'Garden City Ten' – a ten-mile run round the outskirts of Welwyn Garden City which is my only real preparation for the Great North Run in two weeks' time. It's a nice flat course so I managed to trundle across the line in one hour twenty minutes: even, eight-minute miles. I got into running in an attempt to keep my weight down and offset some of the socialising that goes with the job. I am always a stone lighter at the start of the football season compared to the finish.

Monday 4th – Monday 11th

Well, this was the real treat as far as the sabbatical is concerned. A seven-day cruise on the Nile is about as far removed from the broadcasting treadmill as you can get. Originally I was going to Hong Kong, but that fell through and I picked this trip out of a Sunday travel supplement and hoped for the best. As it turned out, I got lucky. Having been flown by Egyptian Airlines from Heathrow to Luxor, I discovered that the *Serenade* is the newest and most luxurious of the hundreds of boats that now populate the Nile. For six days, tombs and temples took over from teams and tactics. Once you force yourself on to a new continent and into a different culture, it's quite difficult not to get life back into perspective. While you are admiring a civilisation 3,000 years old, last night's results tend to slip your mind. Tutankhamun's tomb, the temples at Karnak and Abu Simbel, the statue of Rameses II – they all carry a bit more weight than England v. Colombia.

Tuesday 12th

From one culture shock to another. No sooner had I returned from the Valley of the Kings and Queens, than the names of

Thutmosis and Hatsephut are replaced by the equally obscure Rotor Volgograd and Spartak Vladikavkaz – the land of the Pharaohs giving way to the redrawn map of Eastern Europe and the new football dynasty spawned by the break up of the Soviet Union. This is European week one, and both Liverpool and Manchester United are live and exclusive somewhere today. And that's just the start of it.

Wednesday 13th
Time was when BBC and ITV would alternate their midweek football coverage. It was either 'our' week or 'theirs', and whichever channel governed a particular Wednesday, they would shell out a few thousand pounds to show highlights of one European fixture. Now, millions of pounds change hands for 'live' coverage on three successive nights – the centrepiece being the Champions League. So far, ITV have not had a very lucky return on their investment. Neither Manchester United nor Rangers have managed to progress to the quarter-finals and Blackburn Rovers' opening engagement – a home defeat by Moscow Spartak – suggests little improvement this year. But ITV will attract some good audiences.

Thursday 14th
Today saw the turn of Everton and Celtic in the Cup-Winners Cup. Soon there will be football on television every night of the week, but whether quantity means quality is open to debate. And the debate as this week unfolds is about technique, and how far British players have fallen behind the continentals.

Friday 15th
Personally, I don't think it's ever been a contest. Ever since Puskas left Billy Wright on his backside at Wembley in 1953, overseas players have seemed better at manipulating the ball. The big difference now, as opposed to the seventies and eighties when English clubs ruled Europe, is that the continental teams have become stronger mentally. Not so many years ago, before Heysel and the ban on English clubs that followed, a passionate crowd and a high-octane, sustained attacking performance based on endurance and stamina was sufficient to see the old British bulldog spirit win out. Not now. All the classy overseas stars, especially those who have enhanced the Premiership this

season, have 'bottle' to match their talent. We will know more in two weeks' time, but the signs are ominous – they point inward.

Saturday 16th

North to Newcastle for the Great North Run tomorrow, but a chance today to see Keegan's regenerated team take on Manchester City, who have made a hapless start. Three down and with a man sent off, their cause looked hopeless and the sheer pace of Newcastle's play was sufficient to excite top class athletes Jonathan Edwards and Eamonn Martin in the capacity crowd of 36,000. Both appreciate the link between support and performance, and Eamonn had better declare to the British Board the £100 he won by predicting the correct score and first goalscorer. The only losers were the 12,000 would-be supporters who couldn't get tickets. Newcastle are prisoners of their own success. The stadium is not big enough.

Sunday 17th

The Great North Run is aptly named. There are over 20,000 runners, and they include the great and the good. Where else would you see Graham Kelly rubbing shoulders on the starting line with Frank Bruno? Both were there at the finish, too. Kelly's time would have been better had he not been intercepted by Hazel Irvine and a BBC camera team at the nine mile mark. I could have told him how to dodge them. I prefer my pain to be private. When your time is six or seven minutes down on the previous year, and you finish looking and feeling wrecked, you don't want too many people to know about it.

When a mixture of real athletes and charity runners left the finish at South Shields to return to Newcastle in an open top bus, we caught sight of John Caine the race organiser, pleading with the police to open a road. The guy has just organised one of the biggest events in the world without so much as an administrative hitch, and he couldn't relax even two hours later. But the runners could, and we did – in spectacular fashion. It is late in a night like this, when imagination has taken over, that club runners like Ray Scott of Gateshead Harriers persuade tired and emotional commentators to take part again next year. By the time you wake up in the morning, it's too late to change your mind.

Monday 18th
The day got off to a flying start – or a bumpy one, as it happens.
Travelling to Newcastle Airport in the back of a minibus with
Grete Waitz, I found myself being lectured about diet and
preparation for distance running by a world champion. It's nice
to be in a fantasy world once in a while, and it continued on
landing in London with a request to join the *Daily Telegraph*
Fantasy Football League. I learned a bit about picking a team in
my brief spell as a first-season manager on Frank Skinner and
David Baddiel's BBC programme – which apart from anything
else was the only way you could sit next to Karren Brady,
Mandy Smith and Basil Brush on the same sofa. Quite sensibly,
a laddish programme like this changes its guests every year, so
now I'm helping Jimmy Hill raise some money for charity by
joining the *Telegraph*'s celebrity league. My selection, right up
to the £35 million limit, is as follows: Seaman (Arsenal), Barrett
(Everton), Adams (Arsenal), Weatherall (Leeds), Wilson
(Spurs), Yorke (Aston Villa), Keane (Manchester United), Sher-
wood (Blackburn), Thompson (Bolton), Holdsworth
(Wimbledon), Ferdinand (Newcastle). You are permitted to
make two transfers on three separate occasions during the
season, so we'll see how it goes. The rules are slightly different
to the TV programme, in which I finished third.
    I like the name of Ron Atkinson's team – 'My Son Dalian'.
My son is called Frederick, so I named my fantasy team after
his school – Killigrew Juniors.

Tuesday 19th
All television commentators and reporters get a postbag of one
size or another. Many of the letters are critical, but the ones
that come most often are from schoolboys, college students or
university graduates asking how you got into the media in the
first place. I've already touched on my start as a trainee on the
Barnet Press, but that was followed by a spell as a sports writer
and sub-editor on the *Morning Telegraph* in Sheffield. It was
invaluable experience on a provincial daily, not least in subbing
the copy of Alan Hubbard, then chief sports writer in United
Newspapers London office. He looked after me when the paper
sent me as a raw beginner to cover Wimbledon in the late
sixties, and it has taken me over 25 years to invite him to lunch.
John Goodbody of *The Times* – a college friend of mine when
we were both on local weeklies – also joined us. Alan brought

two writers from the *Observer* where he is sports editor, and John was also well supported by a couple of colleagues. We went to the Viceroy in the City, a favourite haunt of Matthew Harding, whose battle with Ken Bates for control of Chelsea formed a central part of the discussion.

In the evening, I was invited to a demonstration of Fantasy League on the Internet. But it was wasted on me. I haven't even graduated from a portable typewriter to a word processor and until recently I thought a lap top was a mechanical cat that you stroked to calm your nerves.

Wednesday 20th

If I was in charge of English football for a day – or even for five minutes – and was allowed to make one major structural change, it would be to streamline the Coca-Cola Cup. I'm not a great fan of Scottish football, but north of the border they have got that bit absolutely right. The competition is done and dusted before Christmas, and therefore does not encroach into the crowded second half of the season as it does in England. The way they achieve this is quite simple. All matches are settled at the first attempt. There are no replays, and no tedious two-leg ties to cloud the issue. Take the match I attended tonight – Tottenham v. Chester. Even if Spurs had made a mess of the first leg, they get a second chance to put things right. Straight knock-out would be far more exciting for the fans (and television, for that matter) and would give the smaller clubs – whose finances are one reason for the present system – a better opportunity of springing a surprise. We could even introduce 'sudden death' in extra time, whereby the first goal settles the game. There was no need for that at White Hart Lane, however, where Spurs won comfortably (4-0), and the only noteworthy point about the game was that Chris Armstrong scored his first goals for Tottenham after his transfer from Crystal Palace. A lot was made in the newspapers about his lean spell, in the same way that it has taken a little while for Dennis Bergkamp to get off the mark for Arsenal. The only certain thing is that those sequences will end sooner rather than later. So, I hope, will the present format for the Coca-Cola Cup.

Thursday 21st

Back to work, after a fashion. In the morning, some local radio interviews to publicise the latest BBC football video, *25 Years of Goal of the Season.* Since 1987, I have written and narrated about 30 videos for BBC Worldwide, many of them club histories.

Still with the nostalgia theme, in the afternoon there was an interview to be done with Lee Dixon for the BBC2 series *Football, Fussball, Voetball,* which over a nine-week period this autumn is tracing the history of European club and international football as part of the build-up to the European Championship draw in December.

Dennis Waterman's series on the seventies seems to have inspired an autumn almanac of football nostalgia. *Kicking and Screaming* on a Monday night, made by an independent company for the BBC, traces the history of the game with some priceless, previously unseen, archive material, and the UK Gold channel has been showing old *Match of the Day* programmes in their original form. At least one long-serving commentator has been suitably embarrassed by some of the things he said fifteen years ago.

Talking of long-serving broadcasters, Bob Wilson and his wife Megs came to dinner this evening. Bob and I were colleagues at the BBC for twenty years before he was made an excellent offer to front ITV's football after the 1994 World Cup. In the early days, when video recorders were not commonplace, I spent many hours in Bob's front room going over my mistakes. He walked me round Wembley to pass the time before my first Cup Final commentary. I think he was making sure I didn't run away.

Friday 22nd

When I was commentating (it's starting to seem a long time ago now), Fridays were always devoted to research and travelling. One of the reasons I am enjoying the break is that I would never normally have a day like today. Well, not on a Friday, at any rate. This morning I recorded a voice-over for Prudential insurance – it's probably the only time in my life I'll get paid more for a morning's work than Stan Collymore. Not as much as Brian Lara though, whose agents Jonathan Barnett and David Manasseh of Stellar Promotions were kind enough to take me to lunch. It was just an exploratory chat to see if there is any common ground between us. I suppose I've got a reputation for being a bit on the serious side, but they wouldn't have thought that if they had stayed with me for the rest of the day.

John d'Arcy, a friend of mine in the advertising business, was entertaining some friends at Langan's Brasserie. I am not one of the regulars at this popular London lunching venue, but I know a man who is, as they say, and he kept me there until late in the evening. This has got to stop. In two weeks' time, it will be back to the old routine. What I'm missing now is not the work, but some of my friends at the BBC. They have been kind enough to ring occasionally and make sure I'm still around. You can't work somewhere for nearly 25 years and not feel a lot for the place.

Saturday 23rd

If I hadn't been a commentator, I think I would have been a taxi driver. It's a similar sort of 'knowledge' really – names, places, attention to detail. Broadcasting, at the speed we do, is often a case of finding the most expedient route from A to B in the shortest possible time – in a verbal sense, if you see what I mean. Threading my way through the streets of London is still a bit of a challenge, especially when I'm going to Highbury. It's a major decision whether to take the 'red route' through Highgate, Archway and down the Holloway Road or whether to cut through Bounds Green, Muswell Hill, past Alexandra Palace and Crouch Hill Broadway. Yes, my brain definitely needs stimulating now.

Having seen Armstrong break his duck, I decided to try the lucky charm on Bergkamp, who made a few 'first goalscorer' punters happy by coming up with two beauties against Southampton. (The final score was Arsenal 4, Southampton 2.) Bruce Rioch is a neighbour of mine in Harpenden, so after the match I knocked on the door of the manager's office to congratulate him on the result. It was eerie and empty, as though the ghost of George Graham was hovering behind the chair. Obviously Bruce has a different routine on a match day. On the way out, I exchanged pleasantries with Peter Hill-Wood, the Arsenal chairman. He was smoking a big cigar and said how he thinks the team are developing a more entertaining image. I tell him to go easy – he doesn't want Danny Baker dancing down the wing. Anyone remember Danny Clapton?

Sunday 24th

You get a lot of requests in my business to write articles for brochures or to contribute to books and magazines. You try to help where you can, but when Geoff Hurst calls you have to sit up and take notice. Not many people score hat-tricks in World Cup Finals and still look fit enough to play 30 years later. Geoff is raising money for charity by gathering together lots of stories called 'Where I was and what I was doing the day England won the World Cup', and putting them into a book to be published in 1996. My tale isn't all that interesting. I watched the match on television. But I broke a lampshade jumping up when one of his goals went in, and in the evening I had to report a student exchange visit for the *Barnet Press*. It took place in Boreham Wood, and when I got there I discovered that the visiting students were German. Unsurprisingly, none of them thought the ball was over the line.

Monday 25th
This entry needs to be very short indeed. Once a year, the commentators take their boots out of the loft and play a challenge match against the boys of St Albans School, the average age of their team being around 30 years younger than ours. Their football master is David Willacy, erstwhile chairman of the English Schools FA. Quite how we won 7-6 only he can explain.

Tuesday 26th
The man who got me into running (or at my speed maybe we should call it jogging) was Tom McNab. He and I were neighbours in St Albans, and between coaching a string of athletes, lecturing overweight businessmen and writing the bestseller *Flanagan's Run*, he told a few of us in our street that we had better start taking regular exercise or we might not see too many more World Cups. I still have the running diary he published in the early eighties, which got me into the habit of recording every route, distance and time. In the years that have elapsed since, I have tried to average three runs a week. Somebody once said that going for a run should be as automatic as cleaning your teeth. Tom has been a great champion of sports facilities for our area, and today we met at the opening of a spanking new municipal running track at Hemel Hempstead. It's linked to one of those state-of-the-art cinema and supermarket complexes which are supposed to make parking and shopping easier but which can be totally intimidating to the simple man. You virtually need a degree in advanced

science to find your way in and out. Tom probably solved the problem by running there.

Wednesday 27th
We are in the middle of another European week and last night Manchester United went out of the UEFA Cup. Peter Schmeichel came up in desperation and scored a goal late in the game, making the final score 2-2.

But it was another Scandinavian goalkeeper who occupied my thoughts today. I contacted Erik Thorstvedt to get some information about the squad Norway will choose to face England in two weeks' time, because that's my first game back, and as it's in Oslo it won't be the gentle return I was hoping for. Fourteen days and – unfortunately – counting.

Thursday 28th
Football is a common language that opens a lot of doors and eases the strain of many a conversation. It is a currency that never gets devalued. Without it, I doubt whether I would have met Gary Rhodes, in whose restaurant I had lunch today. He wouldn't thank me for calling him the male equivalent to Delia Smith, so I won't, although both are keen football fans. He supports Manchester United; she follows Norwich. Quite whether there is any link between the kitchen and the goalmouth I am not sure, but it's an idle thought while I am passing time in eating houses.

Friday 29th
Canon Copiers asked me to host an exhibition of theirs in Crawley today. Nice work if you can get it. The function was fairly low-key but the people were charming, which was a good thing because I don't understand the first thing about the way these amazing machines work. As I said earlier, I'm still into a typewriter and carbon paper. These wizards can change scripts into colour; make the printing a different size; reprint the page upside down if you wish. We're living in the technological age but sometimes the method defeats the message. On the way home I tried to catch a train at Gatwick and finished up in the airport. Where are the signs for the station?

Saturday 30th
Coventry and Aston Villa have both changed their teams considerably since I last covered them, not to mention their

managers. Ron Atkinson is well known for dispensing post-match hospitality to his friends, and before the match he invited one or two senior players who were with him at Villa, like Andy Townsend and Steve Staunton, in for a drink later. As I left him I wondered whether he might have regretted that decision. Villa won 3-0.

OCTOBER
1995

Sunday 1st
This is the day when Eric Cantona came back after what, effectively, has been an eight-month suspension. Manchester United were playing Liverpool at Old Trafford. You could almost hear the *Match of the Day* music and the voice of David Coleman, so traditional is the fixture. These days, of course, it is a natural for Sky Sports and their 'Super Sunday'.

Mine was satisfying, rather than super. I trawled round the Royal Mail Barnack Ten, a road race organised by the Werrington Joggers, near Peterborough. They told me it was a course through the Fens, which I thought meant it would be flat, but there was one killer of a hill.

On the way home, listening to Cantona's penalty on the radio (the final score was 2-2), I realised it was four months since the Umbro Cup and my last proper working day. I've been very lucky to get so long to recharge the batteries.

Monday 2nd
They Think It's All Over, and even though the sabbatical nearly is, today I recorded an episode of the quiz show that, believe it or not, I could have been presenting. Over twelve months ago I auditioned for what later became Nick Hancock's job – and was offered the part. The BBC sports department, wisely in retrospect, advised me against it. The show has an irreverent edge to it, and that could have caused conflict with sports people who might want to regard me as a serious commentator.

Tuesday 3rd
Well, now it really *is* all over – the recording, I mean – I have got to admit I cheated. Just once, and partly by accident, but I cheated. Coming out of the make-up room behind Gary

Lineker, I caught sight of a script lying on a desk, and at the bottom of the page were the words 'W. G. Grace'. It was obviously the answer to an old-time cricket question, and when it came my way during the programme I tried to look as though I was mulling it over before coming up with the answer. Just to show cheats never prosper, my team, under David Gower, lost by one point! Mind you, it was quite an experience mixing with comedians. Lee Hurst and Rory McGrath are just the same off the set as on it – they never stop delivering one-line gags – while the producers made it easy for me by including a couple of clips where I was the commentator. Also, I had to move round the desk and put on my sheepskin coat to be the 'celebrity guest'. Lineker clocked me from behind his blindfold, but he also made the whole experience easier for me.

Wednesday 4th
Will Buckley of the *Observer*, who also writes for the men's magazine *Maxim*, took me to lunch in Soho. He wants to write a piece about my 'comeback' next week. Anybody would think I had been off the air for years, instead of just missing about six *Match of the Day* programmes. Being a commentator, all sorts of clichés go through my mind – 'Absence makes the heart grow fonder' (doubtful); 'Familiarity breeds contempt' (probably); and a new one coined by me: 'Every match you do is one nearer to your last'.

In the evening I sat next to Fulham chairman Jimmy Hill as they crashed to Wolves in the Coca-Cola Cup at Craven Cottage. I often sit next to Jim in the commentary box, but this was a different experience entirely. He had a seat close to the exit where disgruntled fans gave him pieces of their minds as they filed out, but Jimmy took the criticism on his famous chin.

'Not good enough, Jim,' growled one supporter.

'I quite agree with you,' replied the chairman.

'These new players aren't up to much Jim, are they?'

'No, they were hopeless tonight,' he concurred.

I've learned a lot of little homilies from Jimmy down the years: 'Always praise your enemies'; 'Make sure you get a plus out of a minus', etc, etc. Now he's taught me something else. Disarm your critics with a cheerful smile. He's the most irrepressible man I have ever met. Fulham lost 5-1, but within ten minutes he was lining up speakers for a celebrity dinner.

Thursday 5th
This was a day when you count your blessings and praise God for good health. A long-standing friend of mine, Brian Pitts, was marking 25 years' service with BBC Radio News, but it was a tribute to his courage and fortitude that he was able to attend the party they were giving him in Broadcasting House. Brian has had two operations for cancer of the jaw and is still under the doctors. Notwithstanding that, he made a quite magnificent speech which brought the house down. Later, he took me down the Five Live studio where I made a brief contribution to the John Inverdale programme. I finished up reading the weather report and the travel information, having embarrassed Lynn Bowles into a fit of giggles. She's lovely when you meet her, but I hate her when I'm stuck on the M6 on a Friday afternoon.

Friday 6th
When Terry Venables comes walking towards me off the training pitch, I know it's the moment of no return. Or rather, of my return to work. Bisham Abbey, on the morning the England squad start training for next week's match in Norway, was a busy place to start. I got my knuckles rapped, nicely, at the gate, for not having an England accreditation which all media people now need. You can't go away without them changing the rules, can you? Not for three months, anyway. At least the newspaper boys (and girls) are still using the same pub.

Saturday 7th
No way am I going to attack Norway v. England without a 'dummy run', so I was perched at the back of the Ipswich Town directors' box today, alongside Jack, the club's video man, doing a practice commentary on the Endsleigh League game against Wolves. With no Premiership fixtures today, it wasn't possible for me to fit in a *Match of the Day* before Oslo. Talk about being rusty. When the teams came out there was an Ipswich player I have never even heard of – James Scowcroft – playing up front because Ian Marshall pulled out less than half an hour before the kick off. So much for checking the teams. Then Wolves scored a goal that from where I was sitting could have been credited to any one of three players. Jack had the technology to show me a replay, and I still didn't know. Worse

still, the referee was injured and at half-time handed over to his senior linesman. I didn't even notice. Fortunately, the only person who will ever hear this error-strewn commentary is manager George Burley, who will use the tape for tactical purposes. It will give him a good laugh.

The best part of the day was seeing Bobby Robson – with his surgeon – looking well on the way to recovery. David Sheepshanks took me back to his house for a glass of champagne, and he asked me how it went. If I perform like that on Wednesday, I'll be off for another three months, and this time it won't be my own choice.

Monday 9th

It's like going back to school after the summer holidays. I was quite nervous standing at Luton Airport to link up with the media party travelling to Oslo with the England team. But any curiosity about my reappearance was quickly overtaken by more important events.

Terry Venables announced that during the summer he received an approach from Inter-Milan. This immediately ignited the interest of the daily newspapers, especially as the story had broken in one of the Sundays yesterday.

But this was not the only issue demanding a reaction from the Football Association. They were known to be starting discussions about the appointment of a new technical director.

While others were checking their bags in, I fell into conversation with the FA's chief executive, Graham Kelly, who seemed happy enough to discuss the shortlist. I got the feeling he had a lot of respect for the Frenchman, Gerard Houlier.

Suddenly four of the tabloid journalists led by the relentless Harry Harris of the *Daily Mirror*, spotted Kelly and marched in unison across the departure lounge. Kelly has a lugubrious way of dealing with these situations. He went to the toilet.

When we boarded the plane, it was the usual seating arrangements – the media at the back, the players at the front, and the FA officials (who sometimes number nearly as many) in the middle.

It all started off very civilised, and I was relieved to hear one of the journalists behind me order a lager as soon as we took off. A reasonable enough request at lunchtime, but under the previous England manager, alcoholic drinks were banned on the outward flight. You would be amazed where some of us hid our miniatures.

Alan Mullery, working for Capital Gold, gave me some good-natured ribbing about an article in this morning's *Daily Mail* by their television sports columnist, Neil Wilson.

Many years before, Wilson and I had both worked for United Newspapers, and in his capacity as one of the leading athletics writers he caught up with me a couple of weeks ago at the Great North Run.

I told him about the dummy run I was doing at Ipswich, so he turned it into an item for his Monday column. Mind you, he caught me by surprise by referring to the return of a 'national institution' (I think he must have meant my coat) and by suggesting that, in the fullness of time, my voice might be coming from a different direction – in other words a rival channel to the BBC.

The truth of the matter is that I have twice had exploratory talks with the satellite people, but on neither occasion has anything materialised. The first company no longer exists, and their successors have built their own dedicated team who do things rather differently to the BBC.

Whether a careworn Motson would ever fit into an independent or cable company is a matter of some conjecture. Experience is one thing, but television is moving so fast that my generation of commentators may not last into their seventies the way many of our elders have.

Sitting behind me on the aeroplane were skilful young journalists like Henry Winter of the *Daily Telegraph*. A lot of the senior men who used to intimidate me on my early England trips – hard-hitting writers like Frank McGhee – have either retired or departed the daily scene.

Those who looked after me when I joined the media troupe, like Jeff Powell of the *Mail* and Frank Clough of the *Sun*, moved on to different areas of sports journalism. Looking round the plane, it was hard to spot a kindred spirit who had been there when I first travelled with England over 20 years ago.

Eventually I spotted Steve Curry of the *Daily Express* and Michael Hart of the *Evening Standard*, and made a mental note to have a beer with them in Oslo. Not a difficult rendezvous to set up.

Tuesday 10th
Nearly everybody I meet thinks the overseas travel is the most glamorous part of my job. If only they knew. If they came with

me on an international assignment, they would see two airports, a fleeting glimpse of the city in the dark from a coach window, the inside of a typical, garish chain hotel, at least two training sessions, and finally, a football match. The rest of the time we spend in our rooms preparing for the broadcast.

The Norwegians, like all Scandinavian teams, are obliging and open with the media. They train in public, then all the players mingle with the press for about half an hour. Thorstvedt pointed out the squad players I didn't know.

What wasn't so clever was that in the evening, at the England training, one or two of ours looked less than distinctive. I finally realised I was staring at Gary Neville and Nick Barmby.

Wednesday 11th
Three months I have waited for this – and what happens? A tedious 0-0 draw. Anti-climax. But a commentator's dilemma none the less. To what extent do you criticise the England performance? Norway haven't been beaten at home for five years and it was on this ground where they more or less put us out of the World Cup. Steady on there – Venables is still in the building process. On the plane home he told me how pleased he was with Neville's performance. Have we solved that right back dilemma at last, Terry?

Thursday 12th
Well, I think it is Thursday anyway. The England party finally returned to Luton at 2.30 a.m. – they come back the same night so the players can return to their clubs quickly. Quite what state they are in to train, I'm not sure. If I had my way, we would scrap England games in midweek and play all our internationals on Saturdays, like the Italians do. It would make little difference to the Premiership, because as things stand at present we are cancelling the programme anyway. We could then play the League games the following Wednesday – instead of an international. A straight swap in other words. Sounds too simple, doesn't it? Perhaps that's why we never try it.

Friday 13th
Unlucky for some, and maybe for Manchester City who play at Old Trafford in the derby tomorrow. It's back to the two games a week routine for me, and when I made contact with Alan Ball from the car en route to Manchester, he sounded remarkably

cheerful for a man at the bottom of the League. He gave me his team without an if or a but, then went back to his glass of wine. That's how to deal with pressure.

In the evening, Gary Lineker's *Dreaming of Ajax* programme was screened. In terms of matching *their* production line, English clubs can go on dreaming.

Saturday 14th
A lunchtime interview with Alex Ferguson for *Football Focus*. He told me Cantona wouldn't be playing in the derby, which rather took the edge off the occasion. United scored early (the only goal of the game) through Paul Scholes, although it looked to me like a wicked deflection off Keith Curle. Commentators are supposed to be precise about these things, but nobody else mentioned it so maybe we get over-concerned about detail sometimes. City played better than their position indicates, and Georgiou Kinkladze looks to be an ace signing.

Sunday 15th
There was no point going home, because first thing tomorrow morning I'm off to Denmark with Liverpool for their UEFA Cup tie with Brondby. Time spent away from home is a downside of the job.

I filled in today visiting a family I met on the Nile trip, then moved camp to the Bowler Hat at Birkenhead – that's a hotel, not a casino – where Ray Stubbs joined me for a natter. We have heard a nasty rumour that the BBC may lose the FA Cup contract.

Monday 16th
It's my first trip to Copenhagen – the only European capital I haven't visited – but the Tivoli Gardens were shut. So too, when we got there, was the stadium, but the Brondby people were very hospitable and agreed to remove the glass from our commentary box. If it rains, I wouldn't be able to see the players – and I forgot to bring windscreen wipers.

Tuesday 17th
I don't believe this. Another 0-0 draw. Three matches back, and all I've seen is one deflected goal. Liverpool will be happy enough with the result. Overseas travel has changed a bit since Bill Shankly's time. Ian Rush used his mobile phone at Copen-

hagen Airport to make sure there was somewhere open for us
to have a quick drink when we got back to Merseyside.

Wednesday 18th
It's strange, but there has been an amazing amount of attention
following my appearance on *They Think It's All Over*. More
people have mentioned my being on the show than have ever
reacted to a football commentary. Is somebody trying to tell me
something?

Thursday 19th
What do commentators do the rest of the time? Watch tapes,
mostly. In a week like this, while you have been working for
your own channel, there have probably been three or four other
major matches that you have missed. On my return from
Liverpool, it was catch-up time, and it's taken most of today
and yesterday.

Friday 20th
A sentimental day, this one. The building which has housed
BBC Sport's offices for over twenty years – Kensington House
off Shepherd's Bush Green – is being vacated, and we are
moving in with the grown-ups at Television Centre in Wood
Lane. You get quite attached to the same room and the same
desk if you have been there as long as I have.
    The evening saw the start of the *Voetball* series I mentioned.
Barry Davies kicked off with Spain and Portugal. I hope
viewers are finding enough time to watch all this football – the
game is so fashionable at the moment that it's hard to reconcile
with that period exactly ten years ago when there were no
games on television before Christmas.

Saturday 21st
I like covering matches at West Ham. We used to live in the
area when my late father was superintendent of the East End
Mission in Stepney. I once saw Stanley Matthews play for
Blackpool in a third round Cup tie at Upton Park. The ground
has changed a lot now, of course, and so has the area, but what
remains is the legacy of good football laid down all those years
ago by Ron Greenwood. West Ham never were into media
lunches and brash headlines – they just put the team on the
pitch and got them to pass the ball properly. That's exactly

what happened today, and with a minute left they were leading the champions Blackburn 1-0. Then Julian Dicks slipped and Alan Shearer scored. It's Blackburn's first away point. Without Shearer, where would they be?

Sunday 22nd – Wednesday 25th
To make 40 minutes of television can take several weeks. Documentary-style programmes require careful research, thorough interviews, sensitive editing, and standards of production and voice work of which the BBC is rightly proud. My first responsibility in the *Voetball* series is the story of British clubs in Europe from 1955 to 1975. The producer, Lakviar Singh, has done most of the work, but fitting my words around the original footage is like doing a jigsaw, playing scrabble and trimming a hedge all rolled into one. Eventually, on Wednesday afternoon, we put the words on and the programme was ready. Some of the early archive material will stir a few memories.

Having co-authored a book on the history of the European Cup, with my BBC colleague John Rowlinson, I know a little bit about the background of how it started and why Chelsea, the League Champions in 1955, were advised against entering by the Football League. Can you imagine that happening now?

As things turned out, Matt Busby and Manchester United took a more forceful view a year later, and insisted on pitting the wits of the 'Busby Babes' against Europe's finest.

We managed to unearth some old archive film of their semi-final in the Bernabeu Stadium in 1957. Real Madrid beat United 3-1, with Di Stefano in command and Bobby Charlton an overawed reserve up in the stand, but the second leg was a 2-2 draw, and United reached the semi-final again the following year only for their team to be decimated in the dreadful Munich air disaster on the way back from Belgrade.

In our fresh interviews for the *Voetball* series, Charlton insisted that the Babes would have gone on to win the European Cup. As it was, Manchester United had to wait another decade before they fulfilled their ambition, fittingly with Charlton as captain.

Celtic beat them to it by a year, and it was absorbing to research and listen again to the old interviews with the likes of Busby and Jock Stein.

In those days, television interviews with managers were rare occurrences, and usually lasted a lot longer than they do now.

This is the era of the 'soundbite', and interviewers like me rarely get the chance to probe beyond a second question.

The most satisfying part of the *Voetball* project for me was seeing Bill Nicholson again. Not only was Bill the first manager to win the League and Cup double, but his Super Spurs were also the first English club to win a European trophy – the Cup-Winners Cup in 1963.

At the age of 76, going on 77, Bill was in coherent, comfortable mood as he recalled the days of Blanchflower, White and Mackay. 'The first day Dave Mackay reported for training, everything at the club changed,' he said. Such was Dave's influence; not just on Tottenham, but on Derby County later.

So much a man of principle was Bill Nicholson that he became disillusioned with the way the game went in the early seventies. He never came to terms with the lack of dedication that, in certain cases, accompanied the newly discovered affluence of the highly paid, overhyped professional footballer in the period after the abolition of the maximum wage. Goodness knows what he makes of some of the wages and signing-on fees now.

But what finally precipitated Nicholson's resignation, after sixteen years as manager, was the riot in Rotterdam when Spurs played Feyenoord in the UEFA Cup Final of 1974. As far as some of us are concerned, that was the start of football hooliganism as it festered over the next few years.

A year later, Leeds supporters rioted in the Parc des Princes in Paris, hurling seats on to the pitch after their defeat by Bayern Munich in the European Cup Final. Symbolically, that marked the end of our first *Voetball* episode on the British influence in Europe.

While we are on the subject, I may as well throw in my own twopenneth – not just in hindsight, but very much the way I felt at the time.

The first time I was really scared at a football match was at The Den in 1978, when Millwall played Ipswich in the sixth round of the FA Cup. The crowd invaded the pitch at a point when Ipswich had won a corner, and the referee took both teams off the field until the atmosphere had calmed down and the pitch was cleared.

There was more trouble after the game, when Bobby Robson and the Ipswich players were abused and spat on as they boarded their coach. Later that evening, an emotive Robson said on *Match of the Day* that the offenders should be birched, at best.

He was accused of over-reacting, but in retrospect he was absolutely right. Had a brave Home Secretary attacked the issue at the time as firmly as he should have done, we might have avoided the carnage which followed.

Two years later, I saw the start of the Turin riot in the streets outside the stadium before England played Belgium in the European Championship. Bricks and boulders were being hurled indiscriminately by louts in T-shirts purporting to be England supporters.

Later, the game was stopped because of fighting on the terraces, and the police weighed in with tear gas. England matches overseas subsequently became a convenient battleground for the hooligan element – many of them incited by sinister organisations.

No sooner had the trouble been quelled by the local police and the damage to town or city assessed, than the perpetrators were rapidly ferried back to England without charge – either here or there.

Back at home, if violence flared on one of our League grounds, those arrested usually received a slap on the wrist – either a suspended sentence or a fine with time to pay. The only inconvenience to the offenders was the whipround which followed.

So it was that – with standards of discipline in this country deteriorating at an alarming rate and the punishment rarely fitting the crime – football hooligans were given carte blanche to wreak havoc as they pleased.

The riot at Luton in 1985, after an FA Cup tie against Millwall, was in many ways a forerunner of the Heysel tragedy that followed two months later. People could have been killed at Kenilworth Road – take the word of one who was there.

For many months afterwards, the police went to the BBC to inspect video-tape evidence, trying to identify among others a youth in a white jacket who was standing in the centre circle kicking a policeman repeatedly in the head. I am not sure they ever found him.

The only person to take decisive action was David Evans, the Luton chairman. The following morning, he banned away supporters from the ground.

There were those who protested that the innocent majority

were being punished for the indiscretions of an uncivilised minority, but the malaise had gone much deeper than that. There was an ugly mood on the terraces, in the stands and on the streets in 1985.

A postscript, of course, was the fences that went up at most grounds to prevent further pitch invasions. In a dreadful way it proved exactly that – a final solution. For if there had been no fences, would there have been a Hillsborough tragedy four years later?

Thursday 26th

Having battled with that *Voetball* script all week, I got a day off today. My old mate Ricky George – he who scored the winner for non-League Hereford against Newcastle in 1972 – invited me to lunch with his business partner Jeff Zemmell. Actually, it was a lunch about a lunch, because every Christmas I take Rick out along with a few friends to mark the 'Hereford anniversary'. It was the biggest moment of his career and it sort of got mine off the ground, for a variety of reasons.

I must have bored everybody silly with the Hereford story. It was my first season on *Match of the Day* – I was still on a year's 'trial' from BBC Radio – when I was sent to cover their FA Cup third round replay against First Division Newcastle.

The first match at St James's Park had ended in a 2-2 draw, but so bad was the weather in the west country that the replay was postponed three or four times, and was rearranged for the day of the fourth round.

I travelled down to Hereford on the Friday night with two of their players – George, who had been a junior at Tottenham and who I knew from his Barnet days, and Billy Meadows, a bustling centre forward with a broken nose who thought he had had a bad season if he scored less than 45 goals.

Hereford's player-manager, Colin Addison, was happy for Bill and Rick to live in north London and travel down to matches. Hereford were then in the Southern League and the players were part-time. Nowadays, there are players in the Premiership earning £6,000 a week who live up to 200 miles away from their clubs. The polite word for them is itinerants. The impolite word is mercenaries.

Having said that, you can hardly blame the players. The clubs and their chairmen approve the contracts – but it is a fact that the avalanche of television money that has flooded into the game in the last five years has gone largely on wages and signing-on fees.

Anyway, Ricky and Billy were getting about £25 a week from Hereford – supplementing their income from jobs as sports goods salesman and carpet fitter respectively.

Come to think of it, I doubt whether the Newcastle wages were that much higher in 1972 – we were only a decade past the abolition of the maximum wage.

But they did have Malcolm Macdonald – 'Supermac' in his first season on Tyneside – and the editor of *Match of the Day*, the late Sam Leitch, warned me that if Malcolm was on form the game could be over in the first half, and the highlights might last about eight minutes.

When we arrived at the Green Dragon Hotel in Hereford that Friday evening, we had a meal with John Shrewsbury, the BBC director who was also in his first season as a mainline producer.

About eleven o'clock, John and I introduced Ricky to the late Jackie Milburn, three times a Cup-winner with Newcastle and then working as a journalist in the north-east.

'If you were one of my players,' said Milburn to George, 'you would be in bed by now.'

Ricky protested that he was only the substitute the following day, but Milburn was still adamant.

'Well, if I come on and score the winning goal, will that make any difference to what you have just said?' asked George with a cheeky grin.

What happened less than 24 hours later was a fairy-tale for him, for Hereford, and for me. Most of all, perhaps, for an unknown building worker called Ronnie Radford.

With barely ten minutes left, Macdonald headed his accustomed goal from a cross by on-loan Viv Busby, and the game seemed as good as over.

What everybody forgets is that two minutes later, Supermac was through on his own, with only goalkeeper Fred Potter to beat. He went round him on his favoured left side, and somehow managed to shoot into the side netting.

In between those two incidents, Ricky George had come on as substitute to replace Hereford's right back Roger Griffiths, who was later discovered to have been playing part of the game with a fractured bone in his leg!

Ricky's first contribution came right in front of the makeshift television gantry where I was sitting. He worked a clever dummy on the left wing and fooled two Newcastle players, starting the move from which Radford ultimately picked up the ball some 40 yards out.

It was a heavy pitch and quite how Ronnie struck the ball with such awesome power nobody will ever know. Certainly the Newcastle goalkeeper, Willie McFaul, threw himself full length and must one day expect to see himself save it – so many times has the video been shown. As we all know, the ball flew into the top corner.

What happened next – more than the goal itself – is why I believe this Cup tie sticks in the memory more than any other since the war. Not just in *my* memory, but in those of most of the ten million viewers who then made up the weekly *Match of the Day* audience.

It was the invasion of the pitch by the crowd that did it. Not an ugly, threatening spat of behaviour that was to become commonplace in a year of two, but a spontaneous expression of unconfined joy by young Hereford supporters in anoraks and parkas – some of whom had watched the match standing on empty cider crates.

This was sheer euphoria, and in many ways it marked the end of the age of innocence as far as football was concerned. Look back at the pictures now, and you see no names on shirts, no executive boxes, little perimeter advertising and certainly no sponsors' logo attached to the dear old FA Cup itself.

Since it was a replay, the match went into extra time, and Hereford would not be denied. Certainly not Ricky George, who picked up a pass from Dudley Tyler on the right-hand side of Newcastle's penalty area, got the ball on to his right foot, and squeezed a shot through Bobby Moncur's legs and beyond the diving McFaul.

On they went again, the Hereford hundreds, and as George was submerged under celebrating players and supporters, the bewildered commentator could only stutter, 'Now it will take some time to clear the field.'

Half an hour later, the excitement had subsided and the pitch was clear as George, Radford, Addison and Radford's two young sons went out to be interviewed for *Match of the Day*. It was like talking publicly to your next-door neighbour after he's won the national lottery.

On the way back to London we bought some fish and chips

and went back to Bill and Pat Meadows' house to watch the programme. I remember Rick's wife, another Pat, saying she hoped it would regenerate his career because at 25 he was still the youngest player in the Hereford team.

Pat Meadows had just bought the new cult record, 'American Pie' by Don McLean. The music had only just started to play where *Match of the Day* and this commentator were concerned.

Friday 27th

I am proud of the fact that in my lifetime, my generation aspired to put a man on the moon. I am less proud of the fact that they never found a way of getting people on and off aeroplanes at anything faster than a snail's pace. I could have driven to Manchester in the time it took to reach my seat on the afternoon shuttle, where baggage space was about as rare as Premiership players training twice a day. Why do I get so ratty on Fridays?

Saturday 28th

Today started with lunch alongside Mrs Denise Robson – wife of Bryan – and finished with a bit of a tiff with Alex Ferguson. Just another quiet day in the media circus which operates under the big top called Old Trafford.

Michael Edelson, a director of Manchester United and a good friend to the BBC, had invited me to lunch before the match against Middlesbrough. With a major broadcast just a couple of hours away, lunch for commentators is not quite what it seems. Mrs Robson was charming company, but the waitress in the restaurant knew my mind was on other things and produced a plate with two Yorkshire puddings by themselves – a pre-match meal I've enjoyed before at Old Trafford.

Middlesbrough have just signed Juninho from Brazil, but he's still on his way across the Atlantic, and the biggest cheer of the afternoon was reserved for Mrs Robson's husband – this was his first trip to Old Trafford in his capacity as manager of promoted Boro.

Robson's team seemed overawed by the occasion, and Manchester United won more comfortably than the 2-0 score suggested. However, the match was marred by the sending off of United's Roy Keane, his third red card in seven months.

After the game, I interviewed Alex Ferguson for *Grandstand*

and he said Keane could have no complaints – rule one says never lift your hands on the football pitch.

Match of the Day wanted a more considered interview with the United manager, and expected me to elaborate on Keane's disciplinary record.

'I know you keep disciplinary matters within the club, but is Keane's behaviour on the pitch something you need to address?' I ventured.

Fergie's eyes narrowed and he brought the interview to a swift conclusion. As he walked away he made it clear he was less than happy with Motson's line of questioning.

One or two stewards standing in the tunnel overheard the exchange, and by the time Ferguson got to his next port of call – the press conference – word had spread that he and the BBC commentator had fallen out.

When I got to the airport, the Monday newspaper writers flying back to London had heard about the incident and wanted more details. I decided to play it low key. A simmering row in the tabloids over the next two or three days was not going to help either party, and instinct told me that these flare-ups often die down within a matter of days.

Mind you, it was a reminder that commentators are first and foremost journalists, and sometimes awkward questions have to be asked. If in facing up to your responsibilities as a reporter, you occasionally upset somebody you like, it is one of the less palatable but necessary parts of the job. I even angered the placid Ron Greenwood once, asking him after an England defeat whether he should consider resigning. We were live on the nine o'clock news at the time, and Ron obviously felt the question was out of order; just as Alex Ferguson did today.

But he and I have always got on in the past, and I doubt whether there will be any grudges. Come to think of it, I wonder what he said to Roy Keane?

Sunday 29th
My Sunday morning run with my friends and neighbours, Bob Sims and Andrew Murphy, used to get my Saturday frustrations out of the system. I say used to, because they now get so far ahead of me that I am the butt of many a dog owner's humour. Comments like, 'What were you up to last night?' and 'Your mates are just finishing' don't do the old morale too much good. It's Halloween, and all in all it's been a witches' brew of a weekend.

Monday 30th/Tuesday 31st

In the seventies or early eighties, if Liverpool had secured a 0-0 draw away from home, you could put your house on them winning the tie at Anfield. Now it is different. Apart from the mental strength I mentioned earlier, the continental teams seem to have mastered the knack of getting the all-important 'away goal'. So when Dan Eggen headed in a corner for Brondby, it was exit Liverpool, and from November onwards the only English interest in Europe is maintained by Nottingham Forest. The three foreigners rule has not helped the English cause, but if Jean-Marc Bosman's case is upheld, that could be history by Christmas.

NOVEMBER
1995

Wednesday 1st
The flattering flood of requests from students continues. This afternoon a young woman named Faith Lawrence called with her tape recorder. She has to submit a five-minute interview with a chosen subject for her media course. Because she is cheeky and charming with it, she might just have a chance in our business. But she was disappointed in my assertion that Barry Davies and I are the best of colleagues. Understandably, she was looking for an angle.

Thursday 2nd
When I was leaving Egypt, I got buttonholed by a football fan at Luxor Airport who told me what a wonderful job the English coach Allan Harris had done while he was working in Cairo. He won everything and proved so popular he couldn't go out and walk down the street. Now, after a spell in Turkey, Allan is back home hoping to get a job in England. He is an excellent coach and used to be Terry Venables' assistant at Barcelona and Tottenham, but like a lot of football people, he is finding it difficult to get back on the carousel. Over lunch, he concurred with the current view that the English game is lagging behind when it comes to technique and tactics.

Friday 3rd
Tomorrow's Newcastle v. Liverpool match promises to be one of the best games of the season so far. Even Brendan Foster, who was kind enough to take me out to dinner tonight with some of his colleagues from Nova International, is finding it hard to get tickets. Why on earth didn't Sir John Hall build a bigger stadium?

MOTTY'S DIARY

Saturday 4th

When they told me Newcastle was now one of the top six night spots in Europe, they didn't have to prove it. With a rather sore head I had to interview Kevin Keegan for *Football Focus*, but basically you just ask him the first question and off he goes. Today's theme was the failure of English clubs in Europe and the Newcastle manager warmed to the subject.

The two teams then produced a compelling exhibition of Premiership football. As Keegan says, if you want excitement you maybe have to tolerate the imperfection that goes with it. That's no consolation to Liverpool, who passed the ball around beautifully, but lost to a last-minute goal from Stephen Watson. In my *Grandstand* report I boldly suggested it could be the goal, come the end of the season, that was seen to have won Newcastle the title. Slightly premature that prediction. We've just gone into November.

Sunday 5th

When I started in television, the staple football diet on a Sunday was a programme of regional highlights on ITV. Now, we are spoiled for choice. Italian Serie A on Channel 4; live Endsleigh match on ITV; live Premiership action on Sky; it's all rather more filling than the Sunday roast, but the worst indigestion is surely the Sunday papers. There are so many sections now that the letter box is protesting and the reader is getting intimidated. Thank goodness for Zoë Heller in the *Sunday Times* magazine. Her column from America brightens my day.

Monday 6th – Wednesday 8th

This promises to be a quiet week at work. The midweek football comes from the Coca-Cola Cup (yes, it's replay time) and next Saturday there is a blank Premiership weekend prior to the next England game. Time to write part two of the British story in Europe for the *Voetball* series. We are now into the seventies, and in that prolific period when English clubs won the European Cup six years running, not to mention the success we had in the Cup-Winners and UEFA competitions.

The danger of these programmes is that there is so much that demands inclusion, and you don't want it to seem like a catalogue. There has to be light and shade, and we found a bit of that thanks to an interview with Peter Osgood about Chelsea's victory over Real Madrid in Athens.

48

While our other interviewees concentrated on how the winning goal was scored, why the referee was so bad, or who they swapped shirts with at the end, Ossie revealed that on the intervening day between the first (drawn) match and the replay, he and a group of Chelsea players, including Charlie Cooke and Tommy Baldwin, went into an Athens hotel and got rolling drunk. The following day all starred in Chelsea's memorable victory. So much for pre-match preparation.

Thursday 9th – Saturday 11th
I've only been back at work just over a month, and I cannot remember football ever having a higher profile. More matches, more television programmes, more space in the newspapers – I just hope the product can absorb and justify such colossal exposure. To guard against overindulgence, and fill in a weekend without a Premiership menu, there's an approved diet of horse racing on offer at Cheltenham. They say it's the sport of kings, but if flat racing attracts the royal patronage, then the National Hunt season has an aura and an attraction all of its own. Nestling in the Cotswolds, the race course at Cheltenham has charm and character. There is an orderliness about a race meeting which is comforting if you want to melt into the crowd and let the card unfold, but it can rise to a raucous crescendo on the day of a really big race and that's what we are here for. The Mackeson Gold Cup Handicap is the first major event on the steeplechase calendar. It seems to mark the end of autumn and the start of winter, much in the same way as the first round of the FA Cup, which takes place on the same day. Dublin Flyer lives up to his name by edging out Egypt Mill Prince in the Mackeson, but my friends are more concerned about the performance of their horse Earth Summit, who finishes second to Wilsford in another race on the card.

The same consortium have agreed to buy Earth Summit's half-sister, a four-year-old filly who they are calling Summit Else. There is one share left in the syndicate. Flushed with the proceeds from backing a rare winner, guess who takes it up?

Sunday 12th
Summit Else is stabled at Naunton, near Cheltenham, at the training headquarters of Nigel Twiston-Davies and Peter Scudamore. We called to see her today, although she is only doing light work at present and won't be seen on a race course

until March at the earliest. As the newest member of the group, and knowing less about horses than any of them, I stayed discreetly in the background as they walked her around. Everybody made encouraging noises before she went back into her box. We may not have a Grand National winner on our hands, but we should have some good days out.

Monday 13th

Covering an England match is a three-day exercise, even when it's at Wembley. From a commentator's point of view, the hard work starts with the opposition. If they are a nation you have never seen before, you almost set up camp at their hotel for a couple of days, hoping to familiarise yourself with the names and faces. Even when it's a team like Switzerland, as in this case, it would be foolhardy to attempt the commentary without at least seeing them in training. People sometimes wonder whether all this is necessary – who would know or care if you get the Nigerian centre half and centre forward mixed up – but to adopt such a scornful attitude is rather like leaving the milkman short of money; one day you'll get found out.

Tuesday 14th

Having made contact with Roy Hodgson, the English coach to the Swiss team, it's across to Bisham Abbey for the announcement of the England team after training. When I first covered the national side in the early seventies, the media bandwagon had scarcely started rolling. There were a handful of newspapermen, perhaps two or three from radio and television. Now it's like a scrum. There are more cameras and microphones than players when the FA solemnly open the gates of the training ground at the appointed time. We normally see the last, light-hearted minutes of the training session, then Terry Venables and two or three players repair to a nearby building for what is now grandly called a 'media conference'. This merely means we ask fairly obvious questions and they respond with fairly guarded answers. It's difficult to make an international last a whole week, but that is the unenviable brief given to the leading newspaper writers by their sports editors. They need a 'new England angle' every day. Bearing in mind the match itself lasts only 90 minutes, it's a towering task which they approach with stout endurance. The squad assembled last Thursday night, and they will still be writing about England next Friday morning. By comparison, I'm starting to think the commentator's role is less daunting. All I really had to do was sit and listen, then check on the shirt numbers.

Wednesday 15th
Having said all of that, you know your words will be weighed carefully when you are covering an England game. There is little light or shade – we are either going to be billed as world beaters the following morning in the tabloids, or else some sort of vegetable. I kind of think that's why so many internationals at Wembley end in draws – in reality, England are neither one thing nor the other. And the opposition don't make judgement any easier. All too often they start brightly, settle for the privilege of playing at Wembley, use as many substitutes as possible and go home happy with a prestigious draw. The lack of competitive matches owing to our hosting the European Championship hasn't helped. Playing friendlies is like kissing your sister.

David Pleat is my co-commentator for this one, the BBC bedding him in for Euro 96 when we shall need another summariser besides our regular man, Trevor Brooking. The chemistry in the commentary box is quite important. You don't want to be talking across each other at the same time. Trevor knows from my mannerisms when to come in for a quick comment, otherwise he keeps his microphone on his lap. David holds it up to his face the whole time, so I'm not sure at first when he is going to speak. But when he does his words are carefully manicured. 'England tonight have turned over a polished Stone.' I'm not surprised at his eloquence – Pleat's sister writes television scripts and the family obviously have a nice turn of phrase.

Thursday 16th
Another college student called to see me today, wanting about fifteen minutes on his tape recorder about life in the media. I sometimes wonder what their lecturers make of some of the waffle commentators come out with. Mind you, with more university and college courses in broadcasting and journalism figuring in the curriculum, maybe there's a career there for some of us in our dotage. A school for commentators, perhaps?

I'm in a self-deprecating mood today because tonight I am speaking at a Round Table dinner in Barnet, and they will be expecting a string of anecdotes, howlers and malapropisms that cometh out of the mouths of commentators. You know the sort of thing: 'For those watching in black and white, Spurs are in the yellow shirts' (me); 'Watch out for the Africans in this race – they're the ones with the white tops and black bottoms' (David Coleman, allegedly); 'Here we are in the Holy Land of Israel – a real Mecca for tourists' (David Vine, definitely).

It's a charity dinner so they have agreed to make a donation to the Barnet Sunday League, which my old club Roving Reporters helped to start in the sixties and of which I am now president. The league recently lost about £6,000 owing to a misappropriation of funds, and we're trying to get it back on its feet financially.

Friday 17th
Having lived most of my life in north London, Spurs v. Arsenal matches are occasions to be savoured, and tomorrow the highlights of the north London derby will feature on *Match of the Day*. It gives me the chance to nail a couple of myths. No, I don't support Tottenham, and nor for that matter do I have any boyhood affection for Arsenal. The truth about my team will come out later. The Spurs rumour started in the late eighties, when the BBC lost the rights to League football to ITV for a four-year period, and the Tottenham commercial manager, Mike Rollo, asked me to present the club's telephone news service called 'Spursline'. It involved going to the training ground twice a week to interview the manager and players, which was good practice and kept my face in at a top club while my television work was largely restricted to FA Cup ties and internationals. As soon as Tottenham reached the FA Cup Final in 1991, I told Mike it would be invidious to continue – accusations of bias would prejudice my position as commentator at Wembley. As it turned out, nobody wrote to suggest my performance that day was slanted against Nottingham Forest. The only person who took umbrage was Paul Gascoigne, who seemed uneasy about some of my remarks over his injury. We had a minor rift at the first match of the following season, but later he apologised and I softened him up with a Newcastle United video. It's impossible not to like Gazza.

Anyway, back to today. I had a plan. Since both teams train not far from me, it seemed a good idea to see a few faces. Yes, I should know them, but I've still got Swiss names buzzing around my brain.

It was a bitterly cold morning, and after ten minutes watching Arsenal at London Colney I'd had enough. Players don't miss a thing. As I walked away with hunched shoulders, I knew there would be a few sarcastic remarks at White Hart Lane tomorrow.

Over at Mill Hill, Tottenham started and finished a little later, but seeing me shivering, Gerry Francis suggested I went in for a cup of tea. But it wasn't a wasted exercise – by checking on who was injured and who was in the squads, I came away with a fair idea of what the starting line-ups might be tomorrow.

Saturday 18th
It comes as a surprise to some people when I say that commentators get to a ground three or four hours before a match. They think you just turn up with the crowd, pick up a programme and start talking. I wish. Today I arrived at Tottenham mid-morning just as Clive Wilson failed a fitness test and Teddy Sheringham passed one. My method of preparation involves a chart stuck to a piece of cardboard on which I colour in the players' names and details. Like a race card, if you like. Late changes can be a pain, especially if there is a young substitute you have never heard of, so that's a good reason to get there early, as well as giving yourself a better chance of picking up and absorbing information. It can be a laborious process. Come three o'clock, the game comes and goes in a flash.

But at twenty to five, the most taxing part of my day is still to come. The next hour is sheer purgatory. With the brain still numb from 90 minutes of intense concentration, there are various other duties to be fulfilled. The first one is a succinct, on-the-whistle report for *Grandstand*, who usually want one minute and no more. There is no time to write anything, because often they cue over to me within seconds of my wrapping up the *Match of the Day* commentary. Funnily enough, with the adrenalin still pumping, it's not as difficult as it sounds. The trick, which I learned when I first went out with David Coleman, is to keep it simple. Goalscorers, sendings off, notable saves, outstanding personal performances; what else can you cram into 60 seconds?

Today it was Arsenal's first half and Spurs' second, a classic goal by Bergkamp answered by two from Sheringham and Armstrong. When I handed back to Steve Rider, the teleprinter was clattering away and my first instinct was to watch the rest of *Final Score*. No such luck. From my crow's nest high up in the East Stand – where the former Spurs chairman Irving Scholar designed the highest camera platform in the country until Blackburn found a way of beating it – I had to make a complicated journey to reach the far side of the ground where the winning manager, Gerry Francis, was waiting to be interviewed live for *Grandstand*. If they designed a handicap race for commentators, there are some great courses on Premiership grounds.

At Tottenham, a winding staircase rather like a fireman's ladder, takes one person at a time down to the upper tier level of the stand. At this point, the problem is getting through the crowd who are making their way down the normal stairways. Having reached the main concourse and found an exit which took us to the corner of the ground, we were forbidden to cross the pitch by the ground staff who were busy forking it. Quite how much damage my shoes would have done after Tony Adams had been tearing up and down for 90 minutes was not entirely clear, but rules are rules.

Round the track, clutching briefcase, and finally, breathless, harassed and dishevelled, I made it into the interview room where somebody put a microphone into my hand and Steve Rider announced that 'Gerry Francis is talking to John Motson'. Well, of course, I had a carefully considered list of questions in my mind, the whole interview nicely mapped out, the key incidents neatly packaged for delivery – hadn't I? Not really. I blurted out two or three questions – mostly statements just to get a quick reaction – and Francis, who is in the more thoughtful category of managers when faced with a microphone, made some sense of what we were doing. When he left the room, word came through that *Match of the Day* wanted four further interviews. Over the next half hour, Messrs Rioch, Merson, Sheringham and Armstrong all came in and did their bit.

Outside, there was a constant babble in the corridor as radio reporters grabbed the players they needed as they left the dressing room. My only contact with the outside world at this point is the producer whose voice is in my ear. When he says, 'That's a wrap', it's the best news I have all day.

One thing about working at these grounds for so many years is that you tend to know where the nearest watering hole is. At Tottenham, the best bet is the sponsors' lounge, where some of the players go to collect 'Man of the Match' awards. Tony Adams was clutching an alarm clock or a computer game or something, and asked me whether I had thawed out from the previous day. You have to have a laugh with players or else you come off second best all the time. I told him he's got to be careful – I saw him in the Spurs half today and it wasn't for a corner or a free kick.

Several players who were not picked today were there sipping lagers, looking thoroughly miserable. It's a well-paid, privileged life being a professional footballer, but it must be a lousy feeling not to be in the team.

It's a sharp reminder that if you are being paid for something you love doing, you wouldn't be without it. So as I drove home to watch the programme and spot where I should have done better, I really couldn't think of a better way to have spent this Saturday.

Sunday 19th
There are no days off at the moment. There was time in the morning to run ten miles in Bishop's Stortford – an out and back course – before settling down to turn my attention to Lyon, who play at Nottingham Forest in the UEFA Cup on Tuesday night. I have been sent a tape of their victory against Lazio in the previous round so that took precedence over today's generous portion of live games on television.

Monday 20th
Olympique Lyonaisse, to give them their full title, sound more like a circus act than a football club, and during training on Nottingham Forest's ground this evening, their goalkeeper, Pascal Olmeta, played the part of the clown. Fooling around during shooting practice, he landed awkwardly on his ankle and was carried off. His coach immediately phoned France to arrange for another goalkeeper to fly over in the morning. Lyon seemed to have brought half the town with them – just to the training. The touchline was thronged with people, but it turned out a lot of them were players' wives, radio reporters and journalists. The French invented the World Cup, the European Championship and the idea of European club competitions, so they tend to feel they can do as they like. The coach, Guy Stephan, was courteous and helpful, but won't name his team until tomorrow.

Tuesday 21st
Nobody was talking about football today. Princess Diana's interview on *Panorama* last night was the main topic of conversation as Nottingham Forest went through a light training session in the morning. Frank Clark, as straight a man as you will meet in football, gave me his line-up.

In the afternoon I went to the Lyon hotel and sat around for a couple of hours before Guy Stephan gave me his team just to get rid of me.

The match was uneventful until Forest scored a late goal from a penalty rebound. The French commentator said to me as he left the ground: 'You can bet your life it will be nil-nil in Lyon. There is no way we will score.'

Wednesday 22nd
Having done three matches in seven days, I am hopelessly behind on correspondence, returning messages and phone calls, and family life for that matter. It's only a month to Christmas but there's one present I need not worry about – Frederick will get a copy of the FIFA 96 computer game because Electronic Arts, for whom I did the commentary, have sent us the finished article. Ever since Frederick was two, he has supported Derby County, so we always order a few items from their club shop. It shows you the power of sponsorship. You buy your baby son a pencil case with a Ram on it, and he's a fan for life. Funnily enough, my late father was a Derby supporter too. Why did they miss a generation?

Thursday 23rd
Tom Watt sent me his new book this morning. For a fellow whose first football offering was called *The End* (the closing of the North Bank at Highbury), it seems to me he is only just beginning. This one is called *A Passion for the Game* and he has interviewed just about everybody from lords to laundry ladies. His style reminds me of Nick Hornby's in *Fever Pitch*, and it's no surprise to learn that they are good friends. Since acting is still his proper living, Tom will have a part in *Fever Pitch* when it goes on to the stage later this season. He is just about the most enthusiastic person I have ever met. If you ring him up and he's not there, his answerphone offers you about six alternative numbers, including his girlfriend's mobile. I have so far resisted the temptation to ring his girlfriend.

Today I had lunch with Pat Smith, the deputy chief executive of the Football Association, to discuss, among other things, the plans for Euro 96.

In the evening I spoke at the dinner Jimmy Hill organised at Fulham. There was only a small attendance but it's a club with a heart. Andy McCulloch, once of Sheffield Wednesday and other clubs, was in the audience. He and I finished late at night, trying to name the semi-final team he played in back in 1983. We only got nine players and I've promised to ring him in the morning when I've looked up the two others.

Friday 24th
Newcastle is the place to go just at present. They are storming ahead in the Premiership, and when I arrived at the airport, Billy the cab driver – who calls himself Noda 30 – is revving up for the first Championship since 1927.

I met up with the Channel 4 racing team and I nearly talked my way on to their programme. Andrew Franklin, the producer, is best advised to stick to guests who know something about racing . . . In between all this, I managed to locate Howard Wilkinson, who was a bit cagey as to whether Tomas Brolin would make his debut tomorrow. 'He'll be involved,' said Howard, when he rang back. I took that to mean he would be on the bench.

Saturday 25th
It was only eleven o'clock in the morning and Kevin Keegan was already out on the pitch. Not with his players, but with two athletes, Roger Black and John Regis. Keegan spent so long showing them round St James's Park that he almost missed the *Football Focus* interview. He was wearing a pair of sunglasses because he'd been warned that the preceding item was about David Ginola – currently being parodied for his shades. It was a clever ruse and worked on screen because nobody was expecting it. Not many people wear sunglasses in Newcastle in November.

His view of the Championship is getting clearer, however. Newcastle came from 1-0 down to win with two goals in a minute, one from Rob Lee – who Keegan described on *Grandstand* as the best player in the country just now.

Sunday 26th
This is an opinion which had obviously registered with Terry Venables, who I bumped into at the airport after the game. On

the flight back yesterday, the stewardess gave Terry the front row to himself, whereupon he studiously took out a pen and a pad of paper. On the other side of the aisle, Neil Harman of the *Daily Mail* and I wondered if he was picking the next England squad. (Or maybe he was preparing his next statement to counter all the rumours and allegations he has to put up with.) Either way, it didn't seem to be getting him down. Behind us, Steve Curry of the *Daily Express* was transcribing the interviews he had recorded after the match. When he took off his headphones, he told me the *Evening Standard* magazine the previous night had dressed yours truly up as a warrior with a spear, under the headline: 'No more Mr Nice Guy.' Apparently I have come back to the microphone with a much more critical attitude and am now not afraid to put the boot in. Watch it Terry, I might have grabbed that piece of paper when we got off the plane.

Monday 27th
Seven years ago, it fell to me to be commentating live on *Grandstand* when 96 football supporters lost their lives in the Hillsborough disaster. There is no need to add to the pain and suffering of those bereaved relatives here, except to say that I had a good view of the Leppings Lane end from my commentary position and made my observations known both to Lord Justice Taylor's inquiry and the inquest on the victims. One of them was sixteen-year-old Kester Ball, a St Albans schoolboy whose parents have since become friends of our family. Roger Ball, Kester's father, was carried unconscious out of the ground and woke up to find he had lost a son. After Kester's memorial service, Roger and I decided, along with a banking friend of his called Mike Hide, that we would cement our friendship by meeting for lunch two or three times a year. The pre-Christmas venue is always the Windows of the World restaurant on the top floor of the London Hilton in Park Lane. It has the advantage of an unrivalled view across the capital, besides which you are allowed to drink as much wine as you want for an inclusive price – after which, trying to pick out the floodlights of different football grounds becomes slightly more difficult.

Tuesday 28th
Yesterday's conviviality was put firmly into perspective when I visited Brian Pitts at Middlesex Hospital today. He is very poorly again. My former *Barnet Press* colleague Roger Jones,

a lifelong friend of Brian's, found his condition very upsetting. But Brian's spirit is still strong and he talked with great clarity about watching the 1970 World Cup from Mexico.

Wednesday 29th
Commentators and reporters may be the mouthpiece of the BBC sports department, but its real heroes are those whose work behind the scenes make the programmes possible.

Up to a hundred people are involved, for example, in putting *Match of the Day* on the air each Saturday – a team of 30 or so at each of the two grounds where the featured matches are being played, and at least as many again back in the studio and the video-tape area.

The planning for this coming Saturday started in earnest today. Editors, producers, engineers, production assistants and secretaries all have an important part to play. If there is a weak link in the chain, the programme suffers.

The standards were set by those pioneers who got television sport off and running back in the 1950s, and those of us who joined later were keenly aware of the tradition of a department whose output enhanced the BBC's reputation worldwide.

Strangely enough, we don't have that many pep talks or debriefing sessions. Everybody knows his or her responsibility, and the self-motivation comes from knowing that the competition is getting hotter all the time.

Thursday 30th
As a result of that continuity within the department, promotion normally comes from the BBC's ranks. Just recently, two senior men have been appointed to new positions. After eight years as editor of *Match of the Day* and *Sportsnight*, Brian Barwick took overall responsibility for the day-to-day running of the department under the title Head of Production. Niall Sloane, who had been his assistant, was promptly promoted to editor. Both began their careers as newspaper journalists and are charged with supervising the editorial edge that goes with the highly technical business of television output.

A few of our number have moved on to other channels from time to time, but by and large the BBC has managed to train its own and keep them.

Later next year I will mark 25 years with the outfit, but there are plenty of people in the building who have been there longer.

DECEMBER
1995

Friday 1st

I was supposed to have some new visiting cards delivered today, but somewhere along the way somebody left them in a taxi – which probably means about 400 people in London have now acquired my address and telephone number. At first I thought it was a hoax, because two years ago Noel Edmonds got me bang to rights in a taxi for his 'Gotcha' series. A policeman stepped into the road, assumed control of the cab which was carrying me to what proved to be a fictitious appointment, and told me we had to turn round and chase a villain who was armed and carrying stolen goods. We nipped in and out of side roads, car washes and supermarket car parks – with me getting more and more agitated. All this, of course, was being recorded. Eventually, we turned into a disused airfield where the car in front began to perform all sorts of weird manoeuvres. The actor/policeman got out of the cab, gave me his walkie-talkie, and asked me to describe the action in detail to his headquarters while he went to apprehend the offender. So they got me doing a commentary, didn't they? 'And the policeman is approaching the car now, but what's going on? It's reversing at about twenty miles an hour ...' Ultimately, Noel got out of the car and presented me with the 'Gotcha' trophy.

And now you are wondering why you never saw this episode on television. Well, sadly for the programme, a sound fault in the taxi meant that my voice was not recorded, and so they had to scrap the item.

But Edmonds swore he would get me again. And he will.

Saturday 2nd

This is what Terry Venables calls 'slap round the face time'. Just when things are jogging along nicely, somebody up there decides to even it up. The rumours became fact today when it was announced that the Football Association contract for live FA Cup ties – including the final – would go to ITV from the start of the 1997–98 season. From the BBC's point of view, it will mean the end of half a century of tradition, and it will also mean they will lose the right to cover England's matches at Wembley. The mood among those who work for the corporation is more one of sadness than anger. Nothing, it seems, matters more than money, and everybody knows that in trying to compete with the funds available to other channels, the BBC is fighting with one arm tied behind its back. Added to which, although sport provides something like 22 per cent of the output, the licence fee also has to be spread across other priorities on which the BBC has built a reputation for high quality, public service broadcasting – like news and current affairs, light entertainment and drama.

At Queens Park Rangers today, their hospitable chairman Peter Ellis expressed the widely held view that more and more sport would inevitably drift the way of satellite and cable television. And a few commentators too, he added wryly. I told him the BBC might be two goals down, but we're not out of the game yet. Tonight, an audience of around five million will watch *Match of the Day* at eleven o'clock.

Monday 4th
Staying with that theme, it is to the BBC that the FA turned in asking for a special programme tonight in which to make the draw for the third round of the FA Cup. Everybody agreed last season that the draw needed to be modernised a little for television purposes, so it was made in front of an invited audience by Terry Venables and Denis Law. Trevor Brooking and I weren't there, because we had flown to France for the second leg of Lyon v. Nottingham Forest, but I made a minor contribution by locating the pair of former Hereford heroes, Ronnie Radford and Ricky George, who made the third round headlines nearly 25 years ago.

Tuesday 5th
The French commentator was right at Nottingham. Lyon failed to breach a tight Forest defence and had a man sent off near the end. These off the ball incidents can be a commentator's nightmare. Twice in my career, on overseas grounds where my view has been unclear, a player has been dismissed and I have

not actually realised until he has left the field. On this occasion, I noticed Colin Cooper had fallen to the ground before a free kick had been taken, and Trevor and our producer, Ken Burton, spotted the referee flashing his red card. That sort of teamwork means we can make sense of the incident, although when I had a drink later with the Forest chairman, Fred Reacher, he said quite a few people on his side of the ground never realised a man had been sent off.

Wednesday 6th
Returning to London, the thought of Christmas recurred, and I found a couple of hours to do some shopping. My wife Annie organises the presents for everybody else – just as she organises everything else outside my working life – but I made the annual pilgrimage to W. H. Smith and Boots etc. to buy hers. We are great believers in lots of small gifts rather than one, large expensive one. It means you have more parcels to open on Christmas Day. Childhood habits die hard, thank goodness.

Thursday 7th
Another BBC department is making a documentary about the 1988 FA Cup Final between Wimbledon and Liverpool. They are gathering the thoughts and recollections of all those in- volved for a series about sporting dramas. What made it a different Cup Final for me – apart from the shock result – was that it was the only time I ever finished up in the winners' dressing room. Usually I stay away from all that fuss after completing an exhausting two hours at the microphone, but that day Desmond Lynam grabbed me, pushed me through the crowds in Wembley's corridors, and hammered on the door. We were both welcomed in by Bobby Gould, and I still have the photograph, taken at ten past five, of Lynam, Vinnie Jones and myself holding the FA Cup. I still don't know to this day quite how or why that happened, but then Liverpool haven't worked out what happened that afternoon either.

Friday 8th
I went to Chelsea's training ground at Harlington to interview Ruud Gullit about the Holland match. He said it was too cold to talk outside, so we found a gym that was unoccupied. What Ruud wants, Ruud gets, especially as he is perfectly capable of saying 'no' in four languages.

MOTTY'S DIARY

Two days to go to the BBC's prestigious *Sports Review of the Year* programme, when the viewers' choice of sports personality is announced and we look back over the events of 1995. My task today was to pre-record a short football sequence, which was difficult to write because there is not much room for words between the action. Nobody in our office is allowed a clue as to how the voting is going, but the smart money is on Frank Bruno.

Saturday 9th
Having just finished the Forest tie, and with the Ireland v. Holland play-off coming up next Wednesday, I was afforded the luxury of a Saturday off today. High time I went to Barnet to see my local team, who were playing Bury. The two chairmen, Tony Kleanthous and Terry Robinson, are worried about the forthcoming Endsleigh League extraordinary general meeting and the threat of a First Division breakaway. That would almost certainly mean part-time football for Division Three. Terry is a big, bluff northerner who calls a spade a spade. We put football aside for a moment to discuss the dreadful stabbing of the London headmaster, Philip Lawrence, who was killed when he tried to protect a boy from a gang who were attacking him. When you read about the murders, rapes and drug-related offences in the papers every day, it makes you wonder about a government that came to power (Terry interrupted me here to finish the sentence) 'on a mandate of law and order'.

Sunday 10th
They were wrong. Jonathan Edwards got the vote as BBC Sports Personality of the Year, with Frank Bruno second. The 600-strong audience in the Queen Elizabeth Centre at Westminster seemed delighted with the outcome. They included a galaxy of sports stars from far and wide, officials and administrators, managers and coaches, plus a few BBC top brass past and present. It was quite a night, but with the week coming up in football, not a bad idea to leave early.

Monday 11th
My agent John Hockey had his Christmas party today, with a lot of television friends present, but my mind was not fully there. Brian Pitts has died and his widow Katherine has asked me to speak at his funeral tomorrow – Brian was 49.

Tuesday 12th
Dutch television have kindly sent me a tape of Holland's previous match against Norway. Without it, I would have been lost, because Brian's funeral meant I would probably miss the Dutch training tonight. His family were magnificently strong at the crematorium, and there was a strong BBC presence at what was a short, appropriate service.

When I got to Heathrow, the previous shuttle had been delayed so I got an earlier flight than expected, arriving at Anfield just in time to see the Dutch players file out one by one.

Next, a fast car to the Ireland Hotel at Chester, taking in on the way the radio coverage of England v. Portugal at Wembley and the World Cup draw made in Paris. There was almost too much to absorb, but Jack Charlton was in an affable mood and there was quite a gathering around him at the bar until the early hours of the morning. At times like this, characters from the past tend to drift back into your life like old movie stars. Tony Toms, who was Jack's physiotherapist at Sheffield Wednesday, hasn't changed since I last saw him fifteen years ago. But I refused to shake hands with him. The last time that happened, he crushed three of my fingers, and it's safer to buy him a Bacardi and coke.

Wednesday 13th
Seeing those Dutch players fleetingly was a blessing, because in the first half Holland contrived to have two players both with number six on their shirts. It wouldn't have surprised me to discover they had an extra *man* on the pitch, so comprehensively did they out-pass the Irish. There was no need for the 'sudden death' or 'golden goal' to come into play. Patrick Kluivert's two goals settled the game, and from what he was saying at about two o'clock this morning in the bar, Jack Charlton's future as well.

Thursday 14th
Today was Frederick's school play, which is a highlight of their term at Killigrew. It means his dad had to miss the *Match of the Day* lunch, but in a week like this the family has got to come first. He had a speaking part which went off exceedingly well. As Anne is chairman of the governors, we had to sit on the front row, so I couldn't be seen to doze off.

Friday 15th

Getting this close to Christmas you keep your fingers crossed for a London match, and boy, have I got lucky. Arsenal v. Chelsea fits very nicely into the agenda and from where we live I can just about shout across the garden fence to ask Bruce Rioch his team. No Bergkamp, injured on Wednesday, but no Gullit for Chelsea either. Still, you know the atmosphere at a London derby will carry you along, so there was time to attend a lunch at the Cafe Royal given by Pembury Leisure, a corporate hospitality company. Sue Besser, their managing director, had booked a conjurer, who started by masquerading as a safety officer and telling everybody they had to leave the room owing to fire precautions. Some people's sense of humour takes a bit of sharing, but it was a great lunch.

Saturday 16th

It was so crowded on the camera platform at Arsenal today, I thought one of us was going to fall off. More and more overseas commentators are coming in their midwinter break to cover English matches. Chelsea played like Holland for about an hour – some of their passing was that good – but Lee Dixon dug out a last-minute equaliser for Arsenal. It was what I call a perfect 'highlights' match. It looked a cracking game at about 25 minutes – another reminder that not everything has to be 'live'.

But the most nerve-wracking part of the day came later. Every year, a solicitor friend of mine, Dave Aumayer, organises a dinner at which ten of us from different professions have to forecast the winners of leading sporting events in the coming year. The FA Cup, County Championship, Wimbledon, and so on. The fact that I have won the wooden spoon six years out of seven is a source of great amusement to the others, although this year I avoided it by one point. You should try this idea on your friends: it's amazing how good or bad some predictions look a year later.

Sunday 17th

Desmond Lynam and Gary Lineker picked me up in their chauffeur-driven car at a rendezvous just off the M1, to go to Birmingham for the European Championship draw. They were both working. I was just going to watch and be a nuisance.

It was quite early, and we were all working yesterday, so the conversation was slow until we got past Newport Pagnell. The papers have been saying that UEFA will keep England and Scotland apart, but Lynam, who is more meticulous than his 'laid-back' image suggests, was anxious to nail that before the programme.

Gary is enjoying his presentation work in the studio and has no ambition to be a commentator (that's a relief), because for one thing, he would find it hard to get over-excited when somebody scores. Well, you would, wouldn't you, when you've done it more than 300 times yourself.

I sat next to Barry Davies who was commentating live as the draw was made, while Lynam and Lineker worked the studio. When you are not directly involved, you marvel at how smoothly the operation seems to go. On the way back, there was a big hold-up because of an accident on the M1. Lineker and Lynam put the blame firmly on me. If they hadn't had to drop me off, they would have gone on the M40.

Monday 18th
It was the Ricky George lunch in Camden Town today. All our invited guests managed to make it, and a good time was had by all – at least, that's what the size of the bill suggested. I'm thinking of taking some shares in the Camden Brasserie – the owners are big Uruguay supporters and every time I've been there John Spencer's dad has been mending a door frame or something. Funny how you meet people.

Tuesday 19th
This is the week of Christmas lunches, and today's was an annual event too. Four editors of *Match of the Day* past and present – Mike Murphy, Bob Abrahams, Brian Barwick and Niall Sloane – got into the habit of taking Terry Venables out at Christmas, and even though Terry left us after the *Panorama* business to work for ITV, the 'Gentlemen's Lunch' tradition has been upheld. This year it's the turn of Ray Stubbs and myself to play host, so we invited Brendan Foster as this year's 'Special Guest' and chose a favourite Italian of Terry's, 'Il Falcionere' in the Old Brompton Road. The wine and conversation flowed freely, and everybody knew they could talk off the record without being called to order. I advanced a theory that all FA Cup replays should be abolished this season, so that the England team can play in January and February. We could

introduce the 'sudden death' in extra time at the end of the first match. The clubs would not stand for it, of course, and it's too late now for the FA machinery to change the rules, but it seems ridiculous to me that in the season of Euro 96, where England's success is so paramount to the future of the game, Terry's team will not play between December and March. Can you imagine that happening in any other country? They all shook their heads. I'm not sure whether they agreed with me, or whether I'd bored them rigid.

Wednesday 20th
I told you there was something about me and taxis, didn't I? There I was, taking police advice and leaving my car at home, travelling through Mayfair on my way to a lunch in Victoria, when a woman went through a red light at about 35 mph and crashed into the back of our cab. A few feet the other way and she would have come through the back door. As it was, I finished up on the floor with my back in a spasm and my right ankle throbbing. Luckily, as they got me out, that was the extent of the damage to the passenger, but the cab was a sorry mess. A write-off, I shouldn't wonder. The woman in the car endeared herself to her insurance company by admitting it was entirely her fault for going through the red light. People started to call for the police. I decided discretion was the better part of delay, and gave the taxi driver my name and address. Another cab cruised by and I jumped in, assuming lightning doesn't strike twice. Not at midday in the middle of London, anyway.

I still felt shaken when I reached the restaurant, where Derek Hunt, the MFI chieftain, was entertaining just about everybody from his travel agent to his tailor with lots of others in between.

The only legacy I had of the accident was a broken mobile phone, but on the way back through the streets of London, I stumbled upon a cellular communications shop and the guy replaced the aerial for £20. The phone is working again. As Jimmy Hill says: 'Always get a plus out of a minus.'

Thursday 21st
Will Wyatt, managing director of BBC Television, invited some of us for a Christmas drink in his sixth-floor suite at Television Centre. It was a rare chance to meet Peter O'Sullevan and to marvel again at how he calls those horses with unerring accuracy in his late seventies. There's precious little chance of

my lasting that long but it's a wonderful tribute to him. Peter took more than polite interest in my connection with Summit Else, and assured me, 'You'll have lots of fun.'

We certainly used to do that when the commentators' football team was kicking and screaming a few years ago. Now, we play only once or twice a year, but the lads still get together for a Christmas function at Highbury, within a few hundred yards of the Arsenal ground where once upon a time a few of us used to be allowed to train on a Thursday evening. Our base was the Bank of Friendship in Blackstock Road, and Jim Rosenthal and Alan Parry were already there when I arrived. Later we repaired to Parks Restaurant across the road, and returned to the pub later. Although we work for different channels now, we all came from the same radio background so there's a warm camaraderie between us.

Friday 22nd
The week has caught up with me, so I came home early last night, but apparently some of the others went to a karaoke bar and Alan got the Mike Atherton award for twelve hours at the crease. Or in his case, at the bar.

A pre-Christmas haircut is a sure-fire way of returning to normality, and in this respect I am no longer a creature of habit. I went to a barber near Finchley Central Station for over twenty years of my life, but now the owner has retired and distance means it is harder to get there.

The first team captain of my old Sunday side, Ian Cross, has persuaded me to put what remains of my hair into his capable hands at The Cutting Room in Harpenden. The streets were packed with last-minute shoppers but every year I have the growing feeling that we are rapidly losing the true meaning of Christmas.

So it was nice to make a traditional family start to the season of goodwill by taking Annie and Frederick to the Barbican to see the Royal Shakespeare Company's version of Dickens' *Christmas Carol*, adapted by John Mortimer. We don't go to the theatre or cinema as a family as often as I would like, but the Christmas outing (last year we saw *Wind in the Willows* at the National Theatre) and the summer trip to the open-air theatre in Regents Park (*The Music Man*) are events I much look forward to.

Most weekends when I am working, my wife and son find

themselves something worthwhile to go and see. Hopefully, it means Frederick's edification will be somewhat wider than a football pitch.

Saturday 23rd
Went to Birmingham to watch Tranmere Rovers, whose FA Cup tie against Queens Park Rangers I shall be covering in two weeks' time. With bad weather forecast for the holiday period, this might be my only chance to see them play.

I had not seen the refurbished St Andrew's before, neither had I met the Birmingham chairman, David Sullivan. He didn't appear before the match or at half-time, and I was sipping tea with the Tranmere directors after the game when suddenly the doors of the 'Presidential Suite' opened and Sullivan made a grand entrance flanked by his two co-presidents, the Gold brothers. He is quite a small man, and it was rather like Elton John suddenly appearing on stage protected by two minders. They were all wearing bright silver badges saying BCFC on them. Quite dramatic. David confessed that Birmingham have got 52 professionals on their books but only about eight of them live in the Midlands – the rest of Barry Fry's signings are scattered far and wide. I asked him how they managed to get everybody together for training. 'I don't think we train all that often,' he replied. 'We're always playing matches.'

On the way out, I caught sight of Barry Fry driving through the gates with a Discovery vehicle full of kids. I knew Barry well when he was at Barnet. He's got nearly as many children as he has players. One of his ex-Barnet men, Jonathan Hunt, scored the only goal today, but Tranmere were a bit unlucky. John Aldridge actually missed a good chance, which is like saying Christmas might not happen this year.

Sunday 24th/Monday 25th
More and more people of my generation seem to be spending Christmas at home. When you are travelling most of the year, and you see the weather conditions and the roads at holiday time, the family fireside seems the best bet.

Anne's sister and her family joined us, together with Anne's mother, and we had an old-fashioned Christmas – loads of presents by the tree with the adults doing most of the squealing as they were opened. I got a Rod Stewart cassette for the car, which dates me precisely, and the latest Dick Francis novel *Come to Grief*, which I very nearly did in that taxi last week.

Tuesday 26th

Boxing Day morning in the East End of London, and as I got close to the West Ham ground I couldn't understand why so many people were walking the other way. Then it occurred to me that the match must have been called off. It was a late decision by the referee and I feel sorry for all those fans who came down from Coventry.

On the radio, Ron Jones was saying how bad the pitch is at Southampton, even though they were playing there. It will be a sad day if the West Hams and Southamptons leave the Premiership – both are homely, civilised clubs – but I do feel that under-soil heating should be mandatory in the top League. The view is supported when Aston Villa, one of our biggest clubs, had to call off their game against Liverpool at the last minute.

Wednesday 27th

No doubt about the biggest match of the season so far going ahead. Under-soil heating at Old Trafford gave Manchester United the chance to close the gap on Newcastle with a 2-0 victory, and Sky Sports the opportunity to achieve, presumably, one of their biggest football audiences so far.

Not much else happened. All the racing fell victim to the weather, the King George at Kempton and the Welsh Grand National at Chepstow included. I might have gone there today – Earth Summit was due to run.

Thursday 28th

Back to the BBC where a skeleton staff were starting to think about Saturday's *Match of the Day*. I am scheduled to cover West Ham v. Newcastle but if the Upton Park pitch does not recover, we shall probably switch to Chelsea v. Liverpool. It's an unsettling time for commentators. You don't want to start preparing for one match, only to have to tear it up and begin all over again. London is an eerie place in this phoney period between Christmas and New Year. The lights are on in some of the pubs but they are not open. Most businesses have closed down until the New Year and the way the weather is closing in, the football programme is likely to be decimated. So once again the old chestnut comes up – should we close down for a winter break, as some other European countries do?

Friday 29th
I don't think we should. Not just for the old-fashioned reasons
about football being a winter game, but more because you
cannot legislate for when the bad weather will come; and if it
doesn't, hundreds of thousands of supporters want their football to be part of the Christmas and New Year schedule. You
only have to look at the crowds on Boxing Days past to know
there is a demand, and clubs must meet that. I am far more
concerned about the way football is creeping further and
further into the summer. That's when we need a proper break
– between seasons, when the players can have a longer rest and
everybody can recharge the batteries. Be gone with you, Inter-
Toto Cup, and let's get the start of the Premiership programme
put back to the start of September, like they do in Italy.

Saturday 30th
If we shut down for the winter, we would miss games like the
one at Stamford Bridge today. This might be the moment to
admit that in my teens I was a Chelsea season-ticket holder. I
remember sitting in the 'old' North Stand on the corner and
seeing a seventeen-year-old Jimmy Greaves score four goals
against Portsmouth on Christmas morning. He couldn't have
done that in a midwinter break either. Today I sat in the
camera gantry above the West Stand. The stadium was full –
there are few grounds better for atmosphere on the big
occasion.

Chelsea and Liverpool responded with a stirring 2-2 draw. I
was reading an article by Maureen Lipman in one of the
Sunday magazines last week, in which she said that as an
actress, she is happy with about one stage performance in forty
– when nothing goes badly wrong. I thought we had hit the
jackpot today, until we got down to the interview room after
the match. The camera brought in from the cold steamed up
immediately, and Glenn Hoddle's appearance on *Grandstand*
was ghostly to say the least. Then John Barnes came in for a
Match of the Day interview and the lens steamed up again. He
went away for a drink, we changed the lens, and when he
returned the same thing happened again. One of those technical
hitches nobody can do anything about.

Finally, we went outside into the players' tunnel where the
wind was almost cutting in half the journalists waiting for a
word from Chelsea's two-goal marksman John Spencer. Event-

ually, three more interviews were secured. Colin Hutchinson, Chelsea's managing director, took pity on the commentator at this point and invited him in for a warming drink.

I liked John Barnes's parting comment as he got on the coach. 'It's a good job I was wearing a light suit. Otherwise the camera wouldn't have seen me at all.'

Sunday 31st
Having worked yesterday, I am off tomorrow. The editor shared the matches out between the commentators this weekend, to give everybody a chance to enjoy some part of the New Year celebrations. We invited a few neighbours and old friends over, including BBC reporter Bill Hamilton, with whom I once shared a flat in our early radio days. Bill has since brought the plight of deserted Albanian children to the heart of the nation, and has spent much of this year on special VE Day and VJ Day assignments. He is also a class one referee and keeps a whistle in his pocket at all times. This was very handy when a BBC news crew had to land their helicopter on a football pitch in Albania. When they returned some hours later, the helicopter was still in the centre-circle but 22 impatient players had been waiting over half an hour to start a League match. The crowd were understandably restless. Bill blew his whistle to draw their attention, explained what had happened to the two captains and referee, jumped in the helicopter with his camera crew and as they took off, blew his whistle again to start the match. However, he kept his whistle in his pocket at midnight tonight. We settled for the chimes of Big Ben instead.

JANUARY
1996

Monday 1st
European Championship year starts with the weather getting warmer and part of the Bank Holiday football programme rescued. With no commentary to do, it was a day for sitting with the radio – and later in front of the television – catching up with news from all the grounds. Many clubs in the Premiership were playing for the fourth time over the holiday period, and there's a lot to keep pace with before the FA Cup takes over next weekend. My sympathy is with the newspaper boys – the only day without papers was Christmas Day, and they must have been flat out with publication on Christmas Eve, Boxing Day, New Year's Eve and New Year's Day. Whether we as readers want or need all those newspapers is another matter.

As far as *Match of the Day* is concerned, Stan Collymore inspired a revival against his old club and Liverpool came from 2-0 down to beat Nottingham Forest 4-2.

One of the reasons why the Sky/BBC partnership has worked so well is days like this. Sky Sports had two live games – at Middlesbrough and Tottenham – but *Match of the Day* could show highlights of both, together with the Liverpool match at the end of the evening. Soon we shall know what will happen to the Premiership television contract when it expires at the end of next season. Fingers are being crossed at the BBC that *Match of the Day* survives.

Tuesday 2nd
This is the day the nation is supposedly back at work after the extended Christmas and New Year holiday, but there was nothing on the roads, the schools have not yet gone back, and even parking in London was easy. A few belated Christmas cards were in my post tray at the BBC, mostly from people who got one from me and then had a conscience.

79

From the BBC Television Centre at White City, it was a comfortable stroll round the corner to watch Queens Park Rangers play Chelsea. Ken Bates, whose waspish sense of humour has usually found me an easy target, made a point of telling me he thinks my commentary style has improved since I came back. 'More rounded,' was his exact phrase. Compliments don't come commentators' way very often – not in this direction anyway – so it has to go down as a plus.

The Rangers' chairman, Peter Ellis, was bemoaning the gap that is now developing between the very rich and not-so-rich within the Premiership. I suggested that the only way Queens Park Rangers can match Manchester United in a financial sense is to win this week's national lottery, where the top prize has soared to £40 million. I ask you, who needs that much money? It would be far too sensible, I suppose, to have 40 prizes of one million each, or would that detract from the sheer fantasy angle which drives the ticket sales? It reminds me of the parable of the Rich Young Ruler, and I'm not talking about Richard Thompson, the QPR owner. I'm covering their Cup tie at Tranmere next Saturday, and wondering whether I will ever be able to spot the red numbers on the back of their hooped shirts. Maybe my eyes are not what they were. I've decided to book in for my annual check-up with the specialist: even with my glasses on I am struggling to pick out the players on the far side. And this at Rangers' ground, where you are relatively close to the pitch.

Wednesday 3rd
I always back four teams for the FA Cup, usually after a friendly haggle with my contacts at Ladbrokes over the prices! Last year, Everton at 25 to 1 helped to pay for the summer holiday. This year, I can't see an outsider winning at Wembley in May. In the end, playing safe I backed Liverpool, Tottenham, Aston Villa and Sheffield Wednesday – four clubs who won't win the Premiership but who are playing well enough to be among the prizes elsewhere. Chelsea are having a good run, but one of my wing mirrors got broken when I went there on Saturday, and that's supposed to bring bad luck, isn't it?

Thursday 4th
As I thought, the other nations taking part in the European Championship finals are getting their act together. *France Football*, acknowledged as the best magazine of its kind in the

world, reveals that the French have already arranged a January friendly against Portugal, and another in February against Greece. Here, Terry Venables has managed to organise two 'get-togethers' with his squad, but England won't play again until 27 March. Sometimes I think we get the international team we deserve.

Talking of football magazines, Bryon Butler of the *Daily Telegraph* – my favourite writer – has been into his local branch of W. H. Smith and counted no fewer than 30 different ones on the shelf. All have their place and are mostly well-produced with bags of colour, but somehow in this country we have never had the equivalent to *France Football*. It is utterly comprehensive and its appeal lies in the adult market.

Friday 5th
The Prime Minister was on the BBC's *Breakfast Time* this morning, discussing sporting issues with Rob Bonnet. The subject of sport on television came up, and Rob raised the hot potato of terrestrial as opposed to satellite. Is it fair that so many viewers will now be denied access to major events because they cannot afford (or choose not) to subscribe to satellite or cable? Mr Major played his way out of defence very cleverly. The matter was under discussion, he said, and nothing further would be said until those debating the Broadcasting Bill had completed their findings. It made one wonder whether there was half a chance that his government, with an election maybe a year away, might find a new way of protecting the main events or else giving the BBC access to outside funding. It reminded me of the time the Prime Minister side-stepped me in our only face-to-face meeting, but he had to do so because it was in the toilet at Chelsea and there wasn't that much room. He was very chatty but it didn't seem quite the time to draw him into the politics of television sport. We both had other things on our minds, and he obviously believes in the sweeper system because a security man, or should I say an aide, was standing discreetly behind us. Still, it shows he is a football fan, and it was as near as I will ever get to power, standing in that toilet.

Saturday 6th
The King George VI Tripleprint Chase, postponed at Kempton Park on Boxing Day, was run today instead at Sandown, and I

was content to back the winner, One Man, at 3 to 1. My returns paled slightly in comparison to the prize in the national lottery. Imagine what BBC Sport could do with that kind of money.

The man fighting our corner, Jonathan Martin, was the subject of a pertinent interview in this morning's *Daily Telegraph*. He described sport as a 'shared experience', but said it would not be that in the future if those without satellite television could not see great moments. I quote: 'The commercial channels are buying to secure ownership; they are not buying at market prices. They are paying high prices for things which are not always delivering high audiences. It's like *Reader's Digest* – as long as they're getting the books, it doesn't matter whether they read them or not.' Powerful stuff from the Head of Sport, and good to hear terrestrial television stated its case.

Democratic as ever, *Match of the Day* visited Stoke, Plymouth and Tranmere in the third round of the FA Cup, which gave me the chance to meet up again with one of my favourite characters, John Aldridge. Before the game, which Tranmere lost 2-0, John came out of the dressing room half-naked to debate with me in the corridor about how many goals he had scored in his career. Various statisticians have come up with four or five different totals. We agreed to settle for 430 – roughly correct and a nice round figure. As I said to him, who's going to argue? Only someone crazy enough to count them all.

Sunday 7th

Ray Wilkins, still playing in his 40th year, obviously knows a thing or two about keeping fit, and yesterday he had a gentle dig at this commentator for putting on a few pounds over the holiday period. This spurred me into a slightly longer run this morning, interrupted only by a woman on horseback who asked me whether it was a New Year resolution. It obviously looked like my first attempt on the roads.

The stopwatch doesn't lie, to my chagrin, but it certainly carries a degree of elasticity where our leading referees are concerned. In today's televised Cup ties, Leeds scored twice at Derby in what might generously be called stoppage time, and Newcastle equalised at Chelsea in what appeared to be the 94th minute. Sorry to raise it again, but why can't we all be told how long there is to go? The bad news for Terry Venables was that this tie, along with no fewer than fourteen others, has gone to a replay. Since these are still delayed for ten or eleven days – a police-motivated procedure after Hillsborough which is still in force – what price now a fully attended England get-together? Just to make sure we have enough football, the Coca-Cola quarter-finals are coming up this week, and there is every chance one or two of those will go to a second meeting as well. Meantime, the Premiership managers have started to make noises about the over-burdened fixture list. They want a month's break in January in future. Let's hope, if that comes about, that it forces the issue on the restructuring of the fixture list. If the bad weather had not relented this weekend, the season would be in a sorry mess. My Cup tips already *are* – Sheffield Wednesday lost at Charlton!

Monday 8th
As a commentator, I suppose you tend to take your voice for granted. Slightly dangerous, bearing in mind it's your main asset. I was always getting tonsilitis as a child, but my throat has served me well over the last 25 years. I have never taken much medication to protect it, and the only time I nearly missed a match because I was in danger of losing my voice, the Southampton physio, Don Taylor, made me a special gargle in the treatment room before the game at The Dell and saved the day. It was a few years ago now, but I remember Charlie George nearly falling off the treatment table with laughter.

The value of a decent, recognisable voice was brought to my notice in Soho this afternoon. Young and Rubicam, the advertising agency, asked me to help out with a pilot commercial for Sugar Puffs involving Kevin Keegan. When I came out of the studio, three or four people on mobile phones were standing in Wardour Street marking time. I gathered they are semi-resident West End 'voices' who hang around all day waiting for offers of work. It pays, apparently, to be on hand at short notice.

Whenever I go to that part of London, I can't help noticing how tatty it has become in the last few years. Oxford Street and the surrounding area should be part of London's pride, but it looks unkempt and dowdy. Behind the Soho façades, though, are dozens of little studios where videos and commercials get made. It's a multi-million pound business, and leading sporting personalities like Keegan get well paid for their identification with a well-known product. How much they paid the Honey Monster, I never found out.

Tuesday 9th

After-dinner speaking is not my forte, but it's a lucrative earner for some of my colleagues, who seem to have an endless supply of stories and jokes designed to captivate a boisterous audience at testimonial functions and such like. Lots of flattering invitations come my way, but I only accept those where I think I can cope in front of a live audience. That may sound strange coming from someone who effectively talks to five million people on a weekly basis, but it's different when you can see their faces and hear some of the ripostes. My speaking engagements tend to be more informal. Referees' societies, which most of my colleagues also support, are a good case in point. It is usually an informal evening which develops into a question and answer session. They always offer to pay your expenses, but this is one small way in which we can put something back into the grass roots of a game which, when all's said and done, has given commentators a living as well.

Those who claim to have heard me speak at functions should denote the subtle difference between the role of chairman – in which you merely introduce the speakers with a short comment or two – and guest speaker, where you are expected to bring the house down in merriment. The only exception I think I have made this season was for Jimmy Hill at Fulham, although today I accepted an invitation to talk to the Bromley branch of the Charlton Athletic Supporters' Club. As I saw my first game at Charlton and have a handful of shares in the club, it's the least I can do!

Wednesday 10th

While I was picking Frederick up from school, Terry Venables rang my car phone. He asked me to ring him back at Scribes West, but before I could do so, the FA had held a press conference and announced Venables' decision to quit after the European Championship. Had *Sportsnight* been returning this week rather than next, we would have had a hot story on our hands. However, ITV dropped lucky with Venables as their resident studio expert, since they were covering the Arsenal v. Newcastle Coca-Cola Cup tie live from Highbury tonight. Not that he added anything significant to his statement. Fred Venables, Terry's father, spoke on the radio and hinted that lack of support from the international committee, as much as forthcoming litigation, had been the reason for the decision.

Within hours, most of the leading candidates had said publicly they did not fancy the job. Well, they would, wouldn't they? On the grounds that the FA would strive for some sort of continuity, I expect them to talk to Bryan Robson, although he is in his first season as a Premiership manager.

Thursday 11th
Charlie Sale of the *Daily Express* rang to tell me I had been included in 'Who's Who'. I don't even remember filling in the form. But Charlie, who writes a provocative sports gossip column, was using that as a bit of a smokescreen – he wanted to know who is going to be commentating on the big matches for the BBC at the end of the season. I could tell him with a clear conscience that I honestly don't know, but he will write about it anyway, and says my trip down the Nile might have set me back in the pecking order. I should have told him it was research for the African Cup.

Friday 12th
When it was first selected, tomorrow's match between Tottenham and Manchester City looked a nice comfortable assignment. Now it has become a minefield in terms of events off the field. No sooner has the litigation between Alan Sugar and Terry Venables been cited among the reported reasons behind the England coach's resignation, than Gerry Francis is named as a candidate to succeed him. Then, this afternoon, UEFA banned Spurs from Europe for a year because of their lukewarm approach to the Inter-Toto Cup. It all adds up to a spicy interview with Mr Sugar, if I can find him. The Tottenham chairman is usually accessible to the media through one of his henchmen, but today even they were hard to pin down. 'Fixing' interviews is the responsibility of the commentator, so it was with some relief that I made contact with Sugar's personal secretary at Amstrad, who turned out to be a football fan who watches *Match of the Day*. Frances was kind enough to contact her boss in Denmark, and when he flew back in the evening he rang me to say he will do the interview on all three subjects – but preferably after the match, not before. Fear of losing the subject altogether makes me nervous of trying to persuade him otherwise, but I'm feeling uneasy now, thinking that if we don't get to him before the game, somebody else will.

Saturday 13th

The papers were running the European ban as a lead story, so I made a point of getting to Tottenham earlier than usual. Mike Rollo, the commercial manager, and Nick Bouilli, the chief steward in the directors' car park, were standing outside the Bill Nicholson Suite, where some friends of mine were guests of the sponsors for lunch. They told me that the chairman was coming to the ground at lunchtime after all, to record a special message for the Spurs supporters to be broadcast on the giant video screen in the South Stand. I knew then that the interview couldn't wait until after the game, so I persuaded Claude Littner, the chief executive, to contact Alan Sugar on his car phone and ask him to appear live on *Football Focus*. He said he would think about it, but he didn't arrive at the ground until the programme was finishing. *Grandstand* were aware of the situation, and quickly found a special slot after the news. The interview was used again later in the afternoon, and then had a third outlet in *Match of the Day*. Sugar predicted that when the dust has settled, the European ban will be overturned and Terry Venables may be reappointed as the England coach. Two bold statements from a man who doesn't mess around.

In the box holders' lounge, I bumped into another of that breed – David Evans MP, the former Luton chairman. In a recent article I suggested he would make a suitable Minister of Sport. 'Wrong job, mate, what about chairman of the FA?' asked Evans in typically forthright fashion. I like his style. But somehow I think they might find him too radical for Lancaster Gate.

Sunday 14th

It's that Stephen Watson again. If he didn't settle the Championship with his November goal against Liverpool, he surely did when he got the winner (and only goal) at Coventry today. Keegan's team are nine points clear with a game in hand. The only people who can stop them now are Newcastle themselves.

Monday 15th

It is five months to the start of the European Championship, and the real work starts today. My first draft of the sixteen competing teams, their likely squads, and details of those players, is a laborious exercise designed to focus the mind and give me a tablecloth on which to spread more specific homework nearer the time. There are no short cuts when you are planning for a major tournament. Angus Loughran, 'Statto' from *Fantasy Football* rang to offer me a video of the forthcoming friendly between France and Portugal. It could be invaluable. Later this month, the BBC will announce the 'split' of matches with ITV, and will let me know which games are coming my way.

Tuesday 16th
The BBC programme *How Do They Do That?* is going to feature the FIFA 96 computer game that carries my commentary. Today, they were filming at Electronic Arts' headquarters at Langley, near Slough. It is a boffin's paradise – a network of computer experts testing a whole range of new games about to hit the market. It was the first time I had seen FIFA 96 in its final format. How they managed to condense my 18,000 recorded names and phrases into a sensible sequence is one of the great mysteries of modern technology. But they say the game is top of the charts so let's hope FIFA 97 comes my way.

Wednesday 17th
The annual appointment with the optical specialist. If only those wags in the crowd who shout 'get a new pair of glasses' to the commentator could have seen me. Peering into lights, charts and lenses with a squint in my right eye. The expert opinion is that the good news concerns my left eye. That has got better. The bad news is that the right eye is markedly worse than the left. Dangerous thing for a commentator to admit, especially at the office. So I settled for two new pairs of glasses and hope to hell I can still see the numbers on the Newcastle shirts. The truth of it is, I was struggling to read the menu without my glasses when Anne and I celebrated her birthday with lunch at the Cafe Royal. As London prices go, it's not terribly expensive. At least, it wasn't, until we decided to precede it with half an hour's shopping in Regent Street, designed for me to buy her a present. But I can't walk past Aquascutum without my cheque book making a guest appearance, and I finished up with two cashmere jumpers.

Frederick will be ten in a couple of weeks and I have organised a trip to Electronic Arts for him and his friends to see the computer games being tested for the market. That bit was easy. Trying to find pyjamas for boys is difficult. They all seem to have silly cartoons across the front or else look like ill-fitting tracksuits. There must be a market there for somebody – sensible pyjamas for ten year olds and above. Why I've got pyjamas on the brain I'm not sure – except I am one of those traditionalists who always wears them. Well, nearly always. Ricky George says he first met me in the sixties at a pyjama party in Barnet – but I was wearing a suit and tie.

Thursday 18th
Bryon Butler in his 'Talking Football' column in the *Daily Telegraph* has put his finger on the pulse again. Quote:

> The game is treading water in a sea of words and pictures, criticism and expertise, interviews and analysis, confessions and revelations, profiles and reports, exclusives and follow-ups.
>
> The line between fact and speculation is finer than ever, but the divide between watchers and watched seems greater than ever.
>
> The truth might be that football is now overheating to a point where self-combustion is a real danger. It is a big and pretty balloon which could be deflated by one stab from a small pin. Could high prices or high wages be a threat? Or over-exposure? Or rancorous publicity? Or worst of all, a return of hooliganism?
>
> If crowds began to fall again, as they did in the early eighties, the sound of deserting sponsors, advertisers and even television channels would be deafening. The house would be in danger of collapse.

In my view, that decline is not far away unless somebody puts the brakes on. But Bryon is a whimsical, well-balanced chap, and he finishes with the other point of view.

So much for the Doomsday scenario, an example of newspaper speculation of the most injurious kind. Please ignore it. Far more important is El Tel's successor, the battle for the Premiership, the feud between Wimbledon and referees, Sheffield United's injury problems, Oxford's away form, the plight of Torquay, and Yeovil's push for promotion in the ICIS Premier.

Saturday 3 p.m. Be there.

We will, Bryon, we will.

Friday 19th
The sales force of Virgin Publishing need a little lunchtime relief from their demanding motivational talks and videos. Bad luck on them. They got me. I was terribly nervous for some reason and sipped a vodka and tonic before going in to speak. Nicky the publicity director, frowned slightly and explained that the sales boys were restricted to water and orange. Most of them had had a few drinks the night before anyway, as it turns out, but just for the session I made my drink look like iced water.

They were happy to hear some of my well-worn broadcasting gags: 'It's Arsenal 0, Everton 1, and the longer it stays like that the more you've got to fancy Everton to win' (me); 'British hopes may be disappearing now' (Olympic canoeist upsidedown in the water – another Motson special); 'This Chinese high jumper has a chink in his armour' (definitely Stuart Storey); 'What can I say about Peter Shilton? Peter Shilton is Peter Shilton and he has been Peter Shilton since the year dot' (Bobby Robson in Mexico, 1986).

After this, the sales force were in the mood for some fun. A few pointed questions came out about life in the commentary box, and some good-natured banter ensued.

Then something unexpected happened. Bob from the northeast asked a question about my sheepskin coat (the one that made me look like a scarecrow in the snow at Wycombe), and I admitted it had seen better days. Worse still, the man in Hornchurch who used to make them to measure, and charges the likes of me about a third of the retail value, has moved into another business and hung up his skins.

At this point in the discussion, Nicky was trying to attract my attention. She's waving, winking, giving me sidelong glances like the ones the Princess of Wales used to give Charles in the early days, and basically cracking me up.

We adjourned for lunch, and to everybody's amazement, it turned out that Nicky's aunt makes . . . sheepskin coats. Well, she probably bakes cakes as well, and holds smashing dinner parties, and runs the local school fête, but as far as I'm concerned, it's the coats that win the day. I need a new one – and soon.

Saturday 20th
Today I should have been doing my 1,000th commentary for the BBC. Now, before you think only an anorak like me would

bother to count them, let me tell you how this came about. One of the plethora of football magazines competing for shelf space with *Loaded* and *Maxim* have asked me what souvenirs I keep of games I have covered. Like, do you have the programme, or your commentary notes, or your train ticket, or the club video? Well, the answer is no in every case. I have occasionally stuck a few bits and pieces in a scrapbook when I have done overseas trips, but the Egyptians wouldn't have had much to put in my tomb to help me commentate on the Afterlife League. But what I have done, thinking early on that my next game could be my last, is scribble down on a piece of paper the date and score of the matches I have covered. Occasionally it comes in helpful when somebody says, 'You've not been to our ground for ten years' – then you see you were there two seasons ago.

Anyway, the young buck from the magazine wanted me to pick a great match out of every hundred I had watched, and when I updated the list it came to 999. Not unique, by any means. Brian Moore and Barry Davies, who have been in the business longer than I have, would have exceeded that figure long ago. And the way Sky are going, Martin Tyler and Rob Hawthorne will soon be covering 1,000 matches a season, never mind in a career.

Anyway, it so happens I wasn't commentating today. They gave me a Saturday off to watch Reading, who we are covering in the FA Cup against Manchester United next Saturday. So the 1,000th game will have to wait, and who cares anyway?

Certainly not Uri Geller, a keen Reading supporter whose party piece with spoons meant I never got round to putting any sugar in my tea. Alex Ferguson was also there, spying on his FA Cup opponents. Our earlier misunderstanding was clearly forgotten. In fact, he told me Newcastle were signing Asprilla from Parma – the football grapevine must be working fast because I didn't see any mention of it in the morning papers.

A few of the Reading players, knowing we are taking the cameras next week, asked me how I liked their new-style shirts with big red numbers on the back. ITV's Brian Moore has done us all a favour by persuading the club to change the design so that the numbers can be seen against the blue and white hoops. Bless you, Brian, that will make my job a lot easier.

What was not easy was finding my way in and out of Reading. It is obviously a town that has set its heart on frustrating the motorist. I've made a pledge to leave earlier than usual next week.

Sunday 21st

The Fred Hughes Memorial Run is organised by St Albans Striders athletics club in memory of their former chairman who was killed while riding his bicycle to work. It is a ten-mile course round the lanes of Hertfordshire, or rather *up* the lanes, because you always seem to be struggling with an incline. This can be particularly galling after about seven miles, when you are reduced to a quick walk and find two or three young fillies in Striders tracksuits sweeping past you effortlessly while talking about how many Martinis they had last night. I could have done with one myself by the time we reached the last mile – even the finish was at the top of a hill. I shuffled apologetically over the line in 1 hour 26 minutes and out of habit went to the end of the roped-off area where they usually hand you a souvenir gift – an ashtray or a T-shirt or something. Not today, pal. 'Only if your number ends in seven,' said the figure in the yellow anorak. It was like trying to win the lottery.

Your temper is not too even after a run like this, so I made a less than civilised comment and sulked away to the car. My number was 28 and I had a good mind to write minus one underneath and go back. That's how small-minded I can be. Instead, I got the smell of roast beef and Yorkshire pudding and decided to settle for Sunday lunch and a restorative glass of red wine.

Monday 22nd

They say it's a sign of age when policemen start to look younger. In my case, it was when the optician, the hairdresser and the dentist all retired in the same month.

Trying to find a new dentist, especially, is a pain in the mouth. Those who come well recommended have no space for new patients; taking one on trust adds further discomfort to what is already a nerve-wracking experience; and trying to replace a lady who, in my case, has looked after my teeth splendidly for ten years and more is proving decidedly unsettling. As a child I had all manner of extractions and fillings, and the legacy of those days is the small plate in the top of my mouth to which two of my front teeth are connected. Avril – she who has retired – talked at length about the sophisticated (and expensive) bridge treatment that would render the plate redundant, but I've got so used to it that slipping it in and out is part of getting dressed. They have been all over the world, those false teeth. Indeed, they fell out during one particularly memorable moment of skill from Diego Maradona in Mexico in 1986. I had to rescue the errant plate from beneath the desk of the Dutch commentator alongside me.

The other embarrassing moment was in a restaurant at a Christmas party. To eat a steak without risking biting through the plastic, I sometimes take my teeth out and wrap them in a handkerchief. That day I had a bad cold, and I took out the wrong hanky to blow my nose and sent the teeth scudding across the floor. I never had the nerve to get down on my hands and knees among the diners to find them, and that meant digging out my 'spare' from a drawer in the bedroom.

Knowing how easily something of the sort could happen again, and not wanting to risk lisping my way through the next commentary, I need a new one making, and here at least my guide and mentor had not retired.

In fact, Mike Thornhill, who supports Queens Park Rangers and owns The Denture Laboratory in St Albans (repairs and copy dentures while-u-wait), is one of those guys who looks just the same while the rest of us get older.

Going to see Mike is like going to the dentist without the fear factor. He keeps all his intimidating equipment in a different room, and you sit in a comfortable chair in his office while he goes to work. The process takes about five minutes. He inserts a huge metal plate in your mouth, first top then bottom, and you bite as hard as you can on a spongy liquid which tastes like a cross between taramasalata and peppermint cream. This leaves the impression from which Mike carefully crafts the plate and the teeth. A couple of weeks later you go back and – bingo – it slots into the roof of your mouth like a glove.

Tuesday 23rd

I never thought I would say this, but I am starting to agree with those who say we need a second referee with a video aid to clear up certain incidents. The debate is raging today over a tackle by Julian Dicks on Andy Cole in last night's match at Upton Park. The severity of it was not clear to the referee nor, at first, to the viewer watching on television; but Nicky Butt was sent off seconds later and when Andy Gray and Sky examined the tape from a different angle, Dicks's challenge was seen to be dangerous.

I have never been one for taking responsibility away from the man in the middle, especially if his two linesmen are giving him full support with another opinion where relevant, but the proliferation of cameras are now giving the officials little chance of coming up with the right answer every time. Joe Kinnear, the Wimbledon manager, thinks an independent arbiter in the stand could work without wasting too much time. He proposes a red light and a green light, which will signal to the referee which verdict is confirmed. Well, I always said football wasn't black and white. If Joe wasn't in the running for Jack Charlton's old job, he might be a front runner as a traffic policeman, the way he's talking!

I have always been one of those traditionalists who believes the referee's decision on matters of fact during the game should be final and sacrosanct, be it right or wrong, but now that officials are being asked to look at videos and decide if they want to change their minds about red and yellow cards, we have moved away from their original standpoint anyway. So the man in the stand would only be a quicker way of enabling them to come to the right conclusion.

Wednesday 24th
Two magazine supplements rang today. They come up with a different idea every time. First, there is going to be an A Level in football knowledge, and a reporter fired five questions down the phone at me to help with an angle for his feature. Fortunately, they were pretty easy. If you don't know who scored a hat-trick for England in the World Cup Final you obviously haven't been on this planet. Mind you, he got a bit of a shock when I said Roger Hunt.

Another survey carried the 'Who do you most admire in your profession?' tag. Here I was split between Alan Whicker and David Frost, the two broadcasters I wish in my dreams I could have been. Whicker's interview technique – along with his eye for an unusual story – I have long admired; and I always felt an empathy with Frost since watching *TW3* in the early sixties. He was a Methodist minister's son, like me, but unlike me he had the ability to have been a professional footballer. He clearly felt interviewing presidents, cardinals, world leaders, agitators, celebrities and criminals would be a far more worthwhile exercise. As Christopher Booker said: 'Television was made for him.'

Thursday 25th
Talking about Methodism, my attendance at our church in
Marlborough Road, St Albans, has lapsed badly since we
moved to Harpenden three years ago. I should really have
transferred my membership to a church in our new town, but
old habits die hard, and I still have a lot of affection for the
church I attended for fifteen years and where Frederick was
christened. It's also a church that believes in worship outside of
Sunday, so every Thursday lunchtime there is a short 'business
person's' service in the church foyer. Today the theme was
Christian unity, which as far as Methodists are concerned, is
something of an old chestnut. We have been trying to get
together with the Anglicans for years, but doctrinal differences
always seem to get in the way. It sounds simplistic, but don't
we worship the same God and read the same Bible? Fortunately, the Christians in Sport organisation, which has done much
good work including placing chaplains in most football clubs,
is inter-denominational and concerned more about getting the
message across – which is what Christianity is supposed to be
about, isn't it?

The minister at Marlborough Road, David Monkton, is a
warm, versatile chap who played the piano today as well as
organising the service.

My mother was an accomplished pianist but sadly her only
son is tone deaf and never showed any musical aptitude
whatsoever. That's why I'm glad Frederick is progressing so
well with the violin.

Still on the theme of church music, my next call was to get
my car serviced. Ron Jewell and his son Mark, who own the
Ford main dealership, Jewell of Watford, are good friends of
mine. Ron has a wide range of business interests both in and
out of the motor trade, and on Sundays plays the organ at his
local church. He and Mark are season ticket holders at Tottenham, and just now – like a lot more people – they are getting
very excited about the prospect of Euro 96. It makes me realise
that this football extravaganza is only four months away now
– the biggest thing that has happened here football-wise since
1966. Those fans who did not heed the warning to get their
ticket applications in early may be disappointed – it looks as
though most matches will be a sell-out. Terry Venables is
talking about taking the England team to Hong Kong, or
somewhere like that, for a short tour beforehand. But if he

looks out the window this afternoon, his heart will sink. The bad weather is closing in, and my fears about the season dissolving into fixture chaos look certain to be realised.

Friday 26th
A wretched day for a commentator. Snow, ice and frost have enveloped most of Britain, and one FA Cup tie after another has fallen foul of the worst weather of the winter. Pitch inspections are planned for most grounds tomorrow morning, including Reading where I am due to cover the tie against Manchester United.

The BBC have put two other matches on 'standby' in case mine is off and we can hastily move the cameras elsewhere. So I have put in some emergency homework on Southampton v. Crewe and West Ham v. Grimsby. The two Endsleigh managers concerned, Dario Gradi and Brian Laws, were very helpful about their movements. They appreciated our predicament and gave me the number of the team coach and the hotel where they are staying.

Having said that, it's now bedtime and we're still no nearer knowing which match I will be attending. Everybody is in the hands of the overnight conditions, and the state of the roads means the journey, wherever it has to be made, is going to be as tricky as the match commentary.

Saturday 27th
Our producer at Reading, Martin Webster, rang while I was still in bed reading the papers. The match at Reading has survived an early-morning pitch inspection. What did not survive the early morning snow was the M25, where there were vehicles facing the wrong way in the fast lane on the southbound carriageway, and people risking life and limb by standing next to them and waving the oncoming traffic into the centre lane. It was a recipe for carnage.

Britain being the localised land that it is, everything changed when I reached the M4. It was like a summer's day by comparison, and when I reached Reading they were just rolling back the cover of plastic sheeting that had protected the pitch since Wednesday. When *Grandstand* asked for a weather report at five minutes notice, I was thrust in front of the camera wearing the same sheepskin coat that caught the imagination of the nation in the same arctic conditions at Wycombe five years ago.

In the commentary box at Elm Park, there is a safety restriction allowing only two people – a cameraman and myself. We got a raucous cheer as we climbed up the precarious 'fireman's ladder', sited in the middle of the standing spectators. Because the floor manager was not allowed up, I had to work all the controls myself. After 25 years I should be able to cope with the volume control, but what would have happened if anything technical had gone wrong, I hate to think. So fractured was my preparation for this game that when Paul Parker ran on as a second-half substitute for Manchester United, he wasn't even on my list of players. Had it been anybody less recognisable, the commentator would have had egg on his face, because within a minute Parker smashed in the second goal – only the second he has ever scored for the club. Another lesson in why to always be prepared for the unexpected.

Because there was so little space below the stand, all the post-match interviews for radio, television and newspapers were conducted on the pitch. Ryan Giggs obviously doesn't feel the cold, and stood quite happily in the freezing conditions wearing just his suit. Genius can defy even the elements.

From Reading, it was a comparatively easy journey to the Dormy House Hotel in the Cotswolds for Bob Sims's 50th birthday dinner. He had intended to take 50 guests to Cheltenham for racing, but that too fell victim to the weather. Nevertheless, as a media man should, he exercised his imagination to produce a creative guest list along the lines of a race card, with appropriate form guide for the runners and riders. My own entry was treated with some disdain: 'Motty . . . late starter at the Dormy House. Likely to be freshly coiffured. Shows menopausal tendencies. On the downgrade.'

After a day like today, you can say that again. Anyway it was a cracking party. It's now 4 a.m., and I'll try to be up at 7 to watch the repeat of *Match of the Day*, which I missed for the first time in ages.

Sunday 28th
Some of the revellers made tracks through the snow to Nigel Twiston-Davies's stables at Naunton to see their horses. Not trusting myself on those winding lanes, especially with a sore head, I made straight for home. The BBC's live match between Sheffield United and Aston Villa survived the weather and it was nice sitting in the warm to watch the others work.

Monday 29th
I should have been in Newcastle and Leeds with Brian Moore today, inspecting commentary sites for Euro 96, but because of the hazardous driving conditions in the north, our trip has been postponed. In many ways it was a good thing, because the telephone never stopped ringing all day. One caller was Simon Marsh from Umbro, the England kit manufacturers. He had obviously seen my dilapidated state on the screen when I was reporting from Reading, and wondered whether I could do with what he calls a 'manager's coat'. Since my team is doing very nicely in the *Daily Telegraph* Fantasy League, I may as well try to look the part. Dwight Yorke and Clive Wilson both scored at the weekend, and I have just made two of my permitted 'transfers' – bringing in Dan Petrescu and Steve Stone. When it started, I thought Fantasy Football would be a craze, like skateboarding, that would run its course and go away. How wrong I was.

Tuesday 30th
It hasn't taken long for my Christmas conversation with Terry Venables to come to fruition. 'Tel fury as squad is left in tatters' was this morning's headline in the *Sun*. Rearranged League games and FA Cup ties, together with the semi-finals of the Coca-Cola Cup, mean that up to 20 possible England squad men could be involved with their clubs, making his get-together pointless.

But it's a good day for the BBC in the current debate over sport on television. We have secured the Olympic Games until the year 2008 and exclusive rights to live coverage of the England v. Scotland battle in the European Championship.

That gave me plenty to bite on in my address to the Bromley branch of the Charlton Athletic supporters' club. They were a lively crowd with plenty to say about the merits of their own club and the Endsleigh League. Some 200 fans turned up, which was very flattering, but then they are used to getting Charlton players to the monthly meetings, and they produce one of the best fanzines I have seen, on good quality paper. It brought back some distant but happy memories of the first match my father took me to see – Charlton v. Chelsea at The Valley in 1952. Funny how your early recollections centre on something quite trivial. I remember that the band which used to play before the game (in the days before disco music blared over the loudspeaker) retired to the track beside the pitch when the game started. Benny Fenton, the Charlton right half and later the lovable manager of Millwall, smacked a clearance right into the middle of the big bass drum, sending a resounding thud around the Valley – then the biggest ground in the country. It left a lasting impression on a small boy.

Now Charlton are beating the drum towards the top of Endsleigh Division One and are currently still in the FA Cup. After all their ground-sharing tribulations a few years ago, it's good to see them selling out the all-seater stadium that once held nearly 80,000.

A lot of credit is going to Alan Curbishley's new coach, Les Reed, who I met on an FA Preliminary Badge coaching course over twenty years ago. We both passed, but there the comparisons ended. He went on to become a top coach – I failed the Full Badge two years later.

Wednesday 31st
The end of January, and hopefully the end of the bad weather. The frost has gone and tonight's match between Aston Villa and Liverpool went ahead. It might surprise those who think BBC and ITV are bitter rivals that I travelled to Birmingham with Brian Moore. He was keen to watch Villa from the TV gantry, because he is shortly covering their Coca-Cola Cup semi-final against Arsenal.

Before we left, I nearly lost a car door – in a car wash of all places. I hate sitting in the front while the water does its worst, and normally get out of the car before walking back and pressing the button. This time, the token didn't seem to work, and I was about to get back into the car when the attendant – a Brian Lara lookalike – came screaming out of his cash desk just seconds before the mechanism smashed into the driver's door.

The conditions at Villa Park in the evening were very cold, but a protective cover kept the pitch playable and goals from Collymore and Fowler kept Liverpool in the Championship picture.

FEBRUARY
1996

Thursday 1st
Uri Geller is supposed to be something of a hypnotist, and meeting him at Reading seems to have had a weird effect on me. It is Frederick's tenth birthday on Sunday, and for no apparent reason I have got him *Uri Geller's Mind-Power Kit.* He must have planted the idea in my subconscious at Reading without my realising.

One man whose mind is not easily swayed is Alan Sugar, who came out today with some stinging home truths about what will happen to football clubs if they continue to pay wages they cannot afford. Basically he is repeating what Bryon Butler said in the *Telegraph* – that the game and its obsession with money is now getting so inflated there is a serious danger that it is going to burst.

Sugar is one of the few chairmen who seems to be able to apply the same business principles to football as he does to his shareholders. In other words, what is spent will eventually have to be accounted for. Income is not keeping up with expenditure in football – certainly gate money does not pay the wages or anywhere near it – and Sugar also expresses concern about what it now costs a man to take his two sons to a game. What a few of us would like to know is where football would be without the television money it is now commanding?

Having said all of that, it is easy to delude ourselves into thinking the game has never been in better health. The grounds are full for nearly every Premiership match and it would seem churlish to question the direction the game is taking. However, we shall know more next week when some of our leading clubs meet their European counterparts to discuss the extension of European competitions. Pressure may well be brought to bear to reduce the Premiership to eighteen clubs, which was the original intention in the FA Blueprint for Football and should

101

in my opinion have happened from the start. The clubs, of course, will resist that to the bitter end, because those outside the top three or four fear that relegation would be the first step towards bankruptcy. It need not be. Not if the money now flowing into the game was shared more evenly, as it used to be. That is where we came in, of course. The rich are determined to get richer. The others are just hanging on.

Friday 2nd
There is no stepping back now from the charity running project that I concocted with John Caine, the organiser of the Great North Run. John's company, Nova International, have a series of six runs in the summer, and to those I have added a list of another six events reasonably local to where I live. These are a mixture of five miles, ten kilometres (6.2 miles), ten miles and half marathons. The total mileage comes to just short of 100 miles, but spread over twelve meetings it is hardly daunting. We are going to get as much sponsorship as we can for NCH 'Action for Children', and I am hoping to get some of my *Grandstand* colleagues to run in the big event – the Great North Run on Tyneside next September.

That's where I am today, and a big mark for British Airways. After all I said about the frustration of getting on and off aeroplanes, the front row is the answer. It was a painless flight to Newcastle, and after leaving Heathrow at 4.30 I was sitting in the Gosforth Park Hotel by six o'clock. The reason I had picked this hotel was because Sheffield Wednesday, who are Newcastle's opponents tomorrow, are staying here – and it so happens I have not seen them play this season.

It may seem undignified to hang about a hotel reception area waiting to spot the players you don't know, but that is what had to be done in this case. I had never set eyes on Wednesday's two Yugoslavs, Stefanovic and Kovacevic, who look rather alike anyway. They were terribly polite when I met them, but the exercise lost some of its purpose when David Pleat, the manager, whispered to me that he was thinking of leaving one or both of them out of the side.

One man who will definitely be playing is Chris Waddle, who worked for the BBC during the 1994 World Cup and with whom I shared some good times in places like Detroit, Chicago and New York. He thinks my taste in music begins and ends with the New Seekers and we had a joke about that before he joined the team for dinner. I sat down with John Caine, and Dave Roberts, John's colleague, suggested my diet may need some attention before embarking on this fitness programme. That conversation came back to me later this evening when Clive Page, an old friend of mine from BBC Newcastle days, brought his family out to dinner. I keep reading about fresh fruit and vegetables, but keep eating red meat and chips with loads of bread and butter.

Saturday 3rd
The running story in Newcastle is the on-off transfer of the Colombian Faustino Asprilla, from Parma. Newcastle brought him over for a medical, and transfer talks with his Italian club appeared to have been concluded, when suddenly there was a snag. Nobody seems quite sure what the hitch is, although Asprilla has a history of knee trouble. Fortunately, I fixed up earlier in the week to interview Kevin Keegan for *Grandstand*, and when he talked on *Football Focus*, he said it's his opinion that Asprilla will still come to Newcastle. This quote quickly found its way on to just about every news outlet in the country. It wasn't until afterwards that I learned Keegan has refused to answer any questions about the transfer for the past three days.

While this interview was taking place, Keith Gillespie – who has been out for six weeks with a thigh injury – suddenly appeared for a fitness test that nobody was expecting. An hour later, Keegan included him in the team and Newcastle went on to beat Wednesday and secure their thirteenth home victory in thirteen matches.

For *Match of the Day* we interviewed Waddle and Beardsley together. It seems crazy that they are both playing at top level at the age of 35 when, six years ago, both were discarded after helping England to the World Cup semi-final.

Mark Bright of Sheffield Wednesday was flying back to London so the ever-reliable Billy Wilson (Noda 30) rushed us back to the airport while we listened to the results on the radio.

Bright was one of those late developers who did not become a professional until he was 22. He passed his City and Guilds in hydraulic engineering before he became a full-time footballer, and that may explain why he too is one of those still operating at top level well into his 30s. He is one of a number of footballers who are keen to break into media work.

It's just a shame we can't do it the other way round. As Alan

Parry once said to me: 'Nobody's asked me to play centre forward for Tottenham recently.'

Sunday 4th
Just because Chelsea whack Middlesbrough 5-0, it doesn't necessarily mean that Glenn Hoddle is a better bet for the England job than Bryan Robson, although today's result at Stamford Bridge will make a good line for the tabloids. Mind you, it confirms what I have been thinking since before Christmas; namely that Chelsea are the most progressive side in the Premiership just now. That may seem a contrary view, bearing in mind I have just come back from watching Newcastle consolidate their nine-point lead at the top, but I haven't seen Chelsea produce such intelligent, inventive football since the Dave Sexton days of the late sixties and early seventies.

Their passing is neat, accurate and pleasing to the eye, which comes as no great surprise when you consider Hoddle and his assistant, Peter Shreeves, are steeped in the Tottenham tradition. 'Push and run' was a fifties maxim polished by the old Spurs manager Arthur Rowe, and it seems to me that Chelsea have adapted it to suit the nineties. You sense that Hoddle has laid down a pattern of play throughout the club. I haven't seen the youth team under Graham Rix, but I bet they play exactly the same system. As a mere spectator, I have never been a great fan of the 'three at the back and full backs pushed in' system, because I don't believe the full backs are generally good enough to be natural wingers (watch their crosses sometimes) nor are they always in defensive positions when they should be. In the European Championship semi-final of 1992 in Gothenburg, the Danish coach Richard Moller-Nielsen put his two fastest players out on the touchlines and exposed the fact that Holland were playing without real full backs and with a back three in which the sweeper was slow to get across to cover. Denmark won the game and the Championship.

However, who am I to talk about tactics? Hoddle obviously went a long way to perfecting his system at Swindon, who he took into the Premier League. Funnily enough, Chelsea were the first team in England that I ever saw employ the 'proper' sweeper – when Marvin Hinton played behind a line of four defenders in Tommy Docherty's time as manager in the mid-sixties. Nowadays it's more a question of three central de-

104

fenders, with some clubs rotating them in specific areas without detailing one to be the 'spare man'.

Lawrie McMenemy at Southampton (using Ruben Agboola) and John Toshack at Swansea (with Ante Rajkovic) also employed a sweeper for a time, and I remember Bryan Robson starting a game brilliantly there for Manchester United at Highbury, only for Alex Ferguson to have to move him back into midfield because of an injury.

After what happened to his team at Chelsea today, I'll bet Robson wishes that he had been fit enough to play sweeper for Middlesbrough. They lost 5-0, and part of the reason was a startling display by Ruud Gullit. Perversely, he came to Chelsea to fill the sweeper's role, but at present he is wowing us all from midfield.

Monday 5th
It only occurred to me today, after a conversation with my editor, that one of the disadvantages of writing a diary like this is that once the words are committed to print, there is no chance of a rewrite. In other words, if the thoughts I have put on paper so far are found to be wide of the mark in hindsight, it's just tough luck. A bit like doing a commentary, really. Well no, because the spoken word is usually more quickly forgotten, and rarely dragged up and used as evidence against you more than a few days later. Some of these predictions could make the author seem even more preposterous than usual by next Christmas.

That thought occurred while watching a video of the recent international between France and Portugal – two of the qualifiers for Euro 96. Some of the football the French played was breathtaking. They came back from 1-0 down and 2-1 down to eventually win 3-2, and at this stage their coach is picking a squad without Cantona, Ginola and Papin. Watching players like Marcel Desailly, the captain, Youri Djorkaeff, who scored two brilliant goals, and Christian Karambeu, a younger version of Ruud Gullit, you could have convinced yourself you were watching the European Champions elect.

But then again, we all thought Michel Platini's team were going to go close in the last European Championship in 1992, and what happened? England and France both failed to qualify from their group, while Sweden and Denmark went on to the semi-finals.

Patriotism apart, I would love to see the French win another major tournament. I was there when they became European Champions on their own territory in 1984 and it was a rich experience. They play from the soul, which is as it should be for a nation who invented the World Cup, the European Championship and the European Champions Cup. Sadly, this last one is about to be vandalised by its own guardians. Tomorrow, UEFA are holding a significant meeting about the future of European club football. It looks like more clubs, more matches, and, of course, more money.

On that topic, I saw over half a million pounds raised tonight for a worthy cause – the National Advertising Benevolent Society. Every year they hold a celebrity boxing night, the proceeds from the dinner, auction and programme advertising being donated to a fund for those in the trade who have met personal problems. It is a splendid evening, the highlight of which is invariably Jimmy Hill's performance in the ring. Not fighting (except for the cause), but urging the various agencies and their guests to raise the bidding for a succession of glittering prizes.

Brendan Foster and I were guests of the Grey Agency and very hospitable they were too. The evening started with champagne, and many hours later finished with bacon sandwiches.

Jim Rosenthal, who was a guest on another table, drew me into conversation in the upstairs bar with some members of the National Farmers Union, who were gathered at the hotel for a conference. They were wearing pullovers and jeans because their business did not start until the next day. We were still in our dinner jackets. I will leave you to imagine who looked faintly ridiculous.

Tuesday 6th
What was it I said to Terry Venables at Christmas about dispensing with FA Cup replays in this significant season? We woke up to eight inches of snow this morning; half the country is cut off and the FA Cup is in chaos. The fourth round is so far behind that nobody has a clue who will be playing who in the fifth round, which is just ten days away. Surely the FA Challenge Cup committee has some emergency powers, hidebound though they are by the ten-day police rule.

Had Shrewsbury been allowed to switch their tie to Liverpool, which they originally requested anyway, it would have been played at Anfield on the correct date, 27 January. Because it remains in Shropshire, the match will now take place on 18 February – over three weeks later. No wonder the rest of Europe laughs at our fixture congestion.

But for the moment, European football is in danger of going down the same crowded road. The summit meeting of leading clubs in Geneva has been asked to consider a major restructuring of the three club competitions. No longer would entry to the Champions and Cup-Winners Cup be solely for the previous season's domestic winners. Another team would be admitted, based (loosely) on their recent European record.

In other words, if Feyenoord won the Championship in Holland and qualified for the Champions Cup/League by right, then Ajax would also gain admission by virtue of their recent performances in the competition. Sounds Double Dutch to me.

Wednesday 7th

When Tottenham Hotspur beat Wolverhampton Wanderers in the FA Cup Final of 1921 at Stamford Bridge, a crowd of 72,805 (it would have been more but for wretched weather) paid receipts of £13,414 – a world record for a football match at that time.

When the two clubs met again in a fourth round replay at Molineux tonight, the receipts from a capacity crowd of 28,000 were around £320,000.

It's money that talks in football now, and to be outside the Premiership is equivalent to being the envious schoolboy with his nose pressed against the sweet shop window.

Much as I identify with Wolves' tradition, admire their majestic stadium and recognise their ambition, I remain unconvinced by their team.

Granted there is a perceived chasm between Premiership and Endsleigh anyway, and they also happened to come across a Tottenham side producing one of their most complete performances in recent times.

But I was taken aback by the optimism of their manager, Mark McGhee, when I interviewed him afterwards. He thought his team had done well and shown signs of the change of style he was trying to introduce.

Had there been time to prolong the interview, I would have challenged that view. It was a match Spurs could have won by five or six goals, and what disappointed me about Wolves was that they never aroused the passion of the crowd.

Which brings us to the dubious business of managers switching clubs in mid-season and, sometimes, in mid-contract. It has happened a lot recently and quite apart from the lack of respect for the supporters, it often leaves the team in limbo between two contrasting styles of play – the one they were getting used to under the departing manager, and the new one which his successor is determined to introduce.

Mark McGhee is not the only case in point, although he has left both Reading and Leicester in fairly abrupt circumstances. Then again, there are usually two chairmen involved; one who has been unable to sustain the working relationship with his manager, and one who is quite prepared to approach, albeit indirectly, another club's manager whose job is still only half-completed.

When it's all said and done, are these people and their clubs really any happier? Mike Walker and Norwich seemed a perfectly good match when they were playing in Europe barely two years ago; his departure to Everton did not, in hindsight, benefit any of the parties involved.

No sooner had Norwich got themselves a new, high-profile manager in Martin O'Neill from Wycombe, than he was off to Leicester to replace McGhee. And all this, after Brian Little had left Filbert Street just as suddenly a year earlier.

At best it is an unsettling chain of events. At worst it is a shabby side of the game that does the parties involved and their image very little credit.

The solution is quite simple. Managers should be registered, along with their contracts, and there should be a clause forbidding any movement mid-season. The Premiership clubs have already gone partly down this road with their chairmen agreeing not to 'poach' another club's manager.

You only have to look at the top of the Premiership, where Kevin Keegan is just starting his fifth year at Newcastle and Alex Ferguson is in his tenth year at Manchester United, to see the wisdom of giving a manager *time*. Ferguson once generously said to me, earlier in his reign at Old Trafford, that if any one of his three predecessors had been given more time in the job, they might have won the Championship.

Clubs should stop looking for the quick fix and have a little more patience. But then again, those same chairmen will point out that the first people to lose patience when things go wrong are the supporters.

Above left Blame the Reverend. The author with his clergyman father, the late William Motson, who introduced his son to football as soon as he could walk

Above right Stick to the commentating – cementing the reason why the author never looked like a footballer

Above They talk a good game . . . The commentators' football team, including Jim Rosenthal, Alan Parry and Martin Tyler. Ex-professionals Gordon Riddick, Brian Kinsey, Roger Smith and Peter Kitchen add some respectability

Above Radio days – Desmond Lynam and John Motson first worked together on Radio 2 in 1970 . . .

Below . . . and then they both moved to television sport. This picture of the *Match of the Day* team includes Trevor Brooking, Tony Gubba, Alan Hansen and Ray Stubbs

Right Cup Final commentators. Kenneth Wolstenholme was the BBC's voice behind 21 FA Cup Finals. The author got stuck on 17 (plus 5 replays)

Below Waiting for the World Cup Final of 1986 to start in the Aztec Stadium in Mexico City. Can you spot Trevor Brooking and Lawrie McMenemy in the background?

Above Your turn to pour the tea . . . Annie taking a break from her proper job as chairman of the school governors and part-time statistician

Left A goalkeeper not a commentator. Young Frederick Motson under the watchful eye of the master at Bob Wilson's goalkeeping school

Right No doubt about who has the better coat. Rory Bremner and Motty (or should it be the other way round?) compare notes on their sheepskins

Below Not a glamorous job . . . shivering in the snow at Wycombe in 1990

Above Interviewing Gary Lineker at a Tottenham box holders' function before the England captain retired and joined the BBC team

Below With another of England's 1990 World Cup heroes at a social function

Above The long and the short of it. Bob Willis (*left*), ex-Surrey and England and later chairman of the National Sporting Club with one of his guest speakers, John Toshack (*right*), ex-Liverpool and Wales and later a successful manager in Spain

Left Motty's mileage

Below Over the bar, fulfilling his duties as president of the Roving Reporters. The author's old club are the only surviving founder members of the Barnet and District Sunday League. Their chairman Roger Jones is pulling ears rather than pints

Above Manchester City v. Manchester United, 6 April 1996. Meeting an old World Cup hero is always a pleasure – whether Alan Ball would say the same about doing live interviews before a relegation battle is another matter

Above Checking my commentary notes in the players' tunnel just before the game. The Manchester City programme editor Joanne Parker explains how to pronounce 'Kinkladze' and 'Kavelashvili'

Which just goes to show that football, being the volatile business it now is, comes full of contradictions. As one well-known Premiership manager said after a recent controversial defeat: 'I never criticise referees, and I'm not changing my mind for that prat.'

Thursday 8th
And while we are on the topic of greed and grasping, what about UEFA's monster (or should it be monstrous?) proposal for the recycling of European football?

By now the dust has settled on the Geneva meeting earlier in the week, and most columnists have given it a firm thumbs down.

In simple terms, the European body have come up with a complicated restructuring scheme to placate the Continent's richest clubs who want a guaranteed place in Europe, and if possible in the Champions League, every year.

The veiled threat is a breakaway European League, but my belief is that it is one worth calling the bluff on. David Dein of Arsenal is a prime mover, and has clearly thought his plan through, but Highbury is packed every week as it is. Would Arsenal's supporters prefer to watch Inter-Milan than Tottenham or Manchester United?

As for widening the field for the three European competitions, why should a club finishing tenth in the Premiership, or any other national League for that matter, have any earthly right to play in Europe?

The whole idea of European club football was based on a pursuit of excellence. The cream came to the top, hence the elitism of the Champions Cup. You had to win your League in order to take part.

Once you relax the rules of qualification, you devalue the essence and quality of the competition. Sadly, those values are in danger of being eroded as UEFA – and football in general – goes down a dangerous road where quantity takes over. More clubs, more matches, more money – until supporters start staying away because they cannot afford to go.

Then, of course, that latter-day Cyclops called television comes into the formula. With digital, cable, satellite and goodness knows what else taking technology forward faster than UEFA can think up new competitions, you have the inevitable feeling that if 'Middle of the table United' were playing a team from the Ukraine in the preliminary round of the Inter-something Cup in the first week of July, some channel somewhere would pay for the rights to televise the game.

Friday 9th
Today football and everything else which is a mere indulgence on life's perimeter was put firmly back into perspective by the horror of the IRA bomb in the Docklands.

The device exploded at South Quay, near Canary Wharf, at one minute past seven. Less than fifteen minutes later, I was listening to a swift and accurate account of what had happened on the car radio.

When such outrages first happened, we tended to feel they had rocked the foundations of our society. Now they make us all a bit selfish. Your heart goes out to the families of young children whose faces are disfigured, but deep down you are thanking God it wasn't your own son or daughter.

Saturday 10th
Well, the weather forecasters have got it spectacularly wrong again. Yesterday they were cautioning us against a return of the snow, frost and sleet which has been playing havoc with the roads and football fixtures all week; so what was it like this morning? The thaw had set in, the streets were glistening with little pools of water, and the sun was shining benignly.

Sometimes I think the Ian McCaskills can't see the moon for the mist. Last night after the news he was giving us the *European* weather, mumbling about isobars over Waldhof Mannheim or somewhere. We all find it easy to blame the weather man, don't we?

Come to think of it, with the sheepskin coat on I could probably have a go myself at trying to keep it simple. Something like: 'Tonight it will rain; by tomorrow when you get up the snow will have gone; nearly all the sports fixtures including racing at Newbury will take place.'

Which was precisely what happened, and why I took the family up the motorway to Derby, where Frederick's tenth birthday treat was to see his favourite team play at home to Wolves (yes, them again). As it is my Saturday off, I was content to stay in the background as chauffeur. Here is Frederick's account of the day:

I have been looking forward to today for a long time as I haven't seen Derby play for ages. When we first arrived, I went into the Ramtique and bought a new Derby sweater, some pencils, a baseball cap, a rubber, and a book for my dad with the last 25 years Derby statistics in.

I was then given a brilliant tour of the ground by Steve Bradshaw, the community officer. We went into the dressing rooms and the trophy room, and he let me sit in the dug-out. One of the Derby players, Lee Carsley, said he liked my sweater.

We then had lunch in the Sportsmen's Club, where the manager's name was Ian and I ate a lot of French bread and some tuna steak.

While we were watching the match, I kept thinking it was one of the last I would ever see at the Baseball Ground, because Derby are planning to move to a new stadium at Pride Park.

The match against Wolves was very close, with few scoring opportunities. There were no goals, but as we left Steve Bradshaw gave me a signed football.

On the car radio going home we listened to Ram FM and then to Five Live, who told us that Charlton had won at Watford and closed the gap on Derby to three points.

Which just goes to show that nothing can quite match the thrill that football can bring to a wide-eyed schoolboy – which is exactly what Frederick's father became for a few minutes while his son was being shown round the ground.

As I walked down one of those narrow, creaking corridors which make the Baseball Ground a nostalgic, wooden testament to a time gone by, I bumped into two men who fitted perfectly into the time warp in which I had happily lost myself.

One of them was Ray Wilkins, whose looks belied his age, but we are not dealing with the Queens Park Rangers manager here. Few would know the Derby Ray Wilkins, fewer still the place he holds in the history of Boston United, the club my family supported and where my uncles would take me to watch football when I was enjoying my childhood holidays in Lincolnshire.

Ray's companion at Derby today was another ex-footballer whose name I instantly recognised – Reg Harrison – who like Ray had a spell with County but by 1955 had moved into the Midland League to play for Boston United.

In the second round of the FA Cup, Boston were drawn away to Derby – then in the old Third Division North. A week earlier the Rams had thrashed Darlington 6-2 and looked a good bet for promotion.

Boston were under the player-management of the former Derby goalkeeper, Ray Middleton, so there was plenty of local interest in the tie.

My father was the superintendent minister of the Deptford Methodist Mission at the time, and had a function at the church that afternoon. I remember we bought a copy of the *Star*, one of three London evening classified football papers in the fifties, and were amazed to see in the results section: Derby Co. 1, Boston Utd 6.

'There must be a mistake,' my dad said. Funnily enough, he supported Derby as a boy. 'They must mean one-nil, surely.'

At the age of ten, I had the gumption to turn to the back page of the paper where the half-times were listed in tabulated form. And there was the irrefutable evidence: Derby 1, Boston 3.

So it was that Boston, with Ray Wilkins scoring twice against his old club, recorded one of the most handsome victories in the history of the Cup by a non-League side over a League club. A crowd of 23,757 – boosted by many from Boston – were there as witnesses. That was 6,000 more than Derby could house in the capacity crowd for the Wolves game today.

Wilkins, Harrison and I got into full flow. People were pushing past us with teamsheets, cheese rolls, Ram memorabilia and all sorts, but we had only just got on to the little matter of Boston's visit to Tottenham in the third round.

7 January 1956 – my first ever visit to White Hart Lane. There were 46,000 of us – nearly 10,000 travelled from Boston – to see a third-round tie which Danny Blanchflower's team won with rather more difficulty than the 4-0 score suggests.

I could just remember Reg Harrison going close with a shot which whistled across the goal with the score still 0-0, and with a little prompting from him and Ray, I managed to recite the Boston team (2-3-5 formation of course): Middleton, Robinson, Snade, Don Hazeldine, Miller, Lowder, Harrison, Geoff Hazeldine, Wilkins, Birbeck, Howlett.

I could easily have checked it when I got home. I've still got the programme.

Sunday 11th

Hoddle, Crooks and Lineker were all in great form yesterday. That sounds like an old Tottenham match report, but I'm talking about the BBC's *Football Focus*, which I caught up with on the video when I got home from Derby last night.

Older viewers will remember that when I first joined the BBC team in 1971, the *Grandstand* football spot was called *Sam Leitch's Football Preview*. Sam would combine presenting with his main job as editor of *Match of the Day* and *Sportsnight*.

My early days were largely spent touring the country with producer Bob Abrahams, interviewing managers and players for a three-minute spot on Saturday lunchtime. It was invaluable experience and helped me make lots of contacts.

When Bob Wilson retired as Arsenal goalkeeper and joined the BBC in 1974, it was decided to give the programme a new title and, if I may be immodest, it was yours truly who suggested *Football Focus*. Over twenty years later, that remains the title of the 40-minute football slot that gets *Grandstand* off and running every week.

The programme has changed a lot over the years and it's no secret, even at this stage of the season, that the plan is for Gary Lineker to front the show on his own as from next season.

He'll find it different from being the panellist alongside Steve Rider, but as with his radio show, he will adapt quickly. What I hope he retains is his right to an opinion. This weekend, for example, he put a nice new slant on the issue of players' contractual rights in the light of the Bosman ruling.

'If there were no transfer fees, agents would be less involved, and there would be fewer temptations for bungs. In other words, less sleaze in the game.' Well said, that man.

Even when I am not involved, I never miss the *Focus*, because at our meeting next Tuesday we will all be expected to give an opinion on the various items.

That was where Crooks and Hoddle came in. Glenn can be a bit reticent on camera, but Garth could read his passes when they were playing together, and he read the play perfectly with his Chelsea item.

Hoddle talked candidly about his philosophy. He had told his Chelsea players there were three kinds of pass – the one that was safe, the one that took you forward, and the one that hurt the opposition. Then there was the one Hoddle would never condone – the long ball pumped into space for some unspecified person to chase.

Chelsea will never play that way, certainly not while Ruud Gullit is directing operations. His interview with Crooks produced a revealing moment when the Dutch master spontaneously nominated Eddie Newton as a key player in the Chelsea set-up, comparing him to the Holland midfield player Jan Wouters. I find it quite hard to imagine an English player making such a valid point in a foreign language.

It reminded me of something Peter Shreeves said to me two years ago, when Chelsea reached the FA Cup Final. 'Eddie Newton has got enough ability to play for England.'

Talking of ability, the most compelling moments of the weekend came from Faustino Asprilla when he came on as substitute for Newcastle at Middlesbrough.

He confirmed everything Kevin Keegan had said about him when he insisted that the player would definitely finish up at Newcastle.

While these guys from all over the world are bringing a new dimension to our football, the PFA are opposing the renewal of work permits to Ilie Dumitrescu and Marc Hottiger, who have been transferred to West Ham and Everton respectively. The stupid part is, if they had stayed at Spurs and Newcastle, nobody would have said a word.

Back to today. When you are first making your way in a business like ours, there are one or two people for whose advice and encouragement you remain eternally grateful. In my early days at Barnet, that person was Dexter Adams, the former England amateur international centre half who was Barnet Football Club's manager in the sixties.

Dexter was in charge when Barnet, then in the Athenian League, nearly knocked Howard Kendall and Preston out of the FA Cup, a year after Preston played West Ham at Wembley.

Adams then masterminded Barnet's transition from the amateur ranks to semi-professional football. They joined the Southern League First Division and won it at the first attempt.

Dexter was a man of high principle who as a player had shunned the temptations of under-the-counter payments. He was more concerned about getting on the early coaching courses organised by Walter Winterbottom.

His belief in open, attractive football was reflected in all the teams he built at Barnet, but when they lost to Macclesfield in the semi-final of the FA Trophy in 1970 on his 45th birthday, Dexter decided he had had enough.

On the train back he told the *Barnet Press* reporter, Roger

Jones, that he was finishing at the end of the season, and would never get involved in football again.

In the 25 years that followed, I was the only person to persuade him even to go to a match. But Dexter remained a well-known figure in London advertising circles, working for the *Daily Mirror*, *Capital Radio* and the *Sporting Life*.

Now he is well into retirement, but a more spruce or mentally alert 70 year old I do not know. He and his wife Sheila are moving from Potters Bar to Peterborough to be nearer their daughters, and tonight Roger Jones and his partner Julie held a dinner party to see them off in style.

It brought back a lot of happy memories of the early days at Barnet. Dexter Adams was never employed by the club full-time, but he was so committed he used to take the full players' strip to the local launderette to save them money.

Monday 12th

Granada Television rang today regarding a drama documentary they are making about the Hillsborough disaster. They wanted my permission to use a recording of a private conversation between John Shrewsbury, the BBC producer, and myself at about quarter to three on that fateful afternoon.

We have in the commentary box what we call a 'lazy microphone' which is, in effect, a private line between commentator and director. Once, and thankfully only once, it was mistakenly switched to the 'on air' position, and millions of people heard me ask, 'Can you hear me, Fred?', thinking I was addressing only the director, Fred Viner, during a Cup tie at Liverpool.

On the day of the tragedy in April 1989, Shrewsbury and I were discussing on the 'lazy' our opening sequence of words and pictures, looking for a way of reflecting the vibrant atmosphere which accompanies an FA Cup semi-final.

'I really don't see how I can talk about a capacity crowd when there is so much space at either end of that terrace,' I said to John as I looked to my left at the Leppings Lane end. 'The central sections are full but the two end pens are half-empty. You can still see the steps with nobody standing on them.'

As we all discovered later when the full horror unfolded, hundreds of supporters were still outside. When they were allowed in, they were drawn to the central tunnel and into the pens that were already full.

My chance remark was recorded, and formed part of my evidence as an eye-witness to both the Taylor Report and the inquest on the victims.

At first I was a bit nervous about the idea of the drama documentary. But when I was assured it was being made with the approval of the bereaved families, I saw no reason not to allow them to use the tape.

Tuesday 13th

You are probably wondering by now exactly how much time I spend at the BBC and exactly what I do when I am there. Like most commentators and contributors, my contract as a freelance broadcaster means the BBC have first call on my services, but beyond telling me where they want me, what for and when, they give me the freedom to plan my own schedule and preparation accordingly.

Having said that, Tuesday is the one day in the week when most of the football reporters are seen together at Television Centre in west London.

A lot of the staff who have worked on programmes at the weekend have taken Monday off, so Tuesday is the start of the gearing-up process for the next week of programmes, although a lot of long-term planning has already been done.

We have two important editorial meetings on a Tuesday. The first one, at about 10.30, is to plan the following Saturday's *Football Focus* and to review the previous week's programme.

If I had been a footballer, I would have been one of those who always reported for training on time. All my life it has been a point of principle for me to be punctual, a trait I got from my mother and which some of my friends find mildly irritating.

There must be some truth in the football analogy because Gary Lineker and Garth Crooks are always two of the first to arrive in the *Grandstand* office on a Tuesday morning. We do have the odd latecomer, but footballers like to leave quickly when they finish as well, so we make a point of starting the meeting bang on time.

This week it is difficult to plan because some of the Cup pairings next weekend depend on replays or rearranged ties which take place on Tuesday and Wednesday.

For instance, Manchester United's opponents in the BBC's live match next Sunday won't be known until Manchester City and Coventry replay at Maine Road. If Coventry win, there is obviously a good story to be done with Ron Atkinson, Gordon Strachan and Dion Dublin, all of whom would be treading old ground at Old Trafford.

On the other hand, if City get through, and we find ourselves previewing a Manchester derby, the meeting feels that the best personality profile would be Nigel Clough, who has just joined them from Liverpool. Either way, the camera crew and reporter cannot go into action until Thursday at the earliest.

One thing that is certain is that Huddersfield Town will be playing at home to the winners of the Wimbledon–Middlesbrough replay. Gary Richardson has done some research on Huddersfield and their new state-of-the-art stadium, and we all agree that their manager, Brian Horton, is a good story in himself. That will be a banker item.

Should Ipswich beat Walsall and earn a home tie with Aston Villa, there is an obvious FA Cup parallel between their manager George Burley and veteran defender John Wark. Both played in the 1978 final against Arsenal.

Slowly, a structure starts to fall into place. Andy Clement, the editor of the *Focus*, knows he will have plenty of midweek action, and that he can line up one or two live interviews on Saturday morning from the grounds where our cameras are installed for *Match of the Day*.

Because Steve Rider is introducing *Grandstand* from Cardiff, where Wales are playing Scotland in the Five Nations Championship, Ray Stubbs will front the *Focus* with Lineker in the London studio. Stubbs is a busy man because he also has a rugby union preview to prepare for *Sportsnight*.

Which takes us on to our next meeting at about half-past eleven. This is the more immediate business of *Sportsnight*, which has a two-hour show to fill the following evening.

Again, some of the contents speak for themselves. The highlights of England's first World Cup cricket match, against New Zealand, are high on the agenda, as is the FA Cup replay between Port Vale and the holders, Everton.

Boxing is not what it was, in terms of fights guaranteed to suit the television audience, but it has always had a steady spot on the *Sportsnight* agenda, and this week Britain's Billy Hardy defends his European and Commonwealth featherweight titles against Michael Alldis at Southend.

These live events, or 'outside broadcasts', as they are known in the trade, have already been carefully planned by their respective producers and directors. They are responsible for providing the pictures. The studio end of the operation has the editorial responsibility of slotting them into the programme.

But a television programme has to be flexible. Events can sometimes change the entire shape of the programme at a moment's notice.

Wednesday 14th
It was my intention to spend Valentine's Day in Manchester. Not because I had fallen out with my wife of twenty years – cards and flowers had been exchanged as usual – but in order to see the FA Cup replay between Manchester City and Coventry. Wonder of wonders, this was one match that was not going to be covered by television, so the only way for me to run my eye over the team I would be covering at Old Trafford next Sunday was to jump on a plane and see the game at first hand.

I got halfway to the airport before the BBC contacted my driver, Russell, with an urgent message. Bob Paisley had died.

Without, I hope, sounding morbid or irreverent, it is an unhappy coincidence that a number of leading football personalities have died on a Wednesday. The responsibility for putting together *Sportsnight* obituaries in memory of Bill Shankly, Sir Matt Busby and Bobby Moore came my way at roughly the same short notice.

At times like this, the BBC library moves into overdrive, and the archives are trawled for any number of tapes that may include significant snippets of comment, colour or achievement.

Compiling the available material is one thing, editing it into a sensitive tribute is quite another. The producer on this occasion, Peter Allden, was working against the clock.

Between us we worked out a rough running order for the eight-minute item, starting with Bob's roots in the north-east of England ('still' pictures had to be transferred from books that were hurriedly borrowed) and tracing his distinguished career as player, coach and manager through to his retirement in 1983.

A lot of the action spoke for itself. Liverpool winning six Championships and four European trophies under his management was well documented and the BBC footage not hard to locate.

What is more difficult is to reflect something of the man himself. Fortunately, a profile made by *Sportsnight* some years earlier contained valuable material of Bob working at Anfield – including dressing room shots – and there were some vivid close-ups of him sitting in the directors' box.

The programme editor, Niall Sloane, sensibly decided to keep our piece self-contained, with Ray Stubbs putting together a collection of personal tributes from the likes of Roy Evans, Ronnie Moran and Kenny Dalglish in a separate sequence which followed.

All in all, the first fifteen minutes of the programme served as our testament to a fine man and the most successful manager the English game has ever known.

At times like this, you are also aware that whatever is said will be acutely noticed by family and friends of the deceased, as well as being monitored by other sections of the media. One's words never seem quite adequate, especially as we only finished the item about ten minutes before we went on the air.

Everybody has their own personal memory of a man like Bob Paisley. His great quality was his simplicity. Once, when I interviewed him for a book I was writing on the history of the European Cup, he summed up Liverpool's capacity for fielding the same team week after week.

'We got fewer injuries than other teams because we passed the ball properly. If you give the ball to feet, you don't make the other fellow stretch. That way, you don't get hurt.'

Bob's death will be less hurtful to Liverpool supporters if the club can find some way of erecting a memorial akin to the Shankly Gates. I am sure they will, although whether Bob would have expected it I rather doubt. His self-effacement was best summed up by his comment on his own managerial career: 'I never wanted the job in the first place.'

It makes you wonder what would have happened to Liverpool in the next nine years if he hadn't stepped in after Shankly's retirement. Would they have won 20 trophies under anybody else?

Thursday 15th
Today word came through from the BBC about the allocation of big matches for the end of the season. My package consists of two major events in Euro 96 – the England v. Scotland match and the final itself – together with the FA Cup semi-final. I am very happy about it, not least because it puts an end to a lot of speculation.

One of my neighbours in Harpenden is less concerned about which matches I do, than with what demands they make of me. Being in a totally different business himself, he keeps asking me what goes through my mind when I do a commentary and whether I actually *enjoy* it.

It reminds me of what Pat Jennings used to say about goalkeeping. 'I only ever enjoyed a match when it was over. Until then, I was far too worried about making a mistake.'

I can't speak for other commentators, but for 25 years I have felt very much the same. As Peter O'Sullevan once said to me, 'The only commentary we will be remembered for is the one we got wrong.'

The occasional mistake goes with the territory, of course. There isn't a single commentator around who has never made one – you just hope it doesn't happen during a really big game when it is too late to put it right.

My most nervous moment came when England and Germany reached the penalty shoot-out stage of that World Cup semi-final in Turin in 1990.

I have always found it the ultimate test of concentration, remembering how many kicks each team has taken, how the score stands, and at what point one team will take a winning lead. If one or more of the kicks have been missed, it can test the commentator's maths as well.

My big fear was that in the heat of those nerve-racking moments in Turin, with nearly 20 million people watching, I would blurt out something like: 'England are through to the World Cup Final!' when the Germans still had another kick to take.

Fortunately (or unfortunately in England's case) that scenario did not arise. But what applies to every commentary I do is that same apprehension, which I suppose is a good way of focusing the mind.

Like Pat Jennings, I can only really enjoy it when it's over.

Friday 16th

Alan Ball has named two young players in his squad for Sunday who I have never heard of. To get some information about Chris Beech and Aled Rowlands, who may or may not be substitutes, my prime source of information is Bernard Halford, the secretary at Maine Road, who started at City in the season I joined *Match of the Day*. We have been friends ever since.

I have made two other friends at City – both female – but I have never met either of them. In this job you talk to all sorts of people on the telephone and sometimes never come face to face. So Julia and Jo are just voices to whom one day I hope to put a face. Maybe you can understand people who conduct their friendships on the Internet, after all.

But of all the telephone numbers I know off by heart, the one that comes most readily to mind is that of Albert Sewell, the BBC statistics man christened 'our Albert' by Desmond Lynam.

The *Match of the Day* office would not be the same without the weekly offering that the commentators and the production staff call 'Albert's Notes'. These are a run-down on both teams with pen pictures of all the players.

Albert is so infuriatingly accurate that it behoves me, just once a season, to try to catch him out. We had a bit of fun today about whether Kinkladze is City's most expensive buy. Bernard Halford tells me he cost $3 million, which when converted makes him a cheaper purchase than Keith Curle.

All this might seem mighty irrelevant, but it will save me a few letters if I can clarify it before Sunday. Albert likes my last quiz question before I put the phone down: 'How many German-born players in the Manchester City team?'

Uwe Rosler, Eike Immel and now Michael Frontzeck. That's three, isn't it? Until you spot that Steve Lomas was born in Hanover of an Irish father.

Just in case you think I am biased – and I must admit the price of six to one against City for a victory on Sunday is hard to resist – my attitude towards this derby is strictly neutral.

Radio GMR rang this morning for my thoughts on the game and I predicted a draw. I am hoping that Alex Ferguson didn't hear the interview. Tomorrow I will ring him for some information about the United team.

Saturday 17th
Today was Luton v. Millwall revisited. As I have said already, their meeting in the FA Cup eleven years ago ushered in a horrendous period for football. Heysel followed barely two months later, and in between there was the Bradford fire.

Looking around the all-seater stadium at Kenilworth Road today, and watching the supporters of both clubs sensitively observe the one minute's silence for Bob Paisley, it was a reminder of how far we have come in the last decade.

Crowds in the 1985–86 season were the lowest since the war, as genuine supporters turned their backs on a game blighted by hooliganism. Attendances have risen every season since, and now families are flooding back to football – in some cases unable to get tickets for the big games.

There is a general mood of optimism which extends to the Endsleigh League, worried though their clubs are about the financial gulf between the Premiership and themselves. Take today, for example. When I arrived at Luton, chairman David Kohler and his directors were looking anxiously at the League table. They have been in relegation waters most of the season.

Two hours later, after a 1-0 victory thanks to a disputed penalty, Kohler and Co. were looking at the other end of the table – declaring themselves six points off the play-offs after a run of five wins and a draw in six games under new manager Lennie Lawrence.

Even the chimneys on the roofs of the redbrick houses which give the periphery of the ground at Luton an olde worlde charm seem to be that bit straighter. Like most clubs with old-fashioned stadia, they want to relocate to a modern site, but I would hate to see all our old grounds disappear. They hold so many memories.

On the way home I tuned in to the start of David Mellor's *Six-0-Six* programme, and it made me realise the commentator's work is never done. The first caller was a Manchester United supporter appealing for a dignified observance of the minute's silence for Bob Paisley at Old Trafford tomorrow. Apparently there had been some abusive behaviour when the equivalent tribute had been paid to Sir Matt Busby at a match between Liverpool and Manchester City.

As the commentator on the BBC live match tomorrow, the possibility of the minute's silence being violated had never occurred to me. But there will be eight million or so people watching, and should it happen, the commentator would need to know the reason why. Nasty, but necessary.

Sunday 18th
This turned out to be the day when Zoë Heller declared she wanted to get pregnant; when Eduardo Abazaj ruined my lunch; and when Francis Lee shut me up once and for all – by stuffing a sausage roll into my mouth.

Because the kick-off at Old Trafford had been put back to

four o'clock, I had dispensed with my normal routine of going to Manchester the night before, and decided to brave the British Airways shuttle on Sunday morning.

Never again. Any thoughts of a leisurely flight on a half-empty plane were quickly dispelled. I never realised so many people wanted to fly to Manchester on a Sunday morning with so much baggage. The shute carrying it into the hold developed a fault, and we were delayed by 45 minutes.

Normally I would have been fretting, but the contents page of the *Sunday Times* magazine had my favourite columnist declaring: 'I'm not just broody. I am a great tanker of oestrogen waiting to spill.'

They say you should not meet your heroes or heroines, in case you are disappointed. Well, Zoë Heller can disappoint me any time she likes. At the moment she is trying to buy a house in Los Angeles without success. Back in New York, she has bravely decided to open her heart to her readers.

'I am loonily desperate to have a little sprog of my own. I know there are women having their first babies at 50 these days, and God knows, by the time I get to 50 scientists will probably be able to run up a baby out of DNA and masking tape in five minutes. But I don't care. I want my own, home-made one *now*.'

This is strong stuff with your packaged orange juice on the airline breakfast tray. The next thing I knew we were landing in pouring rain in Manchester, where I was due to meet Des Lynam and the rest of the BBC team for a production lunch at the Copthorne Hotel, just round the corner from Old Trafford.

Meanwhile, a few miles away at Maine Road, I knew Keith Curle, the City captain, was taking a late fitness test on his injured knee. If he failed, Alan Ball would have to reshuffle his whole team. I needed time to absorb that, so I had arranged to ring the City manager on a special number while he was having his own lunch.

I think I have already made it clear that some managers are more co-operative than others. Bally is definitely in the Premier League as far as I am concerned. He confirmed that Curle would play, but for all my efforts over the last 24 hours, he then came up with a substitute he could hardly pronounce.

Eduardo Abazaj (apparently pronounced Ab-ar-zi) is an Albanian defender who has joined City on a short-term contract from Benfica. Obscurely, he seems to have a Portuguese passport and therefore does not need a wok permit.

I tried to digest all this along with the roast beef and Yorkshire pudding, knowing that if the said Eduardo came on and scored the winning goal, it might just be handy to know what he looked like and a bit about him. I have always taken precautions over unexpected substitutes ever since Dieter Muller came on for West Germany in my first European Championship and scored a hat-trick. A lot of people thought it was *Gerd* Muller!

David Pleat, my co-commentator today, was also at the Copthorne, and we discussed the team formations based on the information we had both gathered. Would Giggs start on the right or on the left? Would Nigel Clough play an advanced midfield role or not?

When we got to Old Trafford, Ray Stubbs was interviewing Mick Hucknall of Simply Red in the players' tunnel. He is a big United fan, while the boys from Oasis are confirmed City freaks. There is something about pop groups and the Manchester clubs. Many years ago, when I first covered the big games, I saw a funny little fellow with glasses standing next to me on the camera platform. It turned out he was Freddie Garrity of Freddie and the Dreamers.

Well, this match was 'made for me' and the BBC. City scored first through Uwe Rosler, United equalised with a penalty even more contentious than the one at Luton yesterday, and in the second half Lee Sharpe smashed in the winner.

In the boardroom afterwards, Francis Lee and the City directors were privately fuming about the penalty that, in their view, turned the game.

It's a good thing Alan Wilkie, the referee, couldn't hear some of the things that were being said. The strange thing is, although it looked an innocuous challenge by Frontzeck on Cantona, the referee was standing only about three yards away.

Francis Lee, who has a wicked sense of humour, got a lot closer to me than that. Just as I opened my mouth to add my twopenneth to the debate, he grabbed a sausage roll off a plate and stuck it right between my teeth.

'I've waited over twenty years to shut you up,' he said with a grin. 'Not quite as long as City have waited for a win at Old Trafford,' should have been my reply. But I didn't think it was quite the day to deliver that line.

Monday 19th

Many years ago my cousin Jane and I traced our family history, going back to 1770 or something, with the help not just of Somerset House but old parish registers that we dug out of cupboards in Lincolnshire churches.

Now that my father and most of his family have passed on, I thought the days of Motson family relics were gone, but this morning a gentleman called Bruce Rhodes sent me a letter and an old football team picture from his home in Cheltenham.

It turns out that his father, Len Rhodes, was the goalkeeper in the Boston Albion football team of 1932–33, which also included my father and his brother Stanley. I knew my dad had played a bit locally as a bustling centre forward, but I had never seen this picture. Perhaps he never had a copy when he was alive.

This has all come to light because a surviving member of the team, Sydney Bradshaw, has supplied information which has been published in the local paper in Boston.

The team kit is vintage thirties – lace-up collars on the shirts, thick hooped stockings, and heavy boots with large toe caps and thick leather right up to the ankles. Underneath my father's boots (I reckon he was only about eighteen at the time) Bruce Rhodes wants me to sign my name. He is going to send a signed copy of the photograph to Sydney Bradshaw, who has never seen it.

This was not the only item of interest to reach me from Cheltenham today. David Laddams, one of the members of the Summit Else syndicate, rang to say that our horse may make her racecourse debut in a mare's bumper race at Warwick on Saturday week. He is going to the stables to see her work on Wednesday.

I await developments. Fortunately, I am scheduled to have a day off on that Saturday, so if she runs I can conceivably be there. It will be one of the few times in my life I have ever been to a race meeting in preference to a football match on a Saturday afternoon.

Tuesday 20th

Today I 'won' my first award for 30 years. Not that it had anything at all to do with commentating – there's no danger of that – but it was a presentation by BBC Video (part of BBC Worldwide, the corporation's commercial arm) to mark one million sales of the football videos I have written and narrated.

The football video market is flooded now, many of the cassettes produced on a regular basis by the clubs themselves. But when football was a comparatively new product in the video industry ten years ago, the BBC had some early success owing largely to the depth of archive material in their library.

The market leader was *The Official History of Liverpool*, devised and produced by Brian Barwick, which was released in 1987 and sold nearly 160,000 copies. In fact, it is still selling overseas.

A year later, I was also the voice on *The Official History of Manchester United*. This too easily exceeded the 100,000 figure in sales.

As time went on, other companies and production houses caught on, and soon the major stores were devoting vast shelf space to football videos alone. Ours continued to sell fairly well for a further five years.

Match of the Day was an obvious commercial masthead, and we released separate videos on the sixties, seventies and eighties, culminating in a 30-year history when the programme celebrated that milestone in 1994.

When the Premier League started in 1992, BBC Video obtained the rights for an annual release called *Race for the Title* which, as its name implies, is an account of how the Championship was won through the eyes of *Match of the Day*.

In between, I was involved in a lot of other club histories, and one release which was a favourite of mine, *The Boys from Brazil*, produced by Niall Sloane, sold over 80,000.

Eventually somebody totted up all the sales figures on the computer, and it turned out that my voice had been associated with what the video business calls 'one million units'.

The former head of BBC Video, Mike Diprose (who later moved to VCI) and his marketing manager Paul Holland (now with EMI) arranged before they left for a framed memento to be struck, with two of the covers above a nice inscription.

We had a decent dinner to mark the occasion and the certification now hangs proudly behind my desk at home.

My wife asked me when I last won anything and I decided it was in 1966, when I gained an award from the National Council for the Training of Journalists (I was a trainee on the *Barnet Press* at the time) and also became the Barnet and Potters Bar youth table tennis champion. I've still got the cup somewhere. It's the only one I will ever win.

Wednesday 21st

England should have been playing today. Well, had this been a country where the international team is properly treated they should. Other countries, such as France and Germany, organised friendlies as part of their plans for Euro 96. As I have already bemoaned, Terry Venables' team will not take the field between 12 December and 27 March.

Just for fun I decided to run through the team that, form and fitness permitting, might take the field for the first match of the Championship against Switzerland at Wembley on 8 June. What were they doing tonight, when the likes of Klinsmann and Djorkaeff were sharpening their skills in the international arena?

David Seaman – Busy keeping goal for Arsenal in the second leg of the Coca-Cola cup semi-final. (Why not play this as a straight one-off?)

Rob Jones – Waiting to play for Liverpool against Charlton in the FA Cup, having just completed the previous round at Shrewsbury. (Why was the Shrewsbury match not switched to Anfield three weeks earlier?)

Tony Adams – Injured in training and currently out of action. Hopefully fit in June.

Gary Pallister – Also the victim of a recent 'over use' injury. But busy tonight playing against Everton in a rearranged Premiership match. (If we only had eighteen teams in the league this could be avoided.)

Stuart Pearce – Out of action with a calf injury. With Graeme Le Saux having broken his leg, Venables may find himself looking for a new left back. (The danger is that Pearce may push himself too hard trying to get fit for the UEFA Cup quarter-final against Bayern.)

Darren Anderton – Yet to reappear in first team football after a long-standing groin problem.

David Platt – Returned after injury as a substitute for Arsenal against Aston Villa. Nominally the England captain, he last played an international in June last year (like Anderton, has been able to give Venables no clue to his current form).

Paul Gascoigne – Has recently become a father and been booked for over-celebrating (the two events unconnected). His goal last week against Partick Thistle was vintage Gazza (but it *was* against Partick Thistle).

Robert Lee – Missed Newcastle's rearranged Premiership match at West Ham through injury. (Their defeat means a harder run-in than expected to the Championship race.)

Teddy Sheringham – The abandoned Cup tie at Nottingham Forest this week means Spurs must play there again next Wednesday – with the possibility of a draw and a replay – before we know who meets Aston Villa in the sixth round. (He has to play League games in between, of course.)

Alan Shearer – By the time England next play, it will be eighteen months since he scored an international goal. However, he has scored 30 times for Blackburn this season, and mercifully for his Euro 96 prospects, they are out of all the Cup competitions and the Championship race. (Could he finish up as our freshest player in the summer?)

So there they are, a random selection of eleven of Terry Venables' best men. They may be his finest, but are they his fittest or his freshest?

On the evidence of this wet, woeful Wednesday, with snow on the ground and more to come, the answer is 'hardly'. The Coca-Cola semi-final went to extra time, the two FA Cup ties at Grimsby and Leeds both went to replays, and Bulgaria's visit to Wembley for the next international is still five weeks away.

My ten-year-old son put the final touch to these deliberations. Zapping through the various satellite channels, he discovered that the German station ZDF were showing live coverage of the friendly between Portugal and Germany in Oporto – two countries who obviously had their priorities right.

We were able to forget the congested English fixture list and watch the Germans get their game and minds in gear with a 2-1 victory. Jurgen Klinsmann looked eager and sharp.

So he should. He's just had a two-month winter break.

Thursday 22nd
Forget the nebulous award for video sales I mentioned earlier in the week. Tonight was the real thing for those who make an authentic contribution to television. The Royal Television Society made their annual awards, and the BBC won no fewer than twelve of them.

They were all in the news and sports broadcasting sector, and those of us who have had the privilege of working with him were thrilled that David Coleman's colossal contribution to the business was recognised by a personal award.

In case this sounds like a commercial, let me say straight away that Sky Sports deservedly carried off the prize for outstanding sports broadcast of the year. They broke new ground by covering simultaneously the two matches that settled the Premiership title last May and get full marks for imaginative use of their two dedicated sports channels.

But back to David Coleman and the BBC. His pioneering work as the first presenter of *Grandstand* and *Sportsnight* only touches the perimeter of his influence on the sports department.

When I joined, partly at his behest, in the early seventies, Coleman was in his prime. He was the editorial force behind *Sportsnight with Coleman* and *Match of the Day* – often commentating on the top match in the north of England, and then flying back to front the show in the evening.

His mastery of the athletics scene has been a constant factor for 40 years and more. As I write he is preparing for the Olympic Games in Atlanta – quite an appropriate way to mark his 70th birthday.

Coleman's sense of occasion and economy of words, together with a voice that commanded the viewer's undivided attention, gave him an unparalleled reputation in the annals of BBC sport. Nobody did more to shape its editorial policy or attain such a consistently high level of performance in such a wide area.

Together with Harry Carpenter, who recently retired on attaining the 70 landmark, he gave sports programmes a worthiness and respect which the next generation are seeking to maintain.

And I haven't mentioned until now his favourite pastime. It's called *Question of Sport*, which still commands audiences of over eight million. After a lifetime in the studio and the commentary box, Coleman remains a giant of his trade.

Friday 23rd
Talking of David Coleman reminds me of the four-seater light aircraft that used to transport him, many years ago, to those matches in the north on a Saturday, and then back to London to front *Match of the Day* in the evening.

It was probably quite cost-effective, because it used to set off from Denham airfield, just off the A40, carrying Coleman, the producer Alec Weeks, an intrepid new reporter called Motson and the pilot, who used to bring coffee and sandwiches to soften the bumps as we bobbed and weaved our way to Manchester or Liverpool.

Soon after Jimmy Hill joined us from ITV, he and I flew to Speke Airport on a squally, windy morning, and the flight left us so uncomfortable that we both needed a strong drink to settle our stomachs.

Jimmy made a light joke of this on the air that evening, overlooking the fact that there was a petrol shortage at the time and most of the country was on restricted coupons. The BBC was inundated with letters and telephone calls, complaining about these football men using gallons of valuable fuel when we could easily have got the train.

After that, we never were allowed to use the light aircraft again.

Saturday 24th

Unless you are one of those people who have written to me asking exactly how a commentator spends the day of a match, down to the last detail of what time I arrive at the ground, I suggest you skip this entry. I don't necessarily consider my working day any more taxing or interesting than anybody else's, but for those who have pressed me into a detailed account of what it involves, duty dictates that I include a blow-by-blow account of the ingredients in covering the Premiership match between Southampton and Chelsea at The Dell.

I think I have already said that I consider this to be my 'lucky ground', so undeterred by the bad weather that has again played havoc with the fixtures this week, I set off for Southampton in good heart.

9.00   Fill up with petrol at The Noke in St Albans. Bump into Geoff Shreeves of Sky TV at the garage and congratulate him on their RTS award.

9.30   Pick up our liaison man, Gordon Riddick, at his home in Watford, then a gentle drive to Southampton round the M25 and down the M3. We discuss Graham Taylor's return to his old club which is making a lot of news. Watford are at home to Ipswich today and we agree he needs a good start.

10.55   Arrive at The Dell in pouring rain. The car park attendant, Jack White, is a formidable man unless you have the correct pass. He's even been known to challenge the club secretary, Brian Truscott, before letting him in. But Brian has put us on the official list, and Jack consequently gives us a warm welcome.

11.15   Most of my preparation was done yesterday, but the club programme always prompts an extra thought or two. I give the statistics page a thorough going over, to check my figures are correct for appearances and goalscorers.

Noon   Dave Merrington, Saints' manager, has agreed to an interview for *Football Focus*. Because he likes to have lunch with the players at a nearby hotel, *Grandstand* agreed to pre-record a few minutes before the programme.

    Even though they only want three minutes, I try to get a theme into these segments. Newcastle have just splashed out about £11 million on Asprilla and Batty. Southampton have never paid more than £1.2 million for a player – simply because they cannot afford to. Merrington welcomes the chance to elaborate on this, neatly turning my suggestion that there are now two divisions of the Premiership into his own view that there are three – the top six who can buy the best players; the middle eight who are doing their best to keep pace; and the bottom six who, in a financial sense, cannot compete.

12.20   A television in the deserted press room offers the chance to watch the *Focus*. Clive Tyldesley has put together a challenging item about referees and their current dilemma of having to adopt the FIFA dogma while trying to preserve some individuality and common sense.

1.00   Having cadged a cup of tea and a plate of sandwiches from an obliging lady in the club kitchen, I continue the debate with the match referee, Gerald Ashby, who has just arrived. We agree that the irony of the present situation is that while everybody in the game is crying out for more consistency from referees, that is exactly, albeit in a heavy-handed way, what FIFA are trying to achieve.

1.15   A short meeting with John Shrewsbury, the producer, to discuss how we are going to start our package. We agree to feature Mark Hughes, who is returning from suspension, and Neil Shipperley, Southampton's top scorer and one of three former Chelsea players in the side.

1.30   From now on, the commentator stations himself in the dressing room corridor because the teams are starting to arrive. Some managers and players are talkative, others walk straight past with their minds on the game.

Glenn Hoddle and Peter Shreeves are concerned that the pitch is so heavy, but the players are more worried about sorting out tickets for family and friends.

Deep down, everybody is just going through the motions and passing time before the game. Their minds are somewhere else, including mine, which is ticking off players I can recognise as they walk past.

2.00   The managers come out of their respective dressing rooms with the official team sheets. They have three copies on different coloured paper. One goes to the referee, another to the opposition, and the third to the press and television. There are no late surprises so I shan't need my adhesive labels to make any changes on my chart.

2.15   The last chance to go to the toilet before the game ends. The television gantry at Southampton is above the roof of the main stand and there are no such facilities up there.

2.30   On the way up, I stop at a tea bar and buy a sausage roll and a soft drink. You can do that sort of thing at The Dell, where everything is very civilised. At some of the bigger grounds, I would have been knocked over in the rush.

2.45   The floor manager, Owen Thomas, gives me my headphones and makes sure the microphone is working. John Shrewsbury and I carry out a quick rehearsal and I give the *Match of the Day* office my version of the team formations for our captions which are made up in London. The days of straightforward 4-4-2 seem to have gone – we now have all sorts of fancy variations.

3.00   Gerald Ashby blows his whistle and it is straight into identification of the players. That's why the pre-match planning is so important. You don't get ten minutes to sort everybody out. After seven, Tommy Widdrington, who hardly ever scores, puts Southampton in front. Fortunately, I am at just the right angle to spot a deflection off Chelsea's Nigel Spackman.

3.20   What did I say about Ruud Gullit? I have just called him Glenn Hoddle by mistake – it must be some sort of Freudian slip. The only way out of it is to laugh it off, at which point Wise equalises for Chelsea.

3.30   As the man accused of cramming in too many facts, even I have to smile at this. Monkou (ex-Chelsea) brings down Wise (ex-Wimbledon), who then takes the penalty against Beasant (ex-Chelsea *and* Wimbledon). Mind you, it explains why they stand grinning at each other after the penalty goes into the centre of the goal – exactly where Beasant (saver of a Cup Final penalty!) had been standing.

3.45   The end of a breathless first half, with the score 2-2. But there is no time for a cup of tea. *Grandstand* come across for a live half-time report, at which point our editor in London asks me to look again at Southampton's second goal. I have credited it to Shipperley, but a different camera angle suggests it may have gone in off Mark Hughes. Just to add to the confusion, the press have decided it is an own goal by Steve Clarke! Having coped with plenty of 'dodgy' goals and scorers over 25 years, I am happy that Shipperley will ultimately get his name on it. But we get Gordon Riddick to have a word as the players come out. They confirm our initial thoughts.

4.00   It is one of those games. The second half starts with Watson missing a chance for Southampton, and soon Gullit puts Chelsea back in front. It could have ended 5-5. For good measure, Mr Ashby shows five yellow cards (all justified in my opinion) so there is plenty to keep the cameras and the commentator occupied.

4.50   With so much time added on for stoppages nowadays (what I call 'mystery time'), matches end a lot later than they used to, and this leaves *Grandstand* less time to tidy up the interviews. My first job on the final whistle, sometimes within seconds, is to deliver a short match report, which I can do without leaving my seat.

Now it is a quick dash downstairs to interview the winning manager. Easier said than done. They don't hurry in Hampshire, and a queue of dejected South- ampton supporters are slowly filing out, blocking our path to the interview room.

You have to be quick on your feet and know the geography of grounds at a time like this. We dive through a back door and slip into the first aid room.

5.00 They jam an earpiece into my right ear so that I can hear Steve Rider, and a couple of minutes later, Glenn Hoddle is live on *Grandstand*. The allotted two minutes fly past, but on handing back to the studio I keep Hoddle there so that I can fire a few extra questions for *Match of the Day*.

5.15 Further interviews follow with Dave Merrington and Dennis Wise. In between, I contact the editor on my mobile phone to see whether there is any other angle we need to follow up.

5.30 A couple of press reporters are anxious to know what the replay reveals on Southampton's second goal. We try to help each other at times like this; quite often I need to know from them what has been said in the press conference.

5.45 A welcome retreat to the guest room for a cup of tea where we find Mike Channon and Peter Osgood, colleagues in the Southampton team that won the Cup in 1976. Was it really twenty years ago? Most clubs look after their old players and Southampton are no exception; Ossie also works at Chelsea as a match-day host, and he is anxious to know whether anybody has topped his record of 1970, when he scored for Chelsea in every round of the FA Cup including the final. I promise to check it out for him.

6.00 The traffic will have eased by now so it is time to leave. On the way out, I bump into Chelsea directors Matthew Harding and Colin Hutchinson. It's amaz- ing how superstitious some football people are. Glenn Hoddle has told them Chelsea haven't lost this season when I have been the commentator, so they are quite happy that the BBC have assigned me to their FA Cup replay against Grimsby on Wednesday.

6.15   On the car radio, we hear that Watford have lost after being two up at half-time. Elton John comes on and says the players don't look fit. First job for Graham Taylor.

By a coincidence, when Gordon Riddick and I stop for a beer at Sarratt, we spot the veteran reporter from the *Watford Observer*, Oliver Phillips, who gives us a first-hand account of the events leading up to Taylor's return. According to Oliver, at least one member of the board knew little about it until it happened. It sounds to me as though Watford knew little about the second half today, Ipswich mugged them with three goals.

10.35   Having returned home and had something to eat, I take my seat along with four million others for *Match of the Day*. Top of the bill is the Maine Road meeting of Manchester City and leaders Newcastle, with Faustino Asprilla at the centre of a storm. It is gripping stuff and the graphic pictures tell a story that will run for several days. Our match becomes a lively second feature and there is a bonus in that the 'third' game between Blackburn and Liverpool also produces five goals.

One of them is the most bizarre we shall see this season, when Stan Collymore's shot hits a divot and shoots over Tim Flowers' shoulder. The Blackburn and England goalkeeper has the good grace to come on and explain what happened – or try to.

And finishing on goalkeepers, it is only when I see the edited highlights that I realise how well Kevin Hitchcock played for Chelsea. On reflection, I should have made him Man of the Match in my report, but he never got a mention.

You never get it quite right in this game.

Sunday 25th
An invitation to appear on the Frost programme is not one to be treated lightly, but in my case it was not David Frost who asked me to give up part of my Sunday, but his namesake Rob Frost.

Rob is a Methodist minister who has been seconded to carry out missionary work for the head office of the Methodist Church. He also hosts a three-hour chat and music show on Premier – the London-based Christian radio station.

The station opened in June last year, and broadcasts 24 hours a day on medium wave. *Frost at Night* runs from 9 p.m. to midnight on Sundays, and the studio is staffed largely by volunteers eager to break into broadcasting. Running parallel to the programme, there is a 'Lifeline' service – run on not dissimilar lines to the Samaritans – which takes calls from those seeking help in time of trouble.

Premier Radio is financed partly by donation and partly by advertising. It is still a bit wobbly in terms of a consolidated future, but its declared audience of 250,000 seems a solid base after less than a year.

Rob Frost has a different studio guest for each hour of his show, and augmented my contribution by having Gavin Peacock, the Chelsea player, talk on the telephone about his faith.

As a minister spreading his message, Rob Frost seems to have built a valuable bridge between the sacred and the secular.

Even down to his directions to the studio: 'Near the Pizza Hut, five minutes walk from Victoria Station.'

Monday 26th

Manchester United's 6-0 victory at Bolton has opened things up in the Championship race, and Liverpool are still in touch after winning at Blackburn. Those of us who believed Newcastle were as good as home and dry are being asked to think again. The row over Asprilla's clash with Keith Curle at Maine Road has revived memories of 1972, when Manchester City blew their Championship chance after signing Rodney Marsh. Kevin Keegan has signed not only Asprilla, but also David Batty, which means compared to this time last year the Newcastle team has changed in six positions. In the meantime, Alex Ferguson has made do with what he had, despite losing three players in the summer. And Liverpool are fielding nine Englishmen and two Irishmen with English accents. Three very different approaches to team-building.

What makes the Premiership contest even more absorbing is that although Newcastle still have a four-point lead, with a game in hand, their remaining programme looks a lot tougher on paper than those of Manchester United and Liverpool.

Last season I forecast at Christmas that Blackburn would clinch the title in the last game of the season. This year, I expect Newcastle to leave it nearly as late. But I still think they will win it. Just.

Tuesday 27th
The business press are reporting that Keith Young, the publisher of the Church of England's newspaper and the House of Commons magazine, is planning to launch Britain's first daily football newspaper.

Why have we never had one before? Countries like France, Spain, Italy, and Argentina take a daily sports paper for granted – most of it devoted to football.

One feels the reason it has never taken off here is that the national press cover the game so thoroughly that everything you want to read about the game on a daily basis is already available.

What we do lack, as I have said before, is a grown-up weekly football magazine that provides the sort of classified information which is the hallmark of *France Football*. Mind you, a lot of their pages deal with overseas events, and I feel we may be too parochial to really go for that in a big way.

I wish Mr Young well in his endeavours. But I doubt very much whether he will be successful.

Wednesday 28th
A meeting today with Sybil Ruscoe of Radio Five in Regents Park. Not an intentional one, I hasten to add, but the afternoon presenter was taking a morning constitutional when she came across a group of footballers going through a warm-up routine, and wondered what on earth I was doing watching them.

A good question. It's over a year since I've seen Grimsby Town play, and their FA Cup replay at Chelsea was not a match I was particularly looking forward to. Not after Grimsby's player-manager, Brian Laws, confessed that their shirts were by far the worst he had ever seen and the numbers on the back virtually indecipherable.

The fact that Laws has sacked the kit company, and replaced them with the manufacturers of the Juventus strip, was consolation only for the commentators who may be covering Grimsby *next* season.

For now, I was shivering on a footpath while assistant manager Kenny Swain put the team through a light training session. At this range, the players quickly became familiar. But it was something of an illusion. In their black and white stripes under the Stamford Bridge floodlights, they all looked the same.

After Sybil had passed by, wearing a decidedly puzzled expression even after I tried to explain what was happening, I tagged along with the Grimsby physiotherapist, Gerry Delahunt, who had decided to make an early departure back to the hotel.

Bertie Vogts, the German manager, once said you meet everybody twice. Well, Gerry Delahunt was the York City trainer when they beat Arsenal in a famous cup tie eleven years ago, the game in which Keith Houchen scored the winning goal with a last-minute penalty.

Gerry and Kenny Swain invited me to lunch with the Grimsby team, and the footballers' sense of humour surfaced again. The captain, Paul Groves, had tried to keep quiet the fact that it was his 30th birthday, but his team mates were not going to let that one go easily, and during lunch the hotel staff walked in singing, with a gigantic chocolate birthday cake.

Later, Groves celebrated with a cracking goal, but in a hectic five-minute spell Chelsea replied with three of their own, and finished up winning 4-1.

As for Grimsby's shirts, Brian Laws was quite right. A lot of guessing went on from the commentator, but fortunately they spent most of the game deep in defence.

One of the reasons was another fluent display from Ruud Gullit. When I interviewed him afterwards, he said the Italian League was now envious of the FA Carling Premiership, because so many of the best players were now coming to England.

I don't think it was the Dutchman just being diplomatic. Any thoughts that he had come to Chelsea for the pay cheque were dispelled a while ago, but any lingering doubts have been erased by his last two performances. He covered more ground than anybody else on the pitch and went off tonight to a huge ovation.

So too, no doubt, did Wimbledon, Southampton and Liverpool, all of whom made sure of their place in the last eight. But the one match everybody wanted settled – the rearranged game between Nottingham Forest and Tottenham – ended in a draw and will have to be replayed on the day of the sixth round.

With Forest's forthcoming European commitments, it could even mean one of the semi-finals being delayed. And just for good measure, England's Teddy Sheringham picked up an injury. What a surprise!

Thursday 29th
Nobody proposed to me today, but they wouldn't have found me anyway. I caught the early train from Stevenage to Durham to attend the launch of the Great North Run. This is the moment when the entry list is officially opened and something approaching 30,000 enthusiasts fill in their entry forms.

BBC *Sunday Grandstand* will be covering the event as usual, so it is appropriate that my colleagues Steve Rider, Garth Crooks, Ray Stubbs and Gary Richardson have all agreed to run – although Gary has been suffering from what he fears may be shin splints so at the moment is an injury doubt!

I promised to donate any sponsorship money I could raise to NCH 'Action for Children' (which used to be called the National Children's Home). When I was a child at Sunday school, we used to sell little pictures of homeless children called 'Sunny Smiles' for a shilling a time, so from all my runs this year I am hoping to raise one million old shillings – effectively £50,000.

Bearing in mind I intend to run twelve events totalling a modest 100 miles, I need to receive promises totalling £500 per mile. Sponsorship forms are being circulated forthwith!

MARCH
1996

Friday 1st

We got the charity idea into the public arena thanks to some good publicity in the *Newcastle Journal*. Almost immediately, Neil Wilson of the *Daily Mail* phoned to ask me for more details – he wanted to prepare a piece for his television sports column next Monday.

I thought it only fair to mark Neil's card about the BBC announcement this weekend regarding the allocation of matches at the end of the season.

I couldn't pre-empt their press release by giving him an exclusive, but at least I was able to warn him that the news would come out over the next few days.

Wilson has his own sources of information in our business, which is why he has the most widely read column of its kind. He was not in the least surprised when I mentioned there could be a news item in the offing – in fact, I got the impression he already had wind of it from other people.

What was of greater concern to me was the recurrence of an old groin strain which bothered me when I went for my morning run. The dreadful thought occurred that I could accept pledges of money for Action for Children and then find myself unfit to pound out the mileage. No pun intended.

Saturday 2nd

This was supposed to be my Saturday off, and had been set aside for a trip to Warwick to see Summit Else make her race course debut in a mare's bumper flat race at the end of the card.

I had intended to join the other members of our syndicate so that we could mark the occasion with a decent lunch, but the circuitous route that the FA Cup is taking this season put paid to all that.

The fact that Tottenham and Nottingham Forest now had to

143

replay their fifth round tie on sixth round day meant that only one quarter-final will be played next Saturday – Chelsea against Wimbledon at Stamford Bridge.

Having learned only yesterday that I will be covering that match, I had to go to Selhurst Park today to see the two teams meet in a Premiership match.

The chances are that when clubs come face to face on two successive weekends, there is some sort of 'carry over' from the first game. Certainly I would not have felt comfortable commentating on the Cup tie without knowing at first hand what had happened in the League game.

As things turned out, not a lot *did* happen. Chelsea switched their team around to combat Wimbledon's style, and the Dons were without Dean Holdsworth and Mick Harford – both of whom were expected to play the following week.

The game ended in a tame 1-1 draw, with the players showing almost too much respect for each other. Vinny Jones, who had been sent off against Chelsea earlier in the season, hardly made a tackle.

David Mellor breezed in just before the kick off with his *Six-0-Six* producer. But like a lot of people, they were more concerned about Monday's Championship showdown between Newcastle and Manchester United.

How times have changed. Saturday used to be sacrosanct as 'football day', but on a weekend like this the two biggest games are being played on Sunday (Liverpool v. Aston Villa) and Monday.

Soon rugby's Five Nations Championship will probably change its format due to the demands of television. For now, there are five weekends with two matches on each, and today England beat Scotland at Murrayfield to spoil the Scots' Grand Slam hopes and give themselves a chance to win the Triple Crown.

There were no tries in the match, and on the radio the commentators were giving the England pack grudging praise for dominating the game, while bemoaning the lack of flowing rugby.

It reminded me of the 'boring England' tag that followed Alf Ramsey around for a while after we won the World Cup, and made me wonder how much we would give for Venables' team to win Euro 96 by scraping a series of 1-0 wins.

I am a big admirer of Ian Robertson – the best rugby

broadcaster in my opinion – but today I thought he was very biased on the radio towards Scotland. I made a mental note to have a good-natured pop at him when we meet at Cheltenham next week. On second thoughts, I won't go too strong – he not only knows a lot about rugby but is also a handy tipster on the horses.

Which is where we came in today. All I know after reading the racing results is that Summit Else did not finish in the first three. She finished ninth in a field of 25, apparently overtaking seven or eight other horses in the last three furlongs. In racing parlance, she 'ran on well'.

All being well she will be entered for another bumper before the end of the season, but it will be next autumn before we see her over hurdles.

The next hurdle for England's last survivors in Europe, Nottingham Forest, is a UEFA Cup quarter-final against Bayern Munich. The first leg is in Germany on Tuesday, and we are covering it 'live and exclusive'.

Sunday 3rd

The German equivalent to the BBC, which I can now pick up on a satellite channel, reports that Bayern have gone back to the top of the *Bundesliga* by beating their big city rivals, Munich 1860, 4-2 yesterday in the Olympic Stadium.

It is ominous news for Forest, especially as Jurgen Klinsmann scored twice. In three UEFA Cup rounds, he has already garnered eleven goals and Forest will be without their experienced defender, Colin Cooper, who is suspended.

Keeping up with disciplinary matters in UEFA competitions is a real headache. According to my records, no fewer than fourteen players will start Tuesday's match with one yellow card against their name from an earlier round – nine from Bayern and five Forest men.

This means one or more of them will miss the second leg if they are cautioned again in Munich. I just hope I remember to mention that when the moment arises.

At times like this you need a good contact who can tell you about the overseas team, and the commentator's passport on this occasion was Tony Woodcock, the former Forest and England striker who has been playing and coaching in Germany for the last ten years.

A good thing I checked. Bayern's goalkeeper, Oliver Kahn,

was sent off yesterday. They then took off the captain, Lothar Matthaus, in order to bring on the substitute goalkeeper. Mind you, they were already four goals up by then.

Also ahead of the game was Norman Giller, in the *Sunday Express*. He broke the news regarding our end-of-season match allocation. The fact that the BBC have let the commentators know now, and made it public, means there will not be any mischievous or damaging publicity around the time of the two big Cup Finals. Barry Davies and I will do one each – in what, after all, is a unique season with Euro 96 being held in England.

Monday 4th
David Bryant, head of public relations at BUPA, got my charity running scheme off to a fast start today when he pledged £1,000 as a contribution from the sponsors of the Great North Run.

Neil Wilson did as he promised by giving the project a mention in his *Daily Mail* television sports column. He also revealed that Messrs Rider, Crooks and Stubbs would be running the half marathon with me at Newcastle in September. So now they can't back out – not that I thought they would!

I met Alan Parry and Jim Rosenthal today at an annual lunch staged at Ealing Golf Club by Will and Danny Toye, directors of Allport Freight Ltd. This is purely a social event at which everybody catches up with what has been happening over the last year. Will and Danny were still going strong when I left for the airport to link up with Trevor Brooking for our trip to Munich.

Ray Stubbs had some good news for us. He had discovered that there was a bar in Munich where we could watch the critical Premiership match between Newcastle and Manchester United – a game that would do awfully well to live up to its gigantic billing. Rather like the Bruno–Tyson fight, the previews had been going on for weeks – or so it seemed.

As it turned out it was a smashing evening, not necessarily because Manchester United won and reopened the Championship race, but because we watched the game in the company of some cheerful Nottingham Forest supporters.

It was an Irish bar called Shenanigans (as Frank Skinner would say: 'There was all sorts of Paddy Mulligans going on in there') and the atmosphere was really jumping.

At the final whistle, I thought you had to hand it to Alex

Ferguson. He hadn't spent a penny on his team for over a year, but he was now just one point behind Keegan's team and also through to the quarter-finals of the FA Cup. All that, after selling Hughes, Ince and Kanchelskis and putting his faith in the kids.

When we got back to the hotel, the Forest players had gone to bed but Frank Clark and his staff were still puzzling over a quiz question: Name seventeen Nottingham Forest players who had been capped by England in the last twenty years.

They had sixteen names but were still searching for the last one. I suggested Peter Ward, who came on as substitute for his only cap when England played in Australia just before the 1980 European Championship.

On second thoughts, he was probably still a Brighton player at that time. Clough and Taylor signed him soon afterwards though, so it will do as an answer for now.

Tuesday 5th

In the lobby of the Park Hilton Hotel in Munich this morning, I met the man who could just ruin England's European Championship hopes in June. Perversely, he was born in Barnsley.

Mark Crossley, the Nottingham Forest goalkeeper, had a Scottish grandmother, which means he is apparently eligible to play for either England or Scotland. As his current form is approaching international standard, I wondered if he had made up his mind.

Being a sensible chap, he had worked out that England have got better goalkeepers than Scotland. Well, I could have told him that has been the case since poor Frank Haffey conceded nine goals at Wembley in 1961. When they asked Scotsmen the time that night, the reply was 'Haffey past nine'.

Crossley was far more diplomatic than that, but he declared his allegiance to Scotland and was hoping to play in a 'B' international later in the season.

Thinking further ahead, I mentally pencilled him in as a candidate for their Euro 96 squad and decided to flag him up as their number one keeper in tonight's commentary. I know he speaks with a Yorkshire accent, but he does room with Scot Gemmill so he's doing his best to become the best Anglo-Scottish goalkeeper since Bob Wilson.

Of more concern to Frank Clark, and to Terry Venables for that matter, was the condition of Stuart Pearce, who has missed eight matches with a torn calf muscle sustained in an England training session.

He came through Forest's equivalent without mishap this morning, and only when he reported no ill effects at teatime did Clark confirm that he would play.

Around this time outside Munich's Olympic Stadium, a good old international incident was brewing between German security guards and the English radio and television corps.

Now we all know what happened in the Munich Olympics in 1972 (the breach of security which led to the massacre of Israeli athletes), and it was a fact that some 80 Forest followers had been arrested over the last 48 hours, but there seemed little point in keeping about 30 of us in the freezing cold for an hour while they carried out their umpteenth search of the stadium.

Not even the sizeable figure of Larry Lloyd, the former Forest centre half now working for local radio, could persuade the uniformed guards to give way and let us even as far as the foyer. Quite a few of the radio lads had preview pieces to do and were running out of time to set up their equipment.

Things got so fractious that I half-expected Neville Chamberlain to materialise out of the ether waving a piece of paper. No appeals to the Bayern Munich press officer or the UEFA delegate made any difference.

In the end we were grudgingly admitted to the press area, but I could see a situation where they were going to produce the team sheets about five minutes before the kick off, if we were lucky.

This is the part of the job nobody sees, and really nobody needs to know about. I managed to squeeze through a couple of doors that led to the players' tunnel and was lucky enough to bump into Jurgen Klinsmann, who did some work for the BBC when he was with Tottenham.

Klinsmann was his usual charming self and gave me the Bayern Munich team and their substitutes – something that would have come through the official channels about an hour later.

For all its history and architecture, I find the Olympic Stadium a soulless place. The crowd are a long way from the pitch and people who have played there, like Alan Hansen, all say that it lacks atmosphere.

Even when Klinsmann put Bayern ahead, the cheering could have been coming out of a can, it was so muffled. And a minute later, when Chettle equalised for Forest, the ground was so quiet I actually thought the ball had gone out of play until it appeared in the back of the net.

At this stage two guys in front of us in the commentary seats began to have an argument with one of the aforementioned security men. Great for the concentration, since the players on the far side were like midgets from where we were sitting.

Wednesday 6th
Breakfast this morning was like a news bulletin. Ray Stubbs and Tony Woodcock had gone out for a couple of beers with Larry Lloyd after the match last night and stayed quite late in what the Germans call a 'night cafe'.

Tony was flying back to Cologne and Trevor Brooking and I were getting a midday flight to London, but Ray had intended catching an earlier plane. It appeared he had misread his watch because of the hour time difference, and missed the flight.

But when we got to the airport, there were some Forest fans in a far worse situation. They had missed the coach that was due to take them directly back to Nottingham overnight, and not only had it gone without them – but their passports were on it.

These lads had spent the night at the airport pleading their case, and good old British Airways came to their rescue. One of them was able to borrow the commentator's pen and jot down a few flight details so he could ring his wife and get her to drive down to London from Nottingham to pick them up.

Our good turn done for the day, Brooking and I repaired to the airport bar where he had his usual diet Coke and told me about the conversation he had had in the hotel last night with Forest's Brian Roy.

The Dutchman had been keen to talk about tactics and technique – impressing Trevor with his knowledge and his inquiring mind.

It must be a national trait because word was reaching us, from those who came over on the day of the Munich match, that Ruud Gullit had been a revelation as Sky's analyst on the Newcastle match the night before. Apparently Andy Gray had said, 'Don't ask him to come on again – he knows too much about football.' We already knew about Gullit at the BBC – he joined our team for the Ireland v. Holland play-off in December and plans are afoot to sign him up for the European Championship.

As for Brian Roy and Forest, they were starting to think they had paid Bayern too much respect. On reflection, they could have done better than come away with a 2-1 defeat, and an away goal.

However, they know there is nothing to be afraid of in the second leg. The tie is nicely balanced, but then again, would you back against Klinsmann scoring at Nottingham?

Thursday 7th
Joe Bugner was back in London today. Next week, three days after his 46th birthday, he will fight British and Commonwealth heavyweight champion Scott Welch for the WBO Inter-Continental title.

The British Boxing Board of Control refused Bugner a licence to fight here, but the contest will go ahead in Berlin with Bugner declaring, 'When I beat Henry Cooper in 1971, I beat someone who couldn't even walk in my shadow.'

Well, I was at that fight, reporting for BBC Radio, and I've still got my score card. Like a lot more people, mine did not tally with that of referee Harry Gibbs. I still believe, 25 years later, that Cooper won the fight.

It was on my little Uher (the old, now defunct BBC tape recorder) that Cooper announced his retirement to the radio audience. I can still see him now, walking towards Gibbs at the final bell, and the referee going straight past him to lift the arm of Bugner.

Not that I have anything against Joe. He and his manager, Andy Smith, were regular interviewees in my radio boxing days. Just before he fought Cooper, Joe had a warm-up against a Canadian Bill Drover at the York Hall, Bethnal Green. It was called a draw, but Andy didn't like it when I described it as a diplomatic decision.

Anyway, as we all know, Joe went on to fight for the world title, and good luck to him, although what he's doing making a comeback at the age of 46 only he knows. What is more, there is just the faint possibility his fight might be overshadowed next weekend by another little affray between two heavyweights called Tyson and Bruno.

These deliberations were interrupted by a call from Ray Stubbs, who confessed the real reason he missed the plane from Munich was because he fell asleep in the hotel lobby.

It brings back to mind that story of how long it took some

of the Celtic fans to get back to Glasgow after they won the European Cup in Lisbon in 1967. It is said some are still not accounted for.

Neither are those people who ran on the pitch at Wembley a year earlier and gave Kenneth Wolstenholme the chance to say those immortal words. Ken has now joined forces with a tabloid newspaper to trace them.

Since nobody has discovered who they were after 30 years of playing the tape back, one is left to assume they were German supporters trying to get out of the stadium.

Friday 8th
At last I have got a new coat – and it's the genuine article. A sheepskin a shade lighter in colour than the one about to be cast into mothballs, but of the same shape, size and origin.

Having failed lamentably to find a replacement by appealing on *Grandstand*, and discovering that the leading London stores had none on display, I remembered that when I had mine made to measure all those years ago, our senior floor manager at the BBC, Dave Bowden, also bought one. But whereas I wore my coat out, he kept his in its Cellophane cover and never wore it once.

When we were at a match together recently, I made him a cash offer for it, and because we were standing near our interview camera the conversation was picked up by a sensitive microphone and recorded.

Thus, neither of us could back out of the deal. To his utmost credit, Dave delivered the coat to our house on his journey back from a match, so I added a few pounds for his petrol and solemnly completed the deal.

The coat will make its debut at Stamford Bridge tomorrow, when Chelsea play Wimbledon in the FA Cup sixth round. Fittingly, Dave is on duty and will be tickled pink (or maybe grey) by seeing it in use for the first time.

Traditionally, this was always the weekend when football sheds *its* overcoat and its winter turns into spring. Two games away from Wembley and all that.

But the weather today was foul. Cold, sleeting rain soaked the players and spectators as Killigrew School's 'B' team drew 3-3 with neighbours Windermere.

Despite letting in three goals, including a last-minute equaliser, Killigrew's ten-year-old goalkeeper was praised for his performance. Frederick Motson has learned how to shout at his defenders. Probably by studying Peter Schmeichel.

Saturday 9th

What was I saying about Mark Crossley? Today he saved three penalties in the shoot-out at the end of the Tottenham–Nottingham Forest FA Cup replay. He is also, as my colleague Clive Tyldesley informed the nation, the only goalkeeper to date to have saved a penalty from Matthew Le Tissier, and one of only two to have stopped one in the FA Cup Final (from Gary Lineker, of all people).

So the 1996 version of the FA Cup (or the 'FA Cup in association with Littlewoods Pools', as we media types are now told to call it) stuttered a little bit nearer its penultimate stages. The match at White Hart Lane was a much-delayed fifth round replay, and Forest will now play Aston Villa next Wednesday in a rearranged sixth round tie.

If Leeds and Liverpool draw tomorrow, the FA will make the draw for the semi-final without a single team definitely being through, because my match at Stamford Bridge was also drawn – a south-west London set-to between Chelsea and Wimbledon ending 2-2 with all the goals in the second half.

Peter Osgood, showing sponsors' groups around the ground in his capacity as match-day host, was pleased when I told him, further to his question of two weeks ago, that nobody *had* scored in every round of the FA Cup since he did so in 1970. He was less than pleased when I added that there were about seven players who could still do it this year, depending on this weekend's results.

But the Cup is in a mess. If Forest and Villa draw next Wednesday, their replay will have to take place on semi-final weekend, owing to Forest's European commitment and the long-awaited return to action of the England team later in March.

What with the ten-day police rule, the demands of television, and the proliferation of fixtures anyway, the game is getting itself into a bit of a cul-de-sac. I won't refer again to my conversation with Terry Venables at Christmas, but there was a way round it – for this season anyway.

Still in the 'didn't I tell you so' mode, Dougie Freedman is going great guns at Crystal Palace, who have now been propelled into the promotion frame under new manager Dave Bassett.

Freedman got the winner against West Brom today (his fif-teenth goal since he moved from Barnet), but we will stop short of trying to get Craig Brown to pick him for Scotland in Euro 96. One recommendation is quite enough for this week. And on second thoughts, is Mark Crossley eligible anyway, having won three under-21 caps for England a few years ago?

Sunday 10th
The oldest runner in the Hemel Hempstead ten-mile road race, organised by Dacorum and Tring A.C. and sponsored by Kodak Ltd, was a mere 83 years old.

It was the second year running I had the pleasure of presen-ting her with a special prize. Her young companion, who trotted round just behind her, was only 75.

They were part of a record entry approaching 1,000 runners, the fastest of which skated round the course in just over 50 minutes.

Hemel was the first of the twelve runs I have agreed to enter. It was a calm, fairly warm morning so there were no excuses, apart from my general condition, for the exceedingly moderate time of 1 hour 26 minutes – precisely the same as for the Fred Hughes Memorial at St Albans two months earlier. At least I am not getting any slower – for the time being.

When you get to the super-vets stage, which is the name they give to runners over 50, you need a rest in the afternoon, and the live FA Cup tie between Leeds and Liverpool must have been a useful sedative for many viewers. My BBC colleagues made no attempt to hide the truth – as a spectacle it never got out of the dressing room.

The match apart, the attendance figure of under 25,000 was a trifle disturbing. Two of the country's biggest clubs meeting in the quarter-finals of the most glamorous competition, and the crowd is a full 15,000 below capacity.

Perhaps those absent fans knew something. Or maybe Leeds' recent run of Cup success, with all the attendant matches and replays, has drained their pockets. Then again, a few Liverpool fans probably settled for the television option rather than travelling.

Either way, it showed that sooner or later, the law of diminishing returns will apply to football. At current prices, people can only afford to go to so many matches, and ultimate-ly they will pick and choose.

Managers may disagree, but now that they and the players are picking up such big salaries, there is surely a responsibility to entertain. Jimmy Hill said on television today that spectators watching players who are earning up to £10,000 a week are entitled to see the ball passed properly.

And there were some interesting comments from Terry Venables, when he came back from watching Ajax beat Borussia Dortmund in the Champions League. 'Now we are paying the players three times as much, thanks to television money, are they three times as good?' asked Venables, and gave a negative reply.

The point he was making is that coaching seems to stop once the players have reached a certain age and standard. It certainly hasn't stopped at Ajax.

Frank Clark, whose Forest team were in Munich the same night, said this week that English football will only improve in the long term if and when its new technical director – still to be appointed – breaks the stranglehold the schools have on young talent.

'Take Tony Woodcock and his club in Cologne. They have twenty groups of boys who come to them three nights a week from the age of five upwards. Only recently have we in England been allowed to work with boys at the age of eight.

'We aso need to improve the quality of our coaching. To gain the qualification to work like Woodcock in Germany, you have to complete a six-month residential course.'

All very worthy, and in the long term as truly essential as it is essentially true. But most of all I liked Bryon Butler's comment in the *Daily Telegraph*, when he heard Bruce Rioch praising Dennis Bergkamp for staying out an hour later after training to practise his shooting skills.

'One is entitled to ask the question, where on earth were the other Arsenal players?'

Monday 11th

On the way down to Cheltenham for the National Hunt Festival, we called in at Nigel Twiston-Davies and Peter Scudamore's stables at Naunton, where my travelling companion Bob Sims could only commiserate with his chaser Earth Summit, one-time favourite for the Grand National. He tore a ligament in his last race at Haydock and will be out of action for over a year.

In the next box, Earth Summit's half-sister, Summit Else, looked bigger than when I last saw her. The five-year-old filly came through her first bumper at Warwick very comfortably, according to the stable, but they don't expect her to run again until they put her over hurdles next season. Bob believes her real future is over fences in two years' time.

Manchester United, meantime, are jumping one fence after another. They made it ten wins in a row by beating Southampton at Old Trafford in the FA Cup sixth round.

Eric Cantona scored the first goal and made the second. Again, Ferguson's policies were vindicated. Quite apart from his losing three senior players without replacing them, there was criticism a year ago when he rushed to France to persuade Cantona to continue in English football.

Now, for the third season running, Manchester United are chasing the double. You cannot pick up a newspaper without reading the remaining fixtures for the three leading contenders.

Football apart, what a great week for sport. The National Hunt Festival, the Bruno–Tyson fight, and the climax to the Five Nations tournament in rugby union.

Tuesday 12th
A trio of three former rugby union internationals were the first familiar faces I met at the course on the opening day of Cheltenham.

Ian Robertson, Nigel Starmer-Smith and Chris Rea – all media men of some repute after their playing exploits with England and Scotland – were guests of Guinness, who were sponsoring the Arkle Challenge Trophy Steeple Chase.

Before we sat down to lunch in the Festival Suite, Robertson introduced the leading jockey Richard Dunwoody, who ran through the card with some pointers for the benefit of those like myself whose knowledge beyond the names and colours was sparse.

Very good of him, too. We backed his horse, Ventana Canyon, in the Arkle Chase, and saw it come home ahead of the favourite, Arctic Kinsman.

Between races, we went back inside to keep warm and to chew the fat about our respective sports. Chris Rea's thoughts on the future of rugby union were particularly pointed.

'In soccer, the clubs drive the game. In rugby union, the clubs are driven by the international game. Going professional will mean a hideous overstretch on funds. There is no way rugby clubs are going to find up to one million pounds to pay the wages.'

By the end of the afternoon, it was our own funding that was suffering. But Robertson had a farewell tip for the guests of Guinness. 'The best eight to one shot of the week,' he announced solemnly as they studied their race cards for the umpteenth time. 'Ireland to beat England at Twickenham on Saturday.'

Wednesday 13th
Dunblane. The mention of that one word will chill the hearts of this and future generations like that of Lockerbie, Aberfan, Hillsborough and Hungerford. The massacre of sixteen children and their teacher at a primary school in a peaceful part of Scotland was impossible to comprehend and for the best part of the day, as the shocking news unfolded, the mind almost refused to accept it could have happened.

Some civilisation, when a loner whose peculiarities were well known to his neighbours and to the local police, was allowed to keep a random selection of guns and rifles while bearing an open grudge against society, and one school in particular.

But the inquests will come later. Today you ached for the parents, and for those little lives that were never allowed to flower. And you hugged your own children that little bit tighter, and tried to shoulder your part of the blame for the world we have grown up in, and the standards we have helped shape and come to accept.

Thursday 14th
Gold Cup day at Cheltenham, where the weather is still bitterly cold. Last night over dinner I bumped into Tony Currie, the former England international who is now community officer at his old club, Sheffield United. Why is it that the footballers who were so flamboyant in their playing days seem so conservative by comparison when you meet them later in life?

Currie, with his flowing blond locks and his extravagant style, belonged to that talented group of players in the early seventies who were blessed not only with sublime skills but also a playboy image. His name would get mentioned with those of Hudson, Worthington, Bowles and Osgood.

Yet Tony played for England more often than any of them.

He won a total of seventeen caps under three different managers – Alf Ramsey, Don Revie and Ron Greenwood – over a period of seven years. Now, that fair hair is a lot shorter, the speech is quiet and considered, and the drink is mostly fruit juice. It was his second wife, Jane, who brought up the subject of one of his greatest goals and the strangulated cries of an excitable young commentator.

It took Currie and Motson a little time to work out that it was 21 years ago this month (to the week, in fact) when Tony sent three West Ham players the wrong way with a single sway of the hips and slid the ball casually past Mervyn Day at Bramall Lane. 'A quality goal by a quality player' it was labelled, and I would probably say the same thing now, only in a better tone of voice I hope.

The Cheltenham commentators could be forgiven for losing *theirs* during the run-in to the Gold Cup, in which the Irish horse Imperial Call held off Rough Quest with the odds-on favourite, One Man, labouring back in sixth place.

Some of the behaviour in the parade ring as the winner was led in after the race would have worried the authorities in football or boxing, but this was sheer euphoria which has its place when the Irish win at Cheltenham.

Annie had backed the winner but my own fancy, Dublin Flyer, had faded some way out. Two other winners, Cyborgo and Kibreet, made it seem a decent day.

But it wasn't really. There would not be one person among the 50,000 on the course who was not touched by the Dunblane tragedy. They held a minute's silence at Cheltenham and everything happening at the festival, or anywhere else for that matter, seemed strangely unreal.

Friday 15th
Today John Major and Tony Blair put on a united front as they visited the scene of the massacre. Both were visibly moved by what they found.

It was announced there would be a minute's silence before all tomorrow's football matches – and throughout the nation on Sunday.

But no amount of hand-wringing will bring back one of the sixteen little children whose lives were wiped out almost before they began. Nor will it make any easier the desperate attempt by their families and friends to rebuild their lives.

Saturday 16th

The last day of my spring holiday, and a moment to take stock of where the season stands. Franz Carr's goal for Aston Villa at Nottingham Forest on Wednesday saved a horrendous fixture pile-up in the FA Cup. At least we now know we shall have two semi-finals played on the appointed day.

That's in two weeks' time, but before then I have been allocated four important matches. The second leg of Nottingham Forest v. Bayern Munich on Tuesday; the Wimbledon–Chelsea Cup replay on Wednesday; Arsenal against Newcastle in the Premiership race next Saturday; then England v. Bulgaria in a Wembley friendly four days later.

On paper it looks a tough schedule but they are all big games and the sort that commentators like to be involved in. For today, a quiet visit to Barnet was on the cards. I had not been to my local club since Christmas, and their progress up Division Three begged the question on the lips of so many supporters up and down the country: 'Can we make the play-offs?'

Barnet's opponents today were Torquay, presently propping up the League and hoping like hell that Stevenage win the GM Vauxhall Conference so that nobody will be relegated from the Endsleigh League.

Barnet manager Ray Clemence, down to his last fourteen players owing to injury and suspension, had set his team a target of seven points from their next three games to retain any realistic chance of a play-off position.

They made a solid start by beating Torquay 4-0 and it could have been more. When Sean Devine scored his second and Barnet's fourth goal, a supporter stripped to his underpants, ran on to the pitch and cavorted around so that the re-start was delayed.

Eventually two or three Barnet players intercepted the semi-streaker and manhandled him off the pitch into the arms of the security staff.

The interruption obviously got to the referee, Tony Leake of Darwen. He had no sooner booked the Torquay left back, Steve Winter, for arguing with a linesman, than he collapsed, holding his back.

There were two splendid replacements sitting in the stand – Jack Taylor and Philip Don, who in their different eras have refereed the FA Cup Final and in the World Cup. In the

158

event neither was needed, because Mr Leake made a rapid recovery.

All of this came as a spot of light relief for Tony Kleanthous, the Barnet chairman, who told me that the club was still losing over £15,000 a week and his plans for relocating Barnet to the Copthall Stadium depended very much on overcoming opposition from local residents.

It's a hard slog in the Third Division of the Endsleigh, and remembering what happened earlier in the season, when Barnet sold Dougie Freedman to keep the wolf from the door, I couldn't help but notice the commanding form of their goalkeeper Maik Taylor.

Barnet bought him out of the army for £700, and Kleanthous has already had an offer of over £400,000 from a Premiership club.

Among the scouts at the game was Eddie Baily, Bill Nicholson's old assistant at Tottenham. Quite apart from noting Taylor's performance, he probably spared a thought for Nicholson, who today celebrated the 60th anniversary of his arrival at Spurs as a seventeen-year-old in 1936.

Bill was a guest of the directors but for Tottenham it wasn't a happy occasion. They lost 3-2 to Blackburn, with Alan Shearer completing his hat-trick in 'mystery time'.

At roughly the same moment, elsewhere in London, Eric Cantona saved a point for Manchester United and in doing so probably condemned Queens Park Rangers to relegation. This meant Cantona had scored vital goals in three successive games, and his club had gone top of the Premiership for the first time since September – at least for 48 hours.

But it made me wonder how different the League table might look if games only lasted 90 minutes. This stoppage time thing has become a hobby horse of mine, but it is getting to the stage where a team leading by one goal are entitled to know how much longer they have to play.

Barnet moved up a couple of places, by the way, and when I left the ground they were studying Ceefax to assess their play-off chances. Similar to the people at Luton just four short weeks ago ... but tonight Luton are one from the bottom of Division One with only improving Watford below them.

Three points for a win is not good for the nerves necessarily, but it has made the second half of the season very exciting. Crystal Palace were nowhere a month ago – now under Dave Bassett they are third and climbing.

Sunday 17th

Graham Taylor rang today. A mutual acquaintance of ours, Peter McCrimmon, passed away a few days ago after a long battle against cancer. Graham and Peter had played together as schoolboys in the Scunthorpe Under-15 team.

Happiness is in short supply at the moment, and nowhere more so, Graham Taylor said, than when he arrived for his second spell at Watford. On and off the pitch, morale was low, and in his role as general manager he intended to bring a few smiles back to a club that, in his ten-year partnership with Elton John, had always been community based.

Expectation was going to be a problem. The economics of the game have changed so much that it was unrealistic to assume Taylor or anybody else could take Watford into the never-never land that he achieved in the eighties – second to Liverpool in the Championship, runners-up in the FA Cup at Wembley, and into the third round of the UEFA Cup.

Perhaps his treatment as England manager and his experience at Wolves have made Taylor more cautious, but it sounded to me as though he was not entirely sure whether he had made the right decision in returning to Watford.

But the early signs were encouraging. Yesterday they held leaders Derby on their own ground – only a disputed penalty prevented them winning – and earlier in the week Watford forced a spirited 4-4 draw at West Brom after being three goals down.

They say 'never go back', but then again sometimes a club and a manager are made for each other. I have already said how disturbing it is for supporters when managers keep chopping and changing, and those who jumped ship for whatever reason earlier in the season cannot be too thrilled with the League tables this morning.

Another caller not exactly full of beans today was Mark Bright, my travelling companion of a few weeks ago. He had been left out of the Sheffield Wednesday side as David Pleat rebuilds, and his cause wasn't helped when one of the Yugoslav players jumped into his back during a practice match. Believe it or not they were playing on the same side!

But with a name like Bright you can't be depressed for too long and he offered me £100 towards the charity.

Very generous of him. Wait until I get hold of his former ¹eicester colleague, the versatile Mr Lineker. I shall expect him ⸱ch that – at the very least.

160

Monday 18th

Somebody once said that nobody should be allowed to write another book for ten years, just so we can all catch up on the ones that have already been written.

I am starting to feel the same way about football matches. Gone are the days when it was a Saturday and Wednesday game – now if you are making a cup of tea on a Sunday afternoon you are liable to miss a vital goal, and if you so much as go to the toilet on a Monday night, the Championship picture has probably changed by the time you come back.

Take this weekend for example. Time was when BBC Radio's *Sports Report* and television's *Match of the Day* had wrapped up the day's football news by six o'clock and eleven o'clock respectively. Sunday really was a day of rest for football people, and the only major matches played on Mondays were at West Ham early in the season.

But yesterday, which was Mother's Day, there must have been many mums up and down the country who felt that sport, and football in particular, had sent family life reeling out of the front door.

Much the same way as Mike Tyson left Frank Bruno in the early hours of Sunday morning. Those who went without sleep to 'pay as they viewed' that seven-minute demolition, next turned their weary attention to the World Cup cricket final in which ebullient Sri Lanka overcame Australia.

And that was before a football bill that, if you followed it all the way through, lasted not far short of ten hours.

This time the satellite subscribers needed no extra money to watch Paul Gascoigne play a central role in the Old Firm derby. The 1-1 draw between Rangers and Celtic was followed by a 2-2 result in the Premiership between Leeds and Everton.

Meantime, back in the Endsleigh League, Sunderland were showing the nation why they are the new leaders of Division One by winning at Birmingham in a match screened live by ITV.

Poor old Port Vale. There they were, playing at Wembley for the first time ever, and hardly anybody was watching. A crowd of around 12,000 saw them lose 5-2 to Genoa in the Anglo-Italian Cup Final, but when they went five goals down the English team were probably grateful that this was one Cup Final nobody had the air time to screen.

About and around all this, Sky were repeating and analysing

all the goals scored in yesterday's Premiership programme, while ITV rounded up the rest of the Endsleigh League.

And that was just the *start* of the week. Tonight Newcastle played West Ham and on Tuesday, Wednesday and Thursday we shall have European quarter-finals – with a couple of FA Cup replays thrown in for good measure.

Bloated to the point of needing a change of diet, lunch with Mike Dillon, Ladbrokes' director of public relations, seemed the perfect antidote. Chris Bell, Mike's managing director, and Terry Sherring, Ladbrokes' special events manager, had hosted some excellent hospitality at the National Hunt Festival, but I had a more devious reason for bending Mike's ear today.

It was a long-held ambition of mine to have lunch with the commentator I most admire – Peter O'Sullevan, still calling them past the post in that smooth, murmuring style at the age of 78.

Mike promised to act as Mr Fix-it. Strange how reluctant you are to approach your own heroes even if you are in the same business.

Mind you, Dillon is off to Dubai this week and then directly from there to Aintree. Maybe the football treadmill is not so sapping after all.

With two matches to come in the next 48 hours, I was determined to make the most of a rare day off, and the next stop was the International Book Fair at Olympia, where I had been invited to an early evening drinks party by my publishers.

Have you ever had one of those awful dreams where you keep banging on doors and nobody lets you in? Well, that's how it was at Olympia late this afternoon.

Having been dropped off by the taxi driver at what he presumed was the main entrance, I found not only that door bolted, with grim-faced commissionaires on the inside waving me to the next door, but also the two or three I tried afterwards.

Eventually, after starting to think Noel Edmonds would emerge with the 'Gotcha' trophy, I found a side door by a railway line where my printed invitation was quickly whisked away and replaced by an official badge.

Things got much better after that. The Virgin stand was already invisible among the throng of early evening drinkers – I never realised there were so many people in publishing. I was rescued by two smart young ladies whose names were Wendy and Hannah. At least I think they were. By the time my driver came a couple of hours later, I could have been on Mount Olympus, never mind Olympia.

Tuesday 19th
I heard about a centre forward today who moved from one Endsleigh League club to another, received signing-on fees well in excess of £100,000, and asked for wages of £5,000 a week.

Nothing unusual in that, bearing in mind what some of the Premiership players are earning, but it begs the question, are our footballers overpaid? So much of the money that television has pumped into the game over the last five or six years has finished up in the players' pockets and if Mr Murdoch ever pulled the plug, it makes you wonder whether some clubs would disappear down the hole.

Nobody minds players being paid what they are worth, but we are continually being reminded that football is 'a short career'. Well, there can't be too many careers where you only have to work about two hours on most days of the week, and when you have your afternoons free to study or plan for a future outside the game.

Drive past most Premiership training grounds after lunch-time, and you won't see too many first team players practising their skills. Yet it is in this critical area of individual technique that British players, by common consent, still lag behind the continentals.

The chasm was clearly evident again when Bayern Munich struck five goals past Nottingham Forest, our last survivors in Europe, on their own City Ground. What had started with bright prospects for Frank Clark's team, 2-1 down from the first leg and with an away goal in hand, ended in an embarrassing UEFA Cup exit.

Not one of the six English clubs who qualified for Europe this season got as far as the semi-finals. You can't blame Clark and his fellow managers. They can only work with what they have. But you can blame our system.

Clark, who emerged this week as the latest candidate for the England coaching job after Terry Venables, believes the root cause is that clubs are not allowed to work early enough with schoolboys, implanting the skill factor (as they do on the Continent) from about six years old.

Fair enough. But when a player gets to seventeen and signs

as a professional, should he not continue to practise twice a day? It is easy to blame the fixture list, but as soon as they get a free week a lot of clubs are off on a money-spinning trip abroad to play a friendly.

Half the trouble, as Alan Hansen said after the match tonight, is that the Premiership matches on a Saturday are so exciting that we forget where we stand in comparison to the rest of the world. A long way behind when it comes to inventive, imaginative football.

Hansen's co-panellist Jimmy Hill struck a warning note with regard to the forthcoming European Championship. If our clubs are as badly outclassed as this, what hope for the England team?

The man charged with answering that question, Terry Venables, announces his squad tomorrow for next week's international against Bulgaria. He may need a refresher course on how to use his pencil. He last picked a team over three months ago.

Wednesday 20th
You put yourself at the mercy of Wimbledon's 'Crazy Gang' at your peril, and I should have been on my guard when Andy Thorn invited me for tea and toast with the players before their FA Cup replay against Chelsea at Selhurst Park.

The new sheepskin coat is now fully operational and it was hanging proudly in the corner while I stood at a discreet distance from the rest of the players, trying to identify one or two faces among the squad that were still unfamiliar to me. You tend not to overstay your welcome in this enclosed world, especially when players are building up to a big game, so after a couple of cups of tea I made my excuses and left, knowing there was also a warm welcome in the Wimbledon boardroom.

Stanley Reed, the chairman, is the fittest 88 year old you will ever meet. His mind is sharper than many people half his age and he doesn't miss a trick.

Imagine the commentator's embarrassment then, when I took my hand out of my coat pocket to shake hands and found myself holding about ten plastic spoons. And they kept coming – dozens of them – until the floor and highly polished table were littered with them.

By now a group of guests had gathered around Mr Reed, wondering just what had possessed this kleptomaniac to raid the Wimbledon kitchen. I tried to mumble an explanation but it was too late – I had been mugged.

When I went back upstairs to check the teams, the Wimbledon dressing room was having a good laugh at my expense. The coach, Terry Burton, told me I had been lucky. 'If it was somebody they didn't like, they would have put the marmalade in too.'

As it so happened, a sticky night was in store for the Crazy Gang. Dennis Wise let them off the hook when he failed with a penalty in the first half, but Chelsea scored twice in the last twelve minutes to earn a semi-final against Manchester United.

Ruud Gullit was everything that Jurgen Klinsmann had been 24 hours earlier – stylish, devastatingly effective, and utterly committed to the cause. However much *they* earn, they are worth every penny, because their attitude matches their unique ability.

When Gullit came to Chelsea at the start of the season, the cynics thought he would stroll around in the sweeper's position on an easy meal ticket at the age of 33.

Six months on, he was the most elegant and influential player in a hectic, physically demanding Cup tie, operating in an advanced midfield position just behind Mark Hughes. It brought back memories of the 1988 European Championship, when he led Holland to the title playing a similar role close to Marco Van Basten.

As for Hughes, having scored in both matches against Wimbledon, he proved again that he is the man for the big occasion. He won three FA Cup winners' medals with Manchester United, but even by his standards the semi-final at Villa Park is going to be something else – playing against his old club.

But Chelsea fans need not worry about Hughes having divided loyalties. As a young boy growing up in North Wales, Mark idolised the Chelsea and England goalkeeper Peter Bonetti. He even bought a replica kit. Quite where and why he lost his sympathy for goalkeepers remains unclear. But you wouldn't bet against him putting one past Peter Schmeichel a week next Sunday.

Thursday 21st
From one centre forward to another, and from a man still at the forefront of the game to one adjusting to leaving it.

Alan Smith was a fine striker for Arsenal and, briefly, for England. A tall, unselfish player who came out of non-League football with Alvechurch, learned his trade at Leicester, and played a significant and uncomplaining part in Arsenal's relentless pursuit of trophies under George Graham. In short, the ideal team player.

I remember commentating on the prolonged FA Cup Final between Arsenal and Sheffield Wednesday in 1993, and drawing attention to the fact that Smith's booking was the first yellow card of his career. And he was a striker when defenders were allowed to tackle from behind!

Injury forced Alan into early retirement and he is trying to forge a writing and media career. He rang today to ask me where to send the script for a television play about football which apparently starts with a commentator speaking from Wembley. There could be a place in the theatre for Motson yet.

Mind you, having written his own piece of theatre with Arsenal, Alan Smith doesn't need to fictionalise about scoring in Cup Finals. He struck the goal that mattered when Arsenal beat Parma in the European Cup-Winners Cup Final of 1994 in Copenhagen, and there aren't too many highs like that in anybody's career.

Smith admitted he misses being centre stage. 'Nothing will ever replace playing,' he said, but that goes for everybody who used to be a professional footballer – including those who now manage.

His old club, Arsenal, lost 1-0 at Manchester United last night but are guaranteed a full house at Highbury on Saturday when Newcastle are the visitors.

That match is the lead feature on *Match of the Day* and will complete a busy week for the BBC football team. A live European match on Tuesday, FA Cup replays on Wednesday, the Championship leaders (as well as Liverpool) on Saturday. Who says all the big football is on satellite?

The Arsenal physiotherapist, Gary Lewin, was one of the first to respond to the letters Annie sent out appealing for support for Action for Children. Gary is a bit of a runner himself, and volunteered to give me moral support in a couple of the events.

That's after he has had an operation on his foot in a couple of weeks' time.

Physio . . . heal thyself.

166

Friday 22nd

With the country in the grip of the 'mad cow' crisis, which could mean sales of British beef being banned throughout Europe, it seemed as good a day as any to start the one-month diet which will hopefully see me shed a stone by the middle of April, when the charity runs will start coming thick and fast.

Red meat was always a weakness of mine anyway, together with all the calorific content of a fat-fuelled diet. Biscuits, cakes, cheese and butter go on the banned list as from today, with my alcohol intake limited to one statutory glass of wine per day.

So it was quite ironic to receive a telephone call inquiring about my availability to voice a radio commercial for Burger King. At any other time, I would have happily traded my voice for a few hundred cheeseburgers.

On the subject of voices, one of the BBC's finest will soon be heard no more on the airwaves after an innings lasting well over 40 years. The cricketing analogy is probably inappropriate in the case of Alan Weeks, who announced his retirement today, since that is about the only sport we never heard him cover.

Alan's mellifluous tones were first heard from Brighton Ice Rink in 1951, and he became synonymous with ice skating, gymnastics, ice hockey and swimming. In my early days with *Match of the Day*, he was still working regularly as a football commentator.

We were part of the same team at the 1974 World Cup in Germany, when I was the new boy on the block, and Alan demonstrated his immense versatility and studied professionalism in a way I shall always remember.

He never seemed to get flustered although David Coleman was always teasing him about looking worried. There was a disarming smile on his face most of the time, and we christened him 'Marco Antonio' after a Brazilian defender who Brian Glanville had described as 'ever-smiling'.

Alan Weeks was certainly that when he fronted *Pot Black* at its inception in 1970. A snooker programme that began as a nervous experiment was the forerunner of a huge television audience for a sport which was transformed from a smoker's pastime into a profitable professional circus.

So the world figure skating championships in Edmonton, Alberta, marked the end of an era. Weeks is reckoned to have commentated on 25 different sports in his 45 years at the BBC microphone – a record that will never be challenged, let alone beaten.

Saturday 23rd

Talking of records, some sixth sense told me to check up on Arsenal's record goalscorers before I went to Highbury for today's match against Newcastle, the Premiership leaders.

It turned out that the all-time club record has stood since before the war, when Cliff Bastin, outside left in the great Arsenal team of the thirties, amassed a total of 178 goals.

Ian Wright, who was recently in the news when he asked for a transfer, started the day with a total of 140, but every time you cover an Arsenal match you are conditioned to expect him to score.

Wrighty obliged in the seventeenth minute, cheekily clipping a Winterburn cross over the prostrate goalkeeper and then embarking on one of his prolonged celebrations which symbolise his empathy with the Highbury crowd.

Soon after, Wright had to leave the field with a back injury. Not that it affected Arsenal too much – Newcastle were so poor that those of us who had backed them for the Championship now have serious misgivings.

Asprilla is obviously a brilliant footballer, but he is a free spirit, and it made me wonder whether the integration of the Colombian and David Batty from Blackburn at this stage of the campaign was counterproductive. Quite a few pundits addressed their thoughts on that in Kevin Keegan's direction: 'If it ain't broke, don't fix it.'

But back to Ian Wright. While Keegan, for the first time in my experience, declined a television interview, and Arsenal manager Bruce Rioch cautiously avoided re-opening the debate over Wright's future with Arsenal, Ian presented himself for *Match of the Day* with an apparent change of heart which took me completely by surprise.

'I shall remain an Arsenal player until somebody tells me otherwise. It's always been my ambition to break Cliff Bastin's record. I believe he scored 178 goals?'

This was the guy who a few days earlier had reluctantly accepted the fact that his transfer request was turned down, and agreed to stay 'until we can sort things out at the end of the season'.

Wright is 32 – not a spring chicken when it comes to strikers – but he was late coming into the professional game and like a lot of those players, seems to retain the appetite that some of those who were stars as teenagers have lost.

He has scored his 141 goals in less than five seasons at Highbury. Bastin took nine seasons to reach his record figure. Then again, there was no League Cup or European football in his time.

All this was of no consolation to Wright's friend from days gone by, London-born Les Ferdinand. The Newcastle striker, who wanted one goal to reach his season's best-ever tally but has never scored at Highbury, was almost lost for words when he was asked to explain their lacklustre performance.

He was probably aghast at how Newcastle had managed to hand over the League leadership to Manchester United without their rivals even playing. The 2-0 defeat at Highbury reduced Newcastle's goal difference to 27, which made it inferior by one goal to that of their closest pursuers. Maybe their *only* ones now, because Liverpool were beaten at Nottingham Forest.

It was the Merseysiders' first defeat since November, but it could have put them out of the race.

Sunday 24th
Pete Edwards, the Nottingham Forest fitness expert, phoned today to tell me he has been signed up for a series on *East Midlands Today* – the regional television programme.

He has been asked to pick six 'guinea pigs' from different age groups, walks of life and weight ranges to illustrate how a structured fitness programme can make them more healthy.

He caught me as I was about to face my Sunday lunch – chicken (as opposed to beef) and vegetables, with boiled as opposed to roast potatoes. I am now five days into my self-imposed diet. No starter and no sweet, by the way.

But if you can avoid indigestion one way, then televised football sure makes up for it in another. Those who believe it is a juggernaut out of control, bound to meet itself coming down the opposite carriageway, were given power to their argument this afternoon when the second half of Sky's monster Premiership match between Manchester United and Tottenham collided head-on with the first half of the Coca-Cola Cup Final on ITV, between Leeds and Aston Villa.

The last time Leeds played at Wembley, in the Charity Shield in 1992, Eric Cantona scored a hat-trick in their 4-3 win over Liverpool. Later that season, Howard Wilkinson sold him to Manchester United.

So there was something faintly ironic about today's events. While Leeds were outplayed by Aston Villa at Wembley, Cantona was pulling the proverbial rabbit out of the hat again for Alex Ferguson.

His fifth goal in as many games – four of them match-winners and one a late saver – was hotly contested by Tottenham inasmuch as it came from a goal kick which should have been a corner.

But it delivered the three points by which Manchester United now lead Newcastle. And the next engagement for Keegan's team is away to Liverpool! The chips are well and truly down.

As for Aston Villa, who produced one of the most overwhelming performances seen in a recent Wembley final, they might temper their celebrations by reminding themselves that when they won the same trophy two years ago, spoiling Manchester United's treble bid, their manager Ron Atkinson got the sack before the end of the year.

However, with their comfortable League position and an FA Cup semi-final coming up next weekend, you can't see that happening to Brian Little.

As for his opposite number, Howard Wilkinson looked utterly drained when he was interviewed by Jim Rosenthal after the match. He has been a manager a long time – and it showed.

Monday 25th

Football fans have short memories, or some of them do. It became clear today why Howard Wilkinson looked so stunned after the match. He was roundly abused by a section of Leeds supporters as he walked out of the stadium.

Quite apart from being one of the most dedicated managers in the game – the sort of fellow who never takes a day off – Wilkinson had brought Leeds back out of the old Second Division, won the last old First Division Championship in 1992, and restored European football to Elland Road.

But supporters are impatient for success, and Leeds' performance yesterday clearly upset those who had spent hard-earned cash making the journey to Wembley. But how far do you blame the manager for the lame output of some of his players on a given day?

The subject cropped up again on Sky TV tonight. Ron Atkinson and his old sparring partner Andy Gray, who was Ron's assistant at Aston Villa before moving to television, fell out on the air after Coventry's defeat at Southampton.

It's that time of the season for managers. Quite a few of them are on a short fuse and Ron has had a plateful just lately: intruders broke into his home and tied up his wife, his father Fred is seriously ill in hospital, and Coventry are now ominously in the bottom three.

What happened was that Richard Keys, who besides being Sky's chief presenter is a Coventry fan, challenged Atkinson with a 'Where do Coventry go from here?' question; while Gray suggested that Atkinson's team did not have the stomach for the fight that Southampton had showed.

Whatever the rights and wrongs, it was gripping television. Big Ron probably felt under the hammer, but at least he had the last word. 'Who was the man of the match?' he asked, and when they replied, 'The Southampton goalkeeper, Dave Beasant,' it gave Atkinson the opening to close the debate.

'We must have done something right then.'

The rest of the football world, from Ferenc Puskas downward, took the night off to attend the opening of 'Football, Football' – the new theme restaurant in London's Haymarket.

The first person I saw when Anne and I arrived was Desmond Lynam. He was standing on the far side of the foyer flanked by countless microphones, photographers and television cameras.

Somebody had done a great job publicising the event because just about everyone coming through the door was being interviewed. A lot of the hard work had been done by Brian Marwood of the Professional Footballers Association.

But footballers were not the only guests. There was a wide range of recognisable faces from the entertainment industry, and Lynam's task was to talk to them as they arrived, the conversation being relayed round the building on video screens.

The fact that it worked so well was solely down to the unflappability of Lynam. When you have to deal with a Grand National that has been declared void, I suppose you get used to interviewees being pushed towards you every few seconds, with no time at all to gather your thoughts. I never asked Desmond how much he got paid, but whatever it was he certainly earned his money tonight. The interviews went on all evening, making it a longer and more taxing assignment than introducing *Grandstand*.

Anne and I managed to grab one of the few empty tables from where we could watch the arrival of the many celebrities – major and minor – who make up the glitterati of football.

Somebody was pumping artificial smoke on to the catwalk as the stars emerged to be greeted by Lynam, and there was a generous reception for members of the 1966 World Cup winning team – men like George Cohen, Alan Ball, Geoff Hurst and Martin Peters.

It was a sign of how far football has come, or perhaps how fashionable it has become, in the last 30 years. The nearest thing to a theme restaurant in the sixties would have been Cassetari's Cafe just near the West Ham ground, where Malcolm Allison – who was also at the launch – discussed tactics, using cups and saucers, with the likes of John Bond and Noel Cantwell.

Even meeting up again with Martin Buchan reminded me that it would soon be twenty years since my first FA Cup Final commentary, when he captained the Manchester United team that beat Liverpool.

On that day I had tried to rescue a far from memorable commentary by linking Buchan with the 39 steps that led from the pitch to the royal box. Martin told me tonight that he had heard a radio reporter refer to the 69 steps yesterday – maybe it felt like that to the Leeds team at Wembley when they collected their losers' medals.

Buchan works for Puma these days, and in his trade there is a lot of business tied up in getting star players to wear a certain brand of footwear.

At the moment he has Liverpool's Robbie Fowler under contract, but after scoring over 30 goals for Liverpool this season and getting into the England squad, Fowler has become hot property and is envied by Puma's rivals.

Quite apart from their wages and bonuses paid by the club, top players in this country can now pull in up to £200,000 a year purely from a boot contract.

My near-neighbour who plays for Arsenal, Lee Dixon, may not be quite in that bracket, but he told me tonight he has just signed a new three-year contract that will take him up to ten years with Arsenal and a testimonial.

He also said how disappointed he was in Newcastle at Highbury on Saturday. At one point in the second half, their players were falling out among themselves. Three days earlier, Arsenal had played Manchester United and been lucky to escape with a 1-0 defeat – there is no doubt who the football fraternity think will win the Championship now.

Tuesday 26th
The coldest day of the season, believe it or not. We stood shivering at Bisham Abbey as we watched the last few minutes of a routine England training session before scurrying to the warmth of the building for the traditional Venables press conference and team announcement.

First, the England coach had to face a battery of television cameras. David Davies, the FA's Head of External Affairs, has now introduced a sensible system where one interviewer – in this case Nick Collins of Sky – asks the questions, and all the other channels record Venables' answers for their own output. It means Terry only has to do one interview instead of seven or eight. The same applies to radio, who are next in line in the guise of the BBC's football correspondent, Mike Ingham.

While Venables was otherwise occupied, the scribes from the written press were in another room interviewing selected players – today it was Steve McManaman and Paul Ince who were in demand. Their comments will form part of the feature pieces that will appear in the national papers on the morning of the match.

But the man most in demand was Venables, especially when he announced he was leaving out his erstwhile captain David Platt, and with Alan Shearer injured, pairing Les Ferdinand with Teddy Sheringham. A lot of the press had plumped for Robbie Fowler, who the coach assured them was in line for a substitute appearance.

The two television commentators, Martin Tyler of Sky and yours truly, are always given a ten-minute briefing by Venables on pointers to watch for in the way England intend to play.

Today he told us that Paul Gascoigne was expected to fulfil all the duties of a midfield player, and not go wildly chasing the ball. Steve McManaman would start on the left, but would be given licence to roam as he does for Liverpool.

In return, we told Terry we would furnish him with any relevant information from the Bulgarian camp, which is our next port of call. He goes on to talk to the newspaper correspondents – a session that can last up to an hour.

Bulgaria were staying at the Sopwell House Hotel at St Albans – a favourite haunt for overseas teams – but they only arrived at lunchtime today because most of their squad were playing for their clubs on Sunday.

Although they are probably the most settled of all European teams – Bulgaria named thirteen players in this squad who took part in the World Cup two years ago – they are scattered across Europe playing their club football in Germany, Austria, Greece, Spain, Italy and Cyprus.

They had time for only one training session – at Wembley tonight – so it's another one of those tedious afternoons watching unshaven, tracksuited figures walking between bedroom and restaurant, trying to put a name to all the faces.

When they arrived at Wembley, Bulgaria's talisman Hristo Stoichkov was clearly troubled by injury. He took no real part in the training, wandering off to the dressing room before the others had finished.

Overseas coaches are notoriously guarded about their line-up, a bit like Kenny Dalglish used to be, but after training Dimitar Penev emerged to give us the intended starting team with numbers – declaring that Stoichkov was doubtful but they would know for sure tomorrow.

Wednesday 27th
In the end Stoichkov did not play, although he poignantly laid sixteen red roses in the centre circle before the teams came out, as an act of remembrance on the part of the Bulgarians to those who died at Dunblane.

With Trevor Brooking taking a brief holiday in America, David Pleat was my co-commentator and when we met on the mobile catering bus to discuss the team formations, the last thing we considered was how difficult it might be to identify the England players.

The Bulgarians, who seemed like brothers after the time spent with them yesterday, had priority on the white shirts for the night. England appeared in their new change strip of 'indigo blue' – a polite way of describing unappealing grey.

Under the Wembley floodlights, the red numbers on the back of the shirts were virtually indecipherable. And the colourless strip had an uncanny way of making all the players look the same.

Only once before had I experienced quite such a sinking

feeling before an international – and that was eighteen years ago in Buenos Aires when Argentina came out for their opening game in the World Cup with numbers nobody could make out on the back of their striped shirts.

But this was Wembley, and surely we all knew Gascoigne, Pearce and Sheringham, but how come Gareth Southgate seemed to melt so far into the background that he hardly merited a mention in the first half?

Quite apart from our problems, the match had an unreal feel about it. These Wembley friendlies have run their course. The opposition again seemed pleased to be there, happy to stroke the ball around, but until very late in the day seemingly disinterested in showing the cutting edge that would be there in a competitive game.

Having said that, England did all that could have been asked of them, apart from adding to the early goal expertly taken by Ferdinand from a wonderful diagonal pass by Sheringham.

Venables admitted afterwards that they lacked the killer instinct to finish off the Bulgarians, but he had reason to be pleased with the way the England team functioned. All three units – defence, midfield and attack – performed with credit and in the absence of Adams, Pallister, Anderton, Shearer, Le Saux and Platt (a late substitute), possibly gave the coach a few selection posers before the next game.

Elsewhere in Europe, the likes of Germany, France, Portugal, Croatia and Russia all won friendlies as part of the Euro 96 build-up, confirming the feeling that the competition is going to be red hot.

The good news was that Switzerland lost. England and Scotland will both have to beat them, you feel, to stand a chance of qualifying for the quarter-finals.

Thursday 28th
The first call this morning was predictable. Simon Marsh of Umbro, the suppliers of kit to the England team, rang to say how concerned he was about my remarks last night regarding the indigo blue strip.

I have to declare an interest here and say that over the last few years, when commentators have campaigned consistently for clearer numbers on shirts, Simon and Umbro have been among the most co-operative.

It even got to the stage a couple of years ago, when the

numbers on Sheffield United's striped shirts were giving us problems, of Simon having a special shirt made up to ask our opinion on a new outline for the number.

He was perfectly prepared to take the latest complaint on board and promised to look into a different way of pressing a clearer number on to the new kit. But he left me in no doubt that indigo blue would continue as England's reserve colours.

Others are now taking up the theme. David Seaman's garish new goalkeeper's outfit, which looks as though somebody has spilled a red and yellow paint pot all over him, has come in for some press criticism, as have the team's grey (or indigo blue) shirts in general.

Martin Tyler from Sky also rang, to ask me whether I would join forces with him in asking for better numbers. I said the matter was already under discussion – and it wasn't even half-past nine yet!

Mind you, this was going to be no ordinary day. I was due to do a commentary 'backwards' for the first time, with everything happening in reverse.

It was the basis of a radio advertisement for Nike (one of Umbro's competitors as it happens) who had hit on the idea of the ball starting in the back of the net, coming out past the beaten goalkeeper, returning to the scorer, and so on right back to the start of the move with the referee blowing his whistle for a free kick.

The advertising agency who dreamed up the idea were not quite sure whether they wanted the commentator to start at his highest pitch and then scale the excitement down (in other words the reverse to normal) or whether it would be more effective to sound calm at first and build up the anticipation, even though the play was doing the opposite!

If that sounds thoroughly confusing, that is exactly how I felt until I got the hang of it. All the players mentioned in the ad – Lee Dixon, Les Ferdinand and David Ginola – wore the same brand of boots, and my job was to emphasise that the ball was sticking to Ginola's Nike footwear like a magnet.

When the agency declared themselves happy with my efforts, after about fifteen takes, I did just wonder how the finished product would sound. Bear in mind this was a *radio* advertisement, and there would be no pictures to show the listener what was happening.

However, these advertising boys always seem to know what

they are doing, although my last line of commentary was a shade corny: 'Listen to the crowd OOB.' (In case you still haven't hacked it – BOO).

By now I was OOB myself (out of breath), and arrived just in time to help Jonathan Pearce of Capital Radio to put the finishing touches to the Burger King voice-over we had done earlier in the week.

In this one, Jonathan was the 'manic' commentator and I was the 'calm' voice as we flagged up a holiday competition with tickets for one of the World Cup qualifiers that will be starting soon.

I put the evening aside for a rare event – sitting back and watching television. There was a documentary about Muhammad Ali in the *Reputations* series on BBC2, and an investigation into ticket touts in *Undercover Britain* on Channel 4. Both programmes were disappointing – they lacked shape as well as any originality.

More eye-catching was Julian Wilson's Grand National preview which I caught up with on the tape of *Sportsnight*. It was beautifully shot and made me decide to back Young Hustler and Son of War in the big race on Saturday.

Friday 29th
The first day of spring really arrived – at last. The crocuses were out in the park today and if you looked hard enough you could find daffodils and primroses too.

On days like this you count your blessings as you walk through one of London's parks – 'the lungs of London' as they were described by William Pitt – or if you stay out of town and take a leisurely ploughman's lunch at your local pub.

Living where I do, on the London side of Hertfordshire, it was possible to do both, and for the first time in ages it was refreshing to take a deep breath of fresh air and reflect that the all-consuming football season has now completed its eighth month and will soon be starting its last.

Mind you, somebody at Wembley on Wednesday told me we were now just 70 days away from the start of the European Championship. Funny how the anticipation is building fast for that event as opposed to the Olympic Games, which take place a month later but have so far scarcely had a mention apart from Redgrave and Pinsent.

But there was no need to jump the gun. We were facing

potentially the biggest sporting weekend of the year – the Grand National on Saturday, the FA Cup semi-finals on Sunday, followed by the Brazilian Grand Prix. All covered by BBC Television, incidentally.

Sport, rather like spring, is at its most compelling when the events and the colours are at their most traditional.

Somehow the launch of rugby league's new European Super League concept, for which Sky TV are said to have paid £87 million, seemed a little out of place. Especially as it started in Paris. Prior to this, the 13-a-side game has not spread its gospel very far from the M62.

However, Paris St Germain beat Sheffield Eagles and a new era was underway. So was the new series of *Fantasy Football League*, the first programme ending with Jeff Astle singing 'Rivers Of Babylon'. Some things definitely *don't* change.

Saturday 30th
And one thing that always stays the same is the Grand National. Of all the British sporting institutions, this one captures the public imagination like no other – Cup Final included. Desmond Lynam told the *Grandstand* audience today that something like £60 million had been taken in wagers.

My small contribution to that bookmakers' benefit fund was spread between four horses – and three of them came in the first five. Unfortunately, none of them managed to head the winner, Rough Quest, and the one that could have made me some money – Son of War – unseated his rider at the 24th fence.

I had arranged to meet up with Lynam at the Midlands hotel and golf centre where Chelsea were staying in preparation for the FA Cup semi-final at Villa Park. As things turned out, Chelsea's plans worked a lot better than ours.

It was the first time in 25 years of checking into hotels that I found the room to which I was sent was already occupied. The gentleman and his wife who I disturbed were terribly nice about it, until they realised my intrusion meant their own room key was now invalid. All three of us ended up in the corridor scowling at the porter.

Things got worse when I discovered there was no space in the restaurant. If you can't book a table on arrival, when the hell are you supposed to book it?

Ultimately a harassed manager sorted all these things out,

but Lynam's driver lost his way between Aintree and Birmingham so that our host for this great sporting weekend arrived after midnight – with the clocks going forward this gave him about five hours sleep.

In the meantime, *Match of the Day* again underlined what an impact the foreign players were having on the Premiership. Curcic scored for Bolton, Amokachi and Kanchelskis for Everton, and Kinkladze starred again for Manchester City.

Somehow you felt that Cantona and Gullit – or maybe both – were destined to play a leading role in tomorrow's semi-final.

Glenn Hoddle, who I found sipping a pint of shandy in the cocktail bar, insisted Chelsea would make no special plans for Cantona. 'It's important we worry about our own game, not theirs,' said the Chelsea manager.

Sunday 31st

Chelsea *did* play their own game until both their wing backs were injured. Already without Dan Petrescu, first choice in that position, Hoddle lost his replacement, Steve Clarke, before half-time, and early in the second half, with Chelsea leading by a Ruud Gullit goal, left back Terry Phelan pulled up with a muscle strain as he burst into the attack.

The three minutes that followed were critical. With Phelan reduced to half pace, and Chelsea still debating the substitution, Manchester United carved out two chances down their right flank and took them both. So United go to Wembley for the third year running and sustain their pursuit of a second double.

But it would be too simplistic to leave it there. For a start, Manchester United *also* had three defenders injured, in their case all ruled out before the game. Without Bruce, Pallister and Irwin, they reshuffled their defence and the young players in whom Alex Ferguson had put his faith at the start of the season – the Neville brothers, Butt and Beckham – came up trumps on the day.

It was 26 years since Manchester United had lost an FA Cup semi-final, and this was their ninth success in a row at this stage of the competition. Somehow, in a tight second half, you felt that record gave them an extra bit of belief.

As Gullit said in an interview before the game: 'Everybody has a mother and father. They have a bigger history than us, that's the only difference.'

The difference between Liverpool and Aston Villa in the other semi-final at Old Trafford was a twenty year old called Robbie Fowler, whose two goals in Liverpool's 3-0 win took his total for the season to 33.

Here again, the dilemma of when to replace an injured player was a factor. Gareth Southgate had just returned to the pitch with his injured knee bandaged, when he failed to prevent Fowler reaching Redknapp's free kick for the first goal.

But this again is a mere pin prick on the panorama of a great sporting weekend. Both semi-finals were settled without resorting to a replay – producing a classic final pairing of Liverpool and Manchester United.

Which brought back memories of my first FA Cup Final for the BBC in 1977, when United won at Wembley to prevent Liverpool completing the League and Cup double. Since then, both clubs have done it, but what an irony if Liverpool were in a position to spoil the ambitions of their bitter rivals this time round.

APRIL
1996

Monday 1st

Today was recrimination day. The Football Association was taken to task for their semi-final ticket prices; Glenn Hoddle was criticised for not taking Terry Phelan off sooner; and I was charged with ignoring a volatile incident in the match at Villa Park.

Wonderful thing, hindsight. On a day when those at the sharp end are high profile and accept the public airing of their imperfections, I am reminded of the story of Mozart when he presented the finished version of an opera to Emperor Joseph II.

'My dear Mozart, there are too many notes in it,' was the Emperor's verdict. 'Tell me, your majesty,' Mozart responded politely, 'which notes would you have me take out?'

The two great footballing composers who called the tune yesterday, Cantona and Gullit, were so influential and creative that an incident in which both were involved led to a columnist in the *Daily Mail* suggesting that Trevor Brooking and myself had deliberately steered clear of a more controversial issue.

What happened was this. With just over an hour gone and Manchester United leading 2-1, Gullit broke clear of their defence and was halted by Schmeichel. As the ball came back off the United goalkeeper, little John Spencer volleyed it back for what would have been a Chelsea equaliser, had not Cantona, of all people, headed the ball off the line.

A few moments later, when play was stopped for a foul by Dennis Wise on Phil Neville, our director replayed the incident that everybody – viewers and commentators alike – was itching to see again.

While this gripping action was on the screen, Roy Keane was getting to grips with Dennis Wise, apparently pushing a hand into the Chelsea captain's face. Keane, who had been sent off playing for Ireland five days before, had already been booked

183

in this match, and was risking another dismissal to add to his four in the last twelve months.

A good story for the papers, and an incident seized on by our radio colleagues, Jon Champion and Alan Brazil. But not by the referee, who was closer to the action than any of us, and certainly not distracted by a television replay.

It is nonsense to suggest Trevor Brooking and I would have ignored an offence, had we seen it. Constructive criticism we have come to accept, because you can always act upon it and improve, but sometimes you wish the second guessers would tell you which notes to take out.

Tuesday 2nd

Just to emphasise the point I was making about commentators sometimes being in a 'no-win' situation, I was under fire again today – this time for not getting sufficiently excited.

When I first saw the headline 'Motty Lacking Passion', it struck me what conclusion the readers would have jumped to had this been a tell-all tabloid with a leaning for the lurid story . . .

Instead, it was the football edition of the *Nottingham Evening Post*, whose correspondence column carried a complaint from Mr Peter Kennedy, of Radcliffe-on-Trent, regarding the UEFA Cup quarter-final between Forest and Bayern Munich.

'Why was John Motson not screaming with enthusiasm and joy, as Forest showed Europe the better side to English football?' protested Mr Kennedy.

'We all know the boys were trying hard but couldn't find the net. Yet while all this was going on, Motson continued in a fashion which left you wondering whether he truly wanted the English club to survive.

'Where was the passion and fire offered by foreign commentators rather than the far from unbiased summary given by an Englishman wearing the blue and red of the German team?'

Once I had removed my Bayern Munich replica shirt and thrown away everything in the house that said 'made in Germany', I tried to address the issue in unbiased fashion.

But it was pretty difficult. Here was a commentator who in the past has been accused of overexuberance, incessant chatter, and of having a gung-ho approach to the English cause, now being charged with overidentifying with the Germans.

The fact that Bayern Munich won the match 5-1 had

something to do with it, so did a Forest performance that tapered away after a promising start, allowing Trevor Brooking and myself little opportunity to give English prospects of survival in Europe anything more than a dignified epitaph.

With due respect to the earnest Mr Kennedy, the first thing any commentator must do when he is accused of bias is to check the postmark – or in this case the source of the publication.

I am a regular reader of the *Football Post* and have been for many years, but as befits a provincial paper they are quick to press their local angle. This edition had two articles telling Terry Venables to waste no further time in appointing Stuart Pearce as his captain for the European Championship. Bad luck, David Platt and Tony Adams – you play for a London club!

Had life taken a different turn, I might have been writing this myself. Back in the sixties, when I was out of my apprenticeship with the *Barnet Press*, I was offered a job on the *Evening Post* at Nottingham, but chose to take an opportunity with the *Morning Telegraph* in Sheffield instead.

Either way, I had reason to be grateful to the schooling I received in football reporting from Bill White, my sports editor at Barnet who modestly used to hide behind the by-line 'Argus'.

It was sad to hear that Bill passed away at the weekend after a long illness. He stood for many of the solid values associated with the local reporter who covered his senior club week in, week out – fairness, diligence and a self-effacing willingness to help and advise others.

Bill would have been glad to see his old club keeping their head above water after the trials and tribulations at Barnet in recent years. They beat Cardiff 1-0 tonight in the Endsleigh League Division Three, keeping alive their hopes of reaching the play-offs.

The two managers were Ray Clemence and Phil Neal – once team mates with Liverpool and England. Tomorrow their old club host what is arguably the biggest match of the season so far in the Premiership – Liverpool v. Newcastle.

Wednesday 3rd
With the match at Anfield set aside for live coverage on Sky, I decided to get stuck in to some serious work on the European Championship today. There are 66 days to go to England's first

match of Euro 96 – let's hope the second of those numbers goes down in our football history as significantly as the first.

Starting first thing in the morning and stoically staying in front of the video until late afternoon, I was able to watch the Czech Republic, Russia, Germany and Portugal in recent action. All four figure on my schedule for the first round of matches in June.

By then, England will have new white numbers on those indigo blue shirts. The dogged Simon Marsh of Umbro phoned back today to tell me they had found a way of pressing clearer numbers on to the material.

Whether the likes of Darren Anderton, Gary Pallister and Gareth Southgate will be able to wear them is a matter of some concern to Terry Venables. All three are presently injured, and he could have up to eleven of his squad involved in the FA Cup Final between Liverpool and Manchester United.

Should that go to a replay, those players would be ruled out of England's last home friendly against Hungary less than 48 hours later.

All of which has got the Robbie Fowler lobby insisting that Venables picks him to start the only international before then – at home to Croatia later this month.

With well over 60 goals in less than two seasons, Fowler is quite properly being compared with the young Jimmy Greaves of 30 to 40 years ago.

It is tempting to say he deserves better luck than Jimmy had in 1966, when Alf Ramsey left him out of the final. But Greaves was 26 by then, whereas Fowler won't be 21 until next week.

Which is why I believe his time will come in the build-up to the 1998 World Cup.

Thursday 4th
That opinion lasted exactly 100 seconds when Liverpool played Newcastle last night. That's how long it took the said Fowler to score the first of seven goals in a match which the Liverpool manager, Roy Evans, described as 'kamikaze football'.

Thoroughly entertaining though it was, and the *Daily Mirror* rang this morning to ask me whether it would figure in my top ten matches of all time, there was some dreadful defending, especially by Newcastle.

Liverpool's winning goal, scored in stoppage time, was a good example. Four defenders gathered in the centre to follow the ball, and Stan Collymore had half the penalty area to himself. Even then, his shot went inside Srnicek's near post.

Keegan valiantly defended his team's cavalier style – 'When that goes, I go' – but their fourth defeat in six games meant their destiny was now, for the first time, out of their own hands.

Amidst all the talk about bad defending, the omission of Gillespie, and the integration of new players, those of us who backed Newcastle at the start needed to put on our bravest face today.

My own theories on what has gone wrong are rather different. I thought the Newcastle defence looked happier when playing in front of Hislop – the expensive goalkeeper who lost his place to Srnicek initially through injury. Also the player who sparkled for club and country in the first half of the season, Rob Lee, has not scored since before Christmas.

If Lee regains his old form, then Newcastle can still do it, but at present the confidence factor lies with Manchester United, unbeaten in sixteen games, and Liverpool, who have lost only once since the end of November.

Everybody seemed captivated today by the sheer theatre that was last night's match. It was on my way to lunch with Brian Barwick, BBC Sports head of production, that the *Mirror* rang to ask me to nominate my best ten matches of all time.

It was quite difficult to give them two pages of copy on the spur of the moment on a mobile phone, but they had to be games at which I had been present, so for a variety of reasons I picked the following:

Brazil 2, Italy 3 (World Cup 1982)
France 3, Portugal 2 (European Championship, 1984)
West Germany 4, Yugoslavia 2 (European Championship, 1976)
Brazil 1, France 1 (World Cup 1986 – France won on penalties)
Tottenham 3, Man. City 2 (FA Cup Final replay, 1981)
Everton 0, Liverpool 5 (Ian Rush scored four, 1982)
Hereford 2, Newcastle 1 (1972 – no list complete without it!)
Liverpool 5, Nottm Forest 0 (League match 1988, described by Tom Finney as the best football he had seen in this country since the war)

Tottenham 9, Bristol Rovers 0 (*Match of the Day* record
score 1977 – Colin Lee scored four on his debut)
Arsenal 5, Newcastle 3 (1976 – Malcolm Macdonald scored
a hat-trick against his old club)

I left the *Mirror*'s Ian Gibb to make some sense of my selection,
and only after I switched the phone off did I realise there wasn't
a single Manchester United match among them.

As we sat down I said to Brian that you never fail to see
somebody you know in Langan's Brasserie, and sure enough,
sitting at table number three (there is a pecking order of
importance, starting with table one where Michael Caine's
friends congregate) we spotted George Graham, being interviewed over lunch by Paul McCarthy of the *Sunday Express*.

These two go back some way, to when Graham was manager
of Millwall and McCarthy a reporter on the *South London
Press*.

When Brian Barwick left, having started a discussion about
a new contract, I decided that George Graham looked affluent
enough, in spite of his year's ban, to sign a sponsorship form
for the charity.

This was really a cunning way of getting him to invite me to
join his table – and it worked. McCarthy had finished his
probing for the *Sunday Express* piece, and we were soon into
Graham's views on the game from which he was banned for a
year – a decision I happened to agree with although I also agree
he was surely not the only offender.

He was generous to his successor at Arsenal, Bruce Rioch,
and wasn't being diplomatic when he said they would qualify
for Europe. It was perhaps indicative of something that he
knew Arsenal's fixtures off by heart for the rest of the season.

Graham was not so sure about whether Newcastle's cavalier
style would win the League. He admired Keegan's bravado, but
as you would expect from a man who won two Championships
based on sound defence, he expressed reservations about
throwing caution to the wind.

Being a mate of Terry Venables, he was guarded about the
shape of the England team, but he did think Terry might need
two others in midfield with Gazza, rather than just Paul Ince.

I left Graham on his way to another fashionable London
venue.

'Well, have that from one of the unemployed,' he replied,

and duly signed my sponsorship form. As I said to him: 'Some of us have got work to do.'

Friday 5th
If Terry Venables had been with us at lunch yesterday, he would probably have been throwing the salt over his shoulder. Some more was spilt today when it was announced that Newcastle's Steve Howey would almost certainly miss the rest of the season with a damaged hamstring. With Tony Adams still out of the first team picture after knee surgery, Mark Wright now on the Liverpool injured list, and the absence of Pallister and Southgate discussed earlier, the defenders' casualty list is mounting.

As of today, the only one of Venables' six centre backs clear of injury is Aston Villa's Ugo Ehiogu – and he has yet to win a full cap.

This was precisely the situation some of us feared early in the season. When you ask players to take part in over 50 games at top level, and then stay fresh and fit for the biggest tournament staged here since 1966, you are overloading the machine and some of its parts will suffer damage.

It is misleading and irresponsible for club chairmen and managers to say injuries can happen at any time. It is the overuse of muscles, and the lengthy recovery time, that has robbed England of key players at times like this before.

Going right back to 1980, when England started to qualify again for big tournaments after the barren years of the seventies (not the great decade some would have us believe), our national team have arrived at the final stages of World Cups and European Championships with one or more of the team's key performers ruled out by injury.

Ron Greenwood, manager in the 1980 European Finals in Italy, believed that England would have won the tournament had Trevor Francis not snapped his Achilles' tendon in the first week in May.

Two years later, having guided a better England team to the 1982 World Cup Finals where they remained unbeaten, Greenwood could point to injuries that ruled Kevin Keegan and Trevor Brooking out of the action until the last, desperate quarter of the final game.

When Bobby Robson took over from Greenwood, he inherited a similar scenario of club-related injuries. The prelude to the

1986 World Cup in Mexico was an ode to Bryan Robson's tender shoulder, which collapsed in the second game and ruled him out of a tournament where England had again surprised themselves, recovering from a poor start only to be beaten to the punch by Maradona in the quarter-final.

I know it's tedious, but we can go on. No Terry Butcher or Stuart Pearce for the 1988 European Finals in Germany; Barnes and Beardsley, in Robson's words, 'absolutely spent'; Lineker contracting hepatitis which weakened him from the start.

Then there was Italia 90, when Bobby Robson's team were denied a place in the final only by a penalty shoot-out. But England's cause was not helped by the fact that his namesake and captain Bryan had again gone home injured – equivalent to the Germans losing Matthaus.

Neither should the beleaguered Graham Taylor be prevented from pleading mitigation. Having qualified for the 1992 European Championship in Sweden, and built his team around a defensive system underpinned by Mark Wright as sweeper, he woke up on the morning the team left to discover that Wright had withdrawn through injury. A couple of weeks earlier, he had captained Liverpool in the FA Cup Final.

We arrived in Sweden not only without Wright, but also without a right back. Lee Dixon, Rob Jones and Gary Stevens all went down lame in the build-up to the Finals, and Taylor used three different players in the three matches England played – Keith Curle, Trevor Steven and David Batty. All were converted from their natural positions.

He also lost John Barnes, who sustained an Achilles' injury on a hard pitch in Finland in the last of England's friendlies. No wonder Terry Venables is going to China to check the playing surface of the stadium in Beijing where England are due to wind up their preparations this year.

To complete the sad and sorry saga, there is the painful memory of how England failed to qualify for USA 94. The traumas of Oslo and so on have been well documented, but just remember that Alan Shearer – by common consent our best striker at the time – missed seven of England's ten qualifying matches with a serious knee injury.

So there we are. It sounds like a succession of tame excuses, until you remember that in most other countries, the domestic programme makes generous allowances for international competition.

As a result, most of our rivals arrive at the big events with all their armoury in place and guns blazing. Not since 1970, when Alf Ramsey took a full squad to Mexico, have England been in that privileged position. It would be nice to think it will change in this of all summers, and that Venables will be able to pick his best troops at the peak of their form and fitness.

Saturday 6th
In Alan Sillitoe's story of 'The Match' (from the *Loneliness of the Long Distance Runner*) Lennox knows Notts County are going to lose before he leaves home. I had that feeling about Manchester City this morning as I drove to Maine Road.

The Manchester derby between City and United has been going for over a century, but it remains an uplifting experience even for those whose task is merely to report. Reporting a City victory, however, has been as rare as the sighting of a comet that accompanied the eclipse of the moon this week.

When City lost in the League and Cup at Old Trafford earlier in the season, I mentioned that they had not won there since 1974. Today's statistic was almost as depressing – they had not beaten United at Maine Road for nearly seven years.

Yet City are a warm and lovable club; their support historically derived from the heart of Manchester, their ground sited amidst the terraced houses of Moss Side – by tradition a sprawling suburb on the edge of the city centre.

Although the skyline is now dominated by City's £12 million Kippax Stand, with its 11,000 seats and its restaurant tier towering towards the stars, their supporters still see United as the toffee-nosed Tories from Stretford – the enemy whose glamorous image is constantly cosseted and massaged by a sycophantic media.

The only problem with that argument – and no doubt one of the reasons for it – is that City have not won anything for exactly twenty years. And then it was a solitary League Cup. In that same period, United have been to Wembley no fewer than twelve times, won two Championships in the last three seasons (admittedly after waiting 26 years) and are currently chasing the Double for the third year running.

What Francis Lee has to contend with, as he tries as chairman to rekindle the glory days he enjoyed with City as a player, is the disparity in the finances of the two organisations. It has long been accepted that City's debts are huge – at one time running into millions – while the same adjective can now be applied to United's profits, their merchandising potential fully exploited and reflected in the share price of a thriving public company.

And nobody with any sense of football history can put United's prosperity on the field down to money. Alex Ferguson, like Matt Busby before him, has invested in youth and been handsomely repaid.

City went down the same road a few years ago, winning the FA Youth Cup with a team of high promise, but in the case of most of those players, it failed to materialise.

They will be hoping their next intake from the YTS scheme will pay dividends. For today, their young apprentices stood self-consciously in the players' corridor, chewing their gum with their hands in their pockets, waiting to get Eric Cantona's autograph.

And that's very much how it was on the field, really. City paid United so much respect that they gave them a penalty after six minutes, and despite twice coming back bravely from a goal behind, danced with the devil in defence before allowing Ryan Giggs to strike a memorable winning goal.

Sadly, the commentary did not do it justice. Nobody on our side of the ground thought the ball had gone inside the post, and the place went so quiet that Giggs himself thought the effort had been disallowed.

At about the same time, Peter Beardsley was turning potential defeat into essential victory for Newcastle against Queens Park Rangers. Keegan at last changed his formation to accommodate Gillespie as a substitute. He also replaced Srnicek with Hislop.

Rangers' defeat did nothing to calm Manchester City's nerves in the relegation scramble. Southampton and Coventry both won, suggesting that it will be a duel to the finish, just like the Championship.

After the match, I interviewed Nigel Clough, who with refreshing honesty took part of the blame for United's third goal. I was on the point of asking him how his father was, when he was rushed away to do another interview.

It wasn't until I read the following morning's papers that I realised Brian Clough had been taken to hospital. I had heard reports of him not being well but have not seen him since he retired. That's not to say I haven't missed him though.

Clough was the interviewer's dream. Once you got him, you only had to do two things. Ask him the first question, then listen. He could be belligerent and intimidating, but also incredibly kind.

In my early days as a radio reporter, he came up to the press room at Selhurst Park to do an interview after his Derby team, captained by Dave Mackay, had won at Crystal Palace.

I was afraid he would walk away before we could start, because it took ages for them to read the football results and take in reports of the other games. Sensing the edginess in a beginner, Clough said, 'Just relax, young man. You can't do anything unless you are relaxed.'

That probably explains why, in later years, he was prone to take his team on holiday before a European Cup Final. But the 'young men' he brought up were all impeccably dressed and well behaved, both his players and his family. Standards, on and off the field, were something he implicitly believed in.

One of Cloughie's contemporaries, Malcolm Allison, was one of Francis Lee's guests after the game at Maine Road. I remember him giving me a hard time when I started on television. 'I thought your report today was terrible,' he once said after a game. 'But I'll tell you when you are good.'

For a man well into his 60s, Malcolm looked *very* good indeed. He was debating the highs and lows of the game with a real old-timer, Charlie Mitten, who played for Manchester United in the Cup Final as long ago as 1948.

Malcolm was City's coach when they won the League, the FA Cup, the League Cup and the European Cup-Winners Cup in the space of three seasons between 1968 and 1970.

Francis Lee was leading marksman in that side, and went on to win a second Championship medal at Derby in 1975. That explains why one of his team mates, Welsh international Rod Thomas, was in the boardroom today, along with Des Anderson, who was assistant manager to Dave Mackay.

All in all, it was cracking company at the end of an exhausting day. But I felt a tiny bit guilty sipping a glass of Lee's champagne. After all, I had had this nagging feeling all along that City were going to lose.

But one thing they will never lose is their support. Bernard Halford, the secretary, told me they had sold 8,400 season tickets for *next* season. And the fans don't know yet which League they will be watching.

Sunday 7th

There is a big difference between being a runner and a jogger. You don't notice it so much when you take part in the longer runs, like half-marathons, because everybody tends to start slowly, but most of the contestants in the Chesham 5K race round the town centre this morning treated it like a sprint.

Because it was a small field of under 100 runners, most of them had disappeared from my sight after the first 300 yards. As the distance we had to cover was only just over three miles, my embarrassment was mercifully short-lived.

So will be today's diary entry. The chance to slip away to our cottage in Suffolk only proffers itself once or twice during the season, and driving through Constable country in the spring sunshine was a therapeutic exercise after the hectic demands of the last three weeks.

Monday 8th

I never quite believed the old adage that the Easter programme sorted out the main issues of Championship, promotion and relegation. In the old days, of course, clubs would play three times over the holiday weekend, including Good Friday, but now it is only twice and the season still has a month to run.

However, you would be a brave man to suggest today's events did not determine that Manchester United will win the Premiership title for the third time in four years, and that Newcastle will not recover from seeing a twelve-point lead evaporate into a six-point deficit.

There is always one match that, in retrospect, proves decisive. Last year, it was Blackburn's victory over Newcastle in their penultimate game, and tonight, when the same teams met again at Ewood Park, it looked from teatime onwards as though, to quote again the man with the placard on his back, the moment of judgement was nigh.

Manchester United beat Coventry in the afternoon – a match clouded by a horrific injury to City's David Busst – to open up that six-point lead, albeit having played two games more.

With four minutes to go at Blackburn, Keegan's team were leading by a David Batty goal and looking at a three-point gap with a game in hand – not to mention a forthcoming weekend when they would be at home and Manchester United would play away.

194

It was then the Newcastle fans experienced a traumatic *déjà vu*. The defensive aberrations that cost them the match at Liverpool five days earlier repeated themselves, defenders drawn like locusts towards the ball as an opposing forward – this time the Geordie-born Graham Fenton – took advantage of the sort of space no team with Championship aspirations should concede.

Had Newcastle kept their lead in those two games, they would now be level on points with their rivals with a game to spare. Had they even drawn them, the gap would be four points with still more than a glimmer of hope. As it is, they appear to have fallen on their sword.

But to imply that they stabbed themselves in the heart is to deny proper credit to Manchester United. Unbeaten since New Year's Day, they have won fifteen of their last sixteen matches, a superhuman run by anybody's standards.

If, as the bookies expect, Ferguson's team tie up the title before the closing day, they will have won it because they had a better goalkeeper, a meaner defence, and because they had Eric Cantona.

Tuesday 9th

A question commentators get asked frequently (almost as often as what was the best *match* you ever saw) is who was the best *player* you ever saw? For years, I have mumbled my way through a muddled and ambiguous answer.

Pele, I never saw in the flesh in his prime. When I went to Wembley in 1963 to see England play Brazil in a friendly, he had been injured in a road accident in Germany and the only glimpse I had of him was when he walked round the pitch before the game.

Bobby Charlton, George Best and Denis Law were all in the twilight of their careers when I joined television, and prior to that I had enjoyed only occasional glimpses of Manchester United – usually when they played in London.

Watching Johan Cruyff play for Holland in the 1974 World Cup, and Franz Beckenbauer patrol the pitch from his sweeper's position in that tournament and in the European Championship two years later, makes me believe they are in the top ten of any list compiled by my generation.

The young Jimmy Greaves would certainly be a candidate. I still have scrapbooks from his early days at Chelsea, when scoring four or five goals in a match was one of his more irritating habits, which he continued at Tottenham.

Moving into the eighties, I was privileged to be in Mexico when Diego Maradona led Argentina to the World Cup pretty much single-handed. Never mind what he did to England; his performance in the semi-final against Belgium almost beggared belief.

So did the way Paul Gascoigne manoeuvred Tottenham to the Cup Final in 1991. Although he pressed the self-destruct button in the final, some of us prefer to remember what he did in every round prior to that. Simply, win each game for Spurs with his genius.

A similar word could be used to identify the talents of Kenny Dalglish, Glenn Hoddle, Liam Brady, Peter Osgood, Peter Beardsley, Arnold Muhren and Ossie Ardiles.

You've probably guessed what all this is leading up to. Where do you place Eric Cantona? After another superlative performance by the Frenchman yesterday, described by his manager as 'out of this world', I think I know. Tomorrow, when for once there is no midweek football to speak of, I will attempt to pay him my own inadequate tribute.

Wednesday 10th
Well, you would expect me to start with a statistic, wouldn't you? Cantona has scored in each of Manchester United's last six League games, which until I checked today made me wonder if that was some sort of club record.

In fact, David Herd scored in seven successive League matches for United in the 1964–65 season – when they won the Championship – and twice in his career Bobby Charlton did what Cantona has now done, and registered a goal in six consecutive games.

But the club record is held by the Irishman, Liam 'Billy' Whelan, who died in the Munich air disaster. The previous season, Whelan scored in *eight* League games on the trot.

So much for the figures. But what about the impact the errant French international has had on one of the world's most venerated football institutions?

I was around the weekend that Manchester United signed Cantona from Leeds in November 1992. I remember seeing him sitting in the Sopwell House Hotel at St Albans the following morning and then taking his seat in the stand when United played at Highbury that afternoon. The transfer had happened so quickly, taking everybody including the media by surprise, that he wasn't available to play that afternoon.

After the match I interviewed Alex Ferguson about the thinking behind the transfer and asked him exactly where Cantona was going to play. 'At the moment, I've no idea,' he replied.

But he knew his team required a fresh impetus. On the morning of the Arsenal game, United were lying a moderate eighth in the Premier League, having lost out on the Championship to Leeds the season before.

From the day Eric was signed until the end of the season, United lost only two of their remaining 26 matches – and in one of those defeats Cantona did not play.

The following season, when the Old Trafford outfit completed the League and Cup Double, the phenomenal Frenchman played on the losing side just once.

In his third year, United were handily placed for both League and FA Cup again, when the infamous 'karate kick' incident took place at Selhurst Park at the end of January.

Without Cantona, who was suspended for eight months, the team faltered as they approached both targets. Yet there were those who wanted United to say good riddance to their *enfant terrible* and wash their hands of his flawed temperament.

Ferguson was not among them. Hughes, Ince and Kanchelskis he allowed to leave, but he made a dash to France to persuade a disillusioned Cantona that he still had a future in English football.

Now, only a few months later, the reformed Frenchman is a candidate for the cherished 'Footballer of the Year' accolade, which carries an appreciation of sporting behaviour as well as outstanding form on the field.

Cantona has been cautioned only once this season, and those who thought he looked a subdued figure a few weeks earlier have been lost in admiration for his mercurial contribution to United's run of eighteen unbeaten games – fifteen of them won.

In my humble opinion, Eric Cantona was the ingredient that bestowed again upon Manchester United the greatness they once had, but which they found so hard to rediscover for 25 years and more.

Having been privileged to watch him at close quarters for

three years, I have little hesitation in nominating him as the best player I have ever seen.

Thursday 11th
Whether it is the rapid approach of Euro 96 I am not sure, but I am being asked to do things that have never been on my agenda before.

Today a man whose column I have read many times, Graham Bridgstock, talked to me for about two hours for his 'Me and My Health' column in the *Daily Mail*.

Lovely man that he is, it was a bit like being grilled by a psychotherapist. Refusing to be fazed by my proud boast of not having a day off work with illness for some 30 years, Mr Bridgstock wanted to know whether my birth had been painless, what ailments I had as a child, had I ever needed counselling or mental therapy, did my feet swell in the night, and why I bite my fingernails.

He is the old-fashioned type of journalist who writes everything down rather than using a tape recorder, but when he faxed me a draft of the article it was word perfect in terms of what I had said.

Mind you, I had the nagging feeling that I must be due some sort of physical setback. I seem to have been extraordinarily lucky with my health, and as I don't subscribe to a particularly careful lifestyle there may be some settling up to be done between me and my body.

I spoke too soon. Tonight I fell over while I was looking at a new car on the garage forecourt. The diagnosis is bruised ribs.

Friday 12th
Chris Rea was quite right when he told me at Cheltenham that rugby union was about to face its biggest-ever upheaval.

The row between the English ruling body and the soon to be professional clubs has escalated into a nasty war of words that threatens the game's immediate future. Anybody who has watched how other sports have changed once the proverbial lid has come off the piggy bank could have told them exactly what would happen. It comes under the heading of greed.

The international game apart – and England are risking a split with the other home nations by demanding more money from the Five Nations television contract – there is one big difference between club rugby, in whatever guise, and the FA Carling Premiership.

Simply, that fewer people want to watch it. When Bath and Leicester can attract the sort of crowd that turns up for a routine match at Highbury, then rugby clubs can start calling the tune.

A game that commercially has only just got out of its pram at club level, is advised to learn to walk before it tries to run.

Saturday 13th

Most rugby union clubs would jump at a crowd half the size of that at Southampton – even though the capacity at The Dell is by some way the smallest in the Premiership.

Time was when 31,000 would pack shoulder to shoulder to watch Manchester United there, but today there was room for less than half that figure. They witnessed at first hand what five million *Match of the Day* viewers saw later – a further twist in the Championship tale that means we are likely to be kept on the edge of our seats a little bit longer.

I suppose we should have guessed. Southampton, after all, had managed to score only three goals in their previous eight games; Manchester United had kept a clean sheet in nine of their last twelve.

So the half-time score of 3-0 to the Saints was in keeping with the perversity of the occasion. Especially as the Premiership leaders did something I could not recall any team doing – changing their colours at half-time.

The unappealing grey shirts (or should they be called indigo blue?) were crossly discarded by players who claimed they were not only unlucky, but made it hard to pick out a colleague.

But the replacement set of blue and white brought no improvement in United's poorest performance since the turn of the year. If you had walked into the ground uninformed, you would have thought Southampton were tilting at the title, and their opponents flirting with relegation.

Alex Ferguson was magnanimous in defeat, but after United had left to catch their private charter flight back to Manchester, one Southampton director ruefully reflected on the difference in the daily budget of the two clubs.

'They come here by private plane. We go on a seven-hour coach journey to Newcastle.'

Southampton will go there next week with renewed hope,

but first the nation waits to see whether Keegan's team can take advantage of United's first defeat since New Year's Day.

Sunday 14th

The Ampthill and Flitwick Flyers attracted an entry of over 500 runners for their annual ten-kilometre race in Bedfordshire. It is run over one of the most pleasant courses in my experience, but perhaps I just said that because my time of inside 48 minutes was more respectable than of late. The diet must be working.

Every finisher received a presentation mug at the end, but the Premiership race is making mugs of a lot of people at the moment. For an hour the atmosphere coming out of Newcastle this afternoon seemed as flat and benign as it had been at Flitwick in the morning.

Then Mark Bosnich had a rush of blood that seems to be affecting all goalkeepers at the moment – even Schmeichel. Like his Manchester counterpart yesterday, Villa's goalkeeper came for a cross he failed to reach, and ended up on the wrong side of the forward who put the ball into the net. In this case, Les Ferdinand.

Newcastle's centre forward was apparently feeling unwell at the time, and they had placed some water by the side of the pitch. If the Championship churns the stomach much more than this, they will be providing large brandies.

Monday 15th

It's Greg Norman who needs the large brandy this morning. The nation stayed up until midnight last night to see Nick Faldo turn a six-shot deficit before the final round of the US Masters into a five-shot victory over the Australian who seems to have a mental block when it comes to winning the majors.

In seven of these championships, Norman has either held or shared the lead going into the final round – but won only one of them. And to think they are accusing Keegan and Newcastle of choking on the last lap!

Striking the front early seems designed to bring on a twitchiness that affects even the most assured. Further down the Leagues, it is starting to trouble Stevenage Borough, whose handsome lead in the GM Vauxhall Conference has been cut to a slender two points by their only real pursuers, Woking.

You may remember my writing about Stevenage and their

200

chairman, Victor Green, back in August, when he was debating whether or not to spend considerable capital on their ground in order to bring it up to Football League standard in time for the admission criteria date of 31 December.

Stevenage failed to make that deadline, although their local authority assured the League's management committee that the ground would measure up to all safety standards by the start of next season – should they win promotion.

In this morning's *Daily Telegraph*, Victor Green bemoaned the fact that Stevenage would still be rejected because their stadium falls short of the minimum capacity of 6,000 which the Football League requires. Having been a champion of the cause of Barnet, Wycombe and Boston United when all were trying to break into what many feel is a closed shop, I have some sympathy with Victor's argument, especially as the Endsleigh League have sometimes been slow to make *their* point of view public.

However, rules are rules, and as Kidderminster and Macclesfield have had to concede, the Conference clubs know where they stand at the beginning of the season, and need to show a commitment to prevent last-minute hitches which could leave the Football League with a ground unworthy of its status.

As Green says, football is based on the principle of promotion and relegation, and it is conceivable that no club will be elevated from the Conference (nor lose their Endsleigh position) for the third season running.

Perhaps now the Premiership is moving further away from the rump of the old Football League, it is time for Endsleigh or their successors to start another 'fourth division', and allow all those Conference clubs who can state a worthwhile case to gain admission.

Preferably with a ground capacity of rather less than 6,000 which, as Victor Green points out, is very nearly twice the average crowd in the Third Division at the moment.

Tuesday 16th
Today Desmond Lynam, Andy Gray and I were at Electronic Arts' sound studio at Langley, near Slough, to record commentary for the computer screen game FIFA '97.

The '96 version, in which I was involved last year, was deemed to be a qualified success – it outsold all its competitors – but as we get nearer to 'virtual reality' it was considered a logical step to bring in a presenter and a co-commentator.

My limited knowledge of the secret service tells me that Langley has been used in the past as a debriefing centre for spies and suchlike. Now it is the headquarters of the computer game industry, it is easy to see why. Every road looks very much the same, and every building bristles with anonymity. Even when you get inside, every door has a combination lock and the security bears the hallmark of an Ian Fleming novel.

Inside, the whizzkids of the computer age sit in front of their screens and consoles, toying with images that will harden into the advanced games of tomorrow. Soon, imagination will be declared redundant – you won't just pretend to be Nick Faldo, you will be right inside his frame, playing the same shots.

Whether you would want to be transported into the mind of Terry Venables at the moment is another matter. Today he lost Alan Shearer, at least for the next two internationals, who needs an operation on his groin. It was also confirmed that Tony Adams has had a setback in his recovery from knee surgery, and must be considered a doubt for Euro 96.

The good news was that Mark Wright played for Liverpool against Everton tonight – a 1-1 draw effectively ending his team's title hopes – and Gary Pallister was said to be nearing full fitness again.

Talking of the European Championship, Mr Shishkovsky wants a fax. This is the start of the long process undertaken to try to ensure commentators can see the teams training before they play.

The Russians will be staying at Wigan, and hopefully will hold at least one public training session before their opening match against Italy at Anfield.

If they are as security-conscious as the old Soviet Union teams used to be, I'll probably be hiding behind a pillar while they have breakfast, trying to snatch a glance at their faces.

But Mr Shishkovsky said 'send me a fax'. He is the liaison officer with the Russian team and it seemed appropriate to fax him from the labyrinthian corridors of Langley.

Wednesday 17th

I couldn't understand what was the matter with Dave Merrington. The Southampton manager had been hale and hearty on Saturday, when he had given me his team for the Manchester United match, but now, four days later, he didn't seem to know who I was.

I normally arrange to ring the manager the day before the game, or on the morning of an evening match, to check the names in the squad and see if he will give me some guidance as to the starting line-up.

Merrington and Southampton were staying at the Gosforth Park Hotel in Newcastle, and he was expecting me to call him there after their last training session.

The receptionists at hotels are always wary when you ask if a football club have arrived. 'I'm not allowed to give out that information, sir,' is usually followed by a reluctant change of mind when you explain who you represent and that the manager concerned is expecting the call.

On this occasion, the said Merrington was not in his room, and attempts to page him took a considerable time. Finally, a voice came over the phone that seemed to lack Dave's usual fiery manner.

'Yes, this is Mr Merrington. Who did you say you are?'

'John Motson, Dave.'

'John Motson?'

'Yes, from the BBC.'

'John Motson from the BBC . . .'

'That is Dave Merrington, isn't it?'

'Oh yes, this is Dave.'

At this point, I began to believe I was being 'wound up' by a gaggle of Southampton footballers splitting their sides in the background.

I was just about to say, 'Come on, Dave, stop them fooling around,' or words to that effect, when I tried one more time.

'Look, is that Dave Merrington, the manager of Southampton Football Club?'

'Well, I'm expecting him back any minute. He's been out for about three hours. This is his father speaking.'

How was I to know that David Merrington senior, still resident in the north-east, would be standing in the foyer when his son was paged? Or that he had the same Christian name?

He must have been more confused than I was, and Dave junior made no reference to the call when I caught up with him later.

'We'll go as we did on Saturday.' This was the forthright manager talking now. 'Newcastle looked a bit nervy on Sunday, and they probably expect us to play with a sweeper. But we'll keep the same team and try to go at them.'

It is an unwritten rule with commentators that once having spoken to a manager, you never release any pre-match information to the opposition. You would soon lose confidences, otherwise, and get no help in the future.

Terry McDermott, who I spoke to at Newcastle, told me who would be in the squad and who was injured, but said Keegan would not name the starting line-up until just before the match. But he assured me there would be no surprises.

Brendan Foster met me at the airport and, devoted Newcastle fan that he is, told me how screwed up the Geordie supporters were, never mind the team. I told him to back Rob Lee for the first goal tonight at 12 to 1 – he is certainly due one.

Thursday 18th
After what happened last night, I reckon they ought to stop the Championship now and let Newcastle and Manchester United share it. It has got too close to call, and neither team is producing anything like the quality of football which gave so much pleasure in the first two-thirds of the season.

I couldn't believe how the atmosphere had changed at St James's Park. On all my previous visits up to January, the place was really jumping and the stadium positively shook with exhilaration.

Last night, the mood was nervous, almost to the point of being morbid. It was as if 36,000 people had seen two accidents in quick succession (which, in a football sense, they had) and were dreading the third.

'We are gutsing it out. Nobody can call us entertainers any more,' was Keegan's honest assessment. His team failed to add to the tenth-minute goal with which Lee ended his barren run; they missed a penalty and survived a couple of scares in Southampton's spasmodic attacks.

Over at Old Trafford, it took Roy Keane and Manchester United 71 minutes to score against Leeds, who were reduced to ten men early in the game when their goalkeeper, Mark Beeney, was harshly sent off for handling the ball fractionally outside the penalty area.

The managers reflected the tension. Ferguson said on *Sportsnight* that if Leeds could play as well as that, then their players had been cheating the manager, Howard Wilkinson, in some of the other games.

As for Keegan, he put on a brave face and agreed to sponsor

me at £5 per mile for the Great North Run. He once did it himself pushing a handicapped competitor in a wheelchair, but the Championship race must seem more like two marathons rolled into one just now.

Friday 19th

When people ask whether I ever played football, I say no, but occasionally they used to let me on to the pitch.

This weekend marks the annual tour to Bournemouth for my old Sunday team, Roving Reporters, who play in the Barnet and District Sunday League.

As a founder member, of both club and league, I now hold the privileged position of president of both. That entitles me to go on the tour providing I can get the weekend off.

This year was no problem. The Premiership is idle this weekend, owing to England's friendly against Croatia next week.

I picked up another of our old players, John Watts, and we drove down to the hotel in Boscombe to join a party of 32 – it seems to get bigger every year although a few of the lads come for the crack and have no intention of playing.

John and I had so much to catch up on, having not seen each other for a year, that we missed the turn to Bournemouth and found ourselves lost somewhere near Poole. Perhaps I wouldn't have made a taxi driver after all.

Saturday 20th

It's a long time since I stayed in bed until nearly midday, but that's the effect of a night out with the younger lads when you get to my age.

By the time I surfaced, Roving Reporters had been to Bashley, the club in the New Forest who kindly entertain us every year, and won their friendly 4-2.

I made amends by taking a few of the senior players to watch Bournemouth play Walsall. Both clubs have ensured their safety in the Second Division of the Endsleigh League, so it was a 0-0 draw peppered with some nice passing but without a cutting edge to the game.

However, you don't often see the 'man of the match' sent off. No sooner had the loudspeaker announced that Bournemouth's Russell Beardsmore had received the vote, than he was shown the red card for a second bookable offence. Some of the home supporters near me were miffed by that – he's not a dirty player and the match was running into stoppage time. But as I said, the referee is mandated to apply the laws strictly and they don't give him much flexibility.

Sunday 21st
It's nearly a year since I have stepped on to a football pitch, but the generous use of substitutes in the match against a Bournemouth local radio station persuaded the Roving Reporters' selection committee to offer the president half a game.

I was spared any embarrassment by the fact that we were already 3-0 up, and we went on to win the match 5-1.

It was another salutary reminder of how much pleasure playing football offers to tens of thousands of young people who would never aspire to the professional game. All over this and many other countries this morning, the goal nets would be up and the coin would be tossed. Somebody would win and someone would lose.

It's such a simple game when you think about it. And whatever our misgivings about life at the top, which now seems to be purely about money, there is little wrong with the grass roots of the game.

Afterwards we went to the clubhouse for a beer with our opponents. They promised to play us again next year and the local disc jockey wanted to know if I would be there.

At my age, I told him, you take every year as it comes.

Monday 22nd
Sally Coxon, who handles my freelance work, informed me that the Nike commercial must be done again. This time, the scriptwriters had not only reversed the order of events (with the ball starting in the back of the net) but had actually transposed the commentator's words.

So now I was saying things like: 'Incredible is this! Seaman past net the of back the into. Ginola by shot great. There 1-2 little lovely. Kick free the takes Ferdinand.' And so on.

Apparently commentators in other sports like Stuart Storey and Jim Rosenthal had made similar recordings for the campaign.

Not being an advertising man myself, I started out thinking the whole concept would be too complicated for the listener to understand. But that was the whole point. The creative agency were out to command the attention of the audience by totally confusing them.

The session was a long one by voiceover standards, and when I left it was difficult to take the brain out of reverse gear. I had to meet a friend of mine, who had just announced he was getting married. He looked startled when I greeted him with: 'News great. Girl lucky the is who.'

Tuesday 23rd

Twenty years ago, when players' shirts were plain red or white, the numbers on the back said one to eleven, and the size of the players' wages meant a supporter didn't need to take out a mortgage to buy a season ticket, one of the managers who helped me a lot was Tommy Docherty.

When you rang the Doc for team news on a Friday, there was no messing about. That rasping Scottish voice would come straight back down the phone: 'Number one, Stepney; number two, Forsyth; number three, Albiston; number four, Daly; number five, Greenhoff; number six, Buchan . . .'

I first met Docherty when I was a young Chelsea supporter in the early sixties. He led the club back to the promised land of the old First Division, the season ending in wild celebration when a 7-0 win over Portsmouth at Stamford Bridge clinched promotion when we thought the chance had gone.

The Doc lived in Cockfosters then, right at the end of the Piccadilly Line, and I was a member of East Barnet Methodist Youth Club, which met at the bottom of his road. Once, I walked back with him from the tube station. He had just bought Derek Kevan, who a lot of Chelsea fans thought was a bit of a carthorse. 'He'll get us up,' the Doc promised me, and sure enough, Kevan headed Chelsea in front after just 90 seconds against Portsmouth.

At the end of the match, in which Terry Venables scored from a penalty and Chelsea's record goalscorer Bobby Tambling got four goals, the Doc seized a microphone and addressed the crowd of 54,000 from the centre of the main stand.

My dad and I had season tickets in the adjacent block, and could hear every word he said. He predicted five years of glory for Chelsea in the top flight, and he wasn't far wrong. He took the club into Europe, into three successive FA Cup semi-finals, and laid the foundations for his coach, Dave Sexton, to later return to Stamford Bridge and win the FA Cup and the European Cup-Winners Cup.

Everybody knows that the Doc became a specialist in changing clubs after that. But he found a spiritual home at Old Trafford, protected by his great idol Matt Busby, and when Manchester United won the FA Cup in 1977 it was their first major achievement since Busby had lifted the European Cup in the same stadium nine years earlier.

Docherty, who had been to Wembley seven times before as player or manager and lost each time, was so thrilled at the end that he balanced the lid of the trophy on his head. But contentious to the last, he toppled over himself a few weeks later when he was sacked for having an affair with the wife of the club physiotherapist.

Nineteen years on, Tommy and Mary are still together, and when I phoned him this morning all the old enthusiasm and banter was still there.

'What's this, John, all our yesterdays?' he quipped, and he was absolutely bang to rights. I had suggested to *Grandstand* that on Cup Final day, we should assemble a feature called '1977 Revisited', and talk to a couple of the main characters from the last equivalent meeting of Liverpool and Manchester United.

That was my first FA Cup Final for BBC Television at the tender age of 31, but what a lot of people never realised was that it was also my first 'live' match. Televised football in the seventies was nearly all shown in edited highlights form, with the only live action on BBC or ITV being the Cup Final, the annual England v. Scotland match and the occasional European final.

So, I had a few recollections to chew over with Docherty. Since those early days at Chelsea, the Doc had swapped the Piccadilly Line for Piccadilly Radio, where he is now flexing those Scottish vocal chords with his forthright opinions so valued by the fans in Manchester – although not necessarily by the managers, who he is not afraid to criticise.

By a happy coincidence, Tommy told me he would be at the Bolton v. Southampton match this Saturday, which is where I am working for *Match of the Day*.

No problems setting up the interview then. 'What time do you want me there?' asked the Doc.

'Let's do it at lunchtime, before we get busy with the match,' I suggested.

'I'll be there at twelve, on the dot, ready to go down memory lane.'

Just what the Doctor ordered.

Wednesday 24th
Terry Venables announced a team with only three defenders, and the five midfield players did not include the mandatory 'wing backs' of the modern system.

It wasn't quite as startling as it appeared, although in the light of the opposition from Croatia, who came to Wembley with a growing reputation, it was a bold departure from normal England practice.

Venables had talked all season about pushing one of the back four players into midfield when the shape of the game demanded, and now in Paul Ince he had a combative midfield man who could drop back when required.

Iulian, the chef in a Hertfordshire restaurant who is an expert in East European football affairs, predicted at lunchtime that England would fail to score. He was proved right.

He also believes, just for the record, that Turkey will do surprisingly well in Euro 96 and that Romania, if they can get through a group that includes France and Spain, are capable of getting to the final.

It prompted a lively debate, with the Spanish and Italian waiters chipping in their pesetas and lire. If you look at it on paper, just about all sixteen nations have some sort of chance.

I was having lunch with Mark Jewell, from whom I had just acquired a new car. A red four-wheel drive Mondeo, with sports injection. A bit on the racy side for me, perhaps.

But Mark, who is a season ticket holder at Tottenham and a regular at England matches, had a more serious issue on his mind. He was convinced that however tight our security precautions, there was going to be trouble either in the stadiums or in the streets from rival supporters this summer.

His warning came back to me when Holland played Germany in Rotterdam tonight. There were a lot of arrests before the game, two people were stabbed, and riot police weighed into the crowd with truncheons at the final whistle.

No such hostility at Wembley, either on or off the pitch. The friendly against Croatia petered out into anti-climax, with England carving out five good chances but failing to put them away. Again, the opposition came to stamp a

Wembley appearance on their football passport and pass the ball around gently breaking into a sweat only when it came to swapping shirts on the final whistle.

So much for friendlies. As Barry Davies said in the commentary: 'The real stuff can't start soon enough.'

Thursday 25th

While we are on the subject of BBC commentators, no, I did not win that wretched competition! Ever since I joined *Match of the Day*, those with long memories have associated me with the *Sportsnight* contest to find a new football commentator which the BBC ran over several weeks in 1969.

The prize in what became known as the 'Commentators' Competition' was a trip to the World Cup in Mexico in 1970. It was won by a Welshman named Idwal Robling, although Ian St John was a close second and was defeated only on the casting vote of the then England manager, Sir Alf Ramsey.

I was beavering away in radio at the time, and being a full-time BBC employee, it was doubtful whether I would have been allowed to enter even if I had wanted to. As it was, I was still a couple of months away from my first radio commentary, let alone television.

But time plays tricks with the memory, and two years on, when I joined *Match of the Day*, the 1970 World Cup was still fresh in people's minds. Understandably then, countless people have come up to me over the years with the opening question: 'Didn't you win that competition?'

Quite apart from obscuring my background on the *Barnet Press*, the *Morning Telegraph* at Sheffield, and in BBC Radio Sport, the suggestion slightly amuses me because it gets asked so often, and implies Motson got the job thanks to an alternative version of the National Lottery!

The follow-up usually goes something like: 'Well, what happened to the guy who *did* win it, then?' At this point I patiently explain that Idwal Robling *did* collect his prize, travelling to Mexico in 1970 with the BBC television commentary team, and later doing some domestic matches.

Indeed, memory tells me that on the day of my Hereford v. Newcastle breakthrough – or certainly in the same season – he was the commentator at one of the other FA Cup ties being carried by *Match of the Day*.

Since then, Idwal has been a regular and respected broadcaster on radio and television in Wales. We have never met for over twenty years, but I am sure he is as tired of being asked about the competition as I am. Twenty-five years on, maybe the BBC should think about staging another one.

On second thoughts, perhaps not. They would probably find somebody a lot better than me.

Friday 26th
It is at this stage of the season that Annie's 'red book' is so invaluable. My wife has helped me keep my records since we married in 1976, and quite apart from maintaining an intricate filing system for all my overseas information, she stoically records every result, goalscorer, appearance and attendance in the Premiership.

Annie does not often offer up theories on the game, although she is a keen Newcastle United supporter. But one thing she always says in April, having listed the players in the left-hand column all season, is that it is easy to spot the clubs in trouble. They always use far more players than the successful teams.

Take Bolton Wanderers for example, who for some strange reason I have not covered this season until this weekend, when they play their last home match against Southampton.

Bolton have used no fewer than 28 players in the first team, one more than Coventry and the same number as Manchester City. All three are fighting for their lives near the bottom.

Liverpool, by comparison, have used only eighteen. And Newcastle, significantly perhaps, managed on only fourteen players until halfway through the Premiership campaign.

At the back of the book, Annie sticks in useful newspaper cuttings referring to international squads, transfers and anything else that may be relevant when I am preparing for a game.

Normally I devote the whole of Friday to preparation and travel, but today I had a meeting with Paul Holland, of EMI, who has got an idea for a sound cassette based on my impressions of the European Championship.

We agree it will have potential if England do well, but might not be flavour of the month if we fail to make the semi-final.

Mind you, that also applies to a lot of commercial propositions just now. Asda have renamed their salt and vinegar crisps 'Salt and Venables' ... now that could *certainly* add some flavour to the month.

Saturday 27th
Nat Lofthouse is 70 and Tommy Docherty two years his junior,
but you would never have guessed if you had seen them having
lunch together at Burnden Park today.

Tommy drove from Basingstoke to Bolton this morning,
after fulfilling a speaking engagement down south last night. 'I
only do the odd one now,' he cracked. 'One a night.'

In fact, Docherty makes far more money as a celebrity
after-dinner guest than he ever did as a football manager. In the
interview we did today, he told me his wages when Manchester
United won the FA Cup in 1977 were only £15,000 per
year.

As for Nat, he had been out until four o'clock in the morning
with one of the other Bolton directors, but he looked as though
he could have gone out and played.

He has his own office at Burnden Park, which says 'N.
Lofthouse, President' on the door – and I'm sure they'll give
him another one when they move to their new £25 million
all-seater stadium at Horwich next year.

The atmosphere at Burnden was a bit muted today, because
Bolton were virtually down before the start, and Matt Le
Tissier's goal confirmed their relegation after only a year in the
Premiership.

But they took their disappointment on the chin and when I
left, Colin Todd was already discussing plans for next season
with his chairman, Gordon Hargreaves.

As I walked out a playful foot suddenly came out and tapped
me on the ankle.

'It's a good job he didn't kick you properly,' said Nat.
'That's Roy Hartle.'

You only need a modicum of Bolton history to know that
Hartle was the fearsome right back of the fifties, who won an
FA Cup winners' medal and played on the opposite flank to the
equally menacing Tommy Banks.

There is a ledge on the edge of the pitch at Burnden Park,
with a short drop to the cinder track alongside. 'Tha'd better
not try to get past us unless tha wants gravel rash,' is what
Hartle and Banks apparently used to say to wingers.

I thought about asking Hartle to verify that quote, but he
looked sprightly enough to give me a demonstration so I made
my excuses and left.

Sunday 28th

The main drama on television today was not Manchester United's five-goal demolition of Nottingham Forest – although it did wonders for their goal difference – nor even the German Grand Prix, the World Snooker Championship or Derby County clinching promotion to the Premiership, an achievement which delighted at least one member of the Motson household.

No, the airwaves were trembling with the first part of Dennis Potter's *Karaoke*. That and his other – and last – television play, *Cold Lazarus*, are being screened in a joint arrangement between BBC1 and Channel 4, which Potter requested before he died.

It is impossible to be ambivalent about this powerful playwright. In the *Sunday Times* culture section this morning, he was torn apart by A. A. Gill, who mimicked a Potter character whose speech was plagued by spoonerisms to rechristen the master 'Pennis Dotter'.

Gill, who is an amusing and trenchant reviewer, doesn't believe Potter, or Dotter, was a master at all. He dismissed him as some sort of self-obsessed eccentric, whose work has been rescued by skilful producers, sensitive acting, and compliant television moguls who had broken the rules for him alone.

After such a thunderous build-up in this and many other widely respected arts columns, *Karaoke* part one was compulsive viewing tonight.

And I must say I found it absorbing. Brutally frank it surely is, and Potter has obviously invested a lot of his own angst and sickness in his leading character Daniel Feeld, played by Albert Finney. But some of the lighter touches and personal confrontations – such as the face-off in the restaurant between Finney and the splendidly casted Anna Chancellor – were real life brought to the screen, which when you cut out all the turgid analysis that a series like this invokes, is surely what television drama is supposed to be about.

Monday 29th

An ambition fulfilled today when Peter O'Sullevan was my guest at lunch. We chose a restaurant he likes near his home in Chelsea and talked on a personal level for the first time since I interviewed him thirteen years ago for Ludovic Kennedy's *Did You See* programme.

For a man in his 79th year who still performs with unerring consistency at high speed, Peter could be forgiven for thinking he has cracked our trade. Nothing could be further from the truth.

Having spoken in French to the waiters to ensure we were drinking the very best red wine, 'The Voice' (as he is known in the racing industry), then admitted to the same sense of loneliness and insecurity that, even at the best of times, bugs most commentators.

O'Sullevan is coming up to his 50th Grand National as a broadcaster, but probably does more homework now than ever before. Rather like yours truly, he isn't always where he wants to be. This coming weekend, he will be commentating for the BBC at Haydock Park while the first Classics of the flat racing season – the 1,000 and 2,000 Guineas – are screened from Newmarket on the rival Channel 4.

Mike Dillon of Ladbrokes was also at the table, and took a sporting bet from Peter on the Guineas. 'I'll probably be watching that on my portable on the platform at Warrington Station on my way back from Haydock,' said O'Sullevan. (You mean to say he still travels by *train*?)

His charm and modesty prevented Peter from delivering his best line until he politely left us to record a telephone interview for BBC Radio Newcastle.

'I had tea with the Queen Mother at Sandown on Saturday,' he murmured. 'At least, I went into her box to have tea, but she suggested we had champagne instead.'

Tuesday 30th

The face-off between Sky's studio presenters and Ron Atkinson a few weeks ago paled beside Kevin Keegan's emotional outburst at their microphone last night, when he took exception to comments his rival Alex Ferguson had made about the attitude Newcastle's opponents might show in their remaining games.

Being in the business, I suppose I should say it was good television, but Keegan was wound up to the point where it made you realise just how much tension those involved are under now that the Championship is well and truly on the line.

Even Richard Keys and Andy Gray looked taken aback by the passionate nature of his response. Wisely in the circumstances, they let Kevin have his say and did not interrupt or aggravate what was obviously a tender situation.

We have come a long way in terms of post-match interviews since Kevin Keegan joined Liverpool as a player in my first season with *Match of the Day*.

In those days, Bill Shankly or his opposite number would come out to face two or three straightforward questions about the game they had just won, and that would be the extent of their responsibilities to the spoken media.

Nowadays, there is a trail of microphones and cameras ready to intercept them the moment they leave the dressing room. Managers and players have to accept that this is very much part of the job, especially when television money is largely paying their wages, but you can understand it if they feel they should be allowed a cooling-off period before they speak.

Talking of television contracts for football, we are just about to enter the month of May when my agent, John Hockey, believes the new deal for Premiership football will be sorted out.

Discussions have been going on for some time with regard to what happens when the existing arrangements run out at the end of next season, and everybody at the BBC obviously hopes *Match of the Day* will survive to show recorded highlights as we have for the past five years.

John reminded me today of the words of the former Luton chairman, David Evans, when he spoke to me about the future of football on television well over ten years ago.

'In the end every club will have its own channel, show its own matches, and employ its own commentator.'

MAY
1996

Wednesday 1st

Just when I was starting to think I might have gone a bit strong in praising Chelsea earlier in the diary, Glenn Hoddle was offered the job of England coach.

His other obvious qualifications notwithstanding, the way his team have played this season surely has something to do with the outcome of the FA's prolonged deliberations.

So Chelsea are not in the Championship race, haven't reached a Cup Final, and won't be playing in Europe, but had they had a Robbie Fowler or an Ian Wright in their side they would probably have been involved in all three.

I remember taking issue with Hoddle over his sweeper system in a friendly discussion at Swindon a few years ago, but he was adamant about the way he wanted his team to play, and he has carried that through with Chelsea and now, it appears, is poised to do so with England.

Without retreading old ground with regard to the pitfalls in the job, the one thing the England manager needs to be is his own man at all times. Hoddle fulfils that criterion, but he will need a lot of support when it comes to coping with the demands of the media.

Starting with his first press conference, which is scheduled for tomorrow.

Thursday 2nd

His first media appointment was very harmonious. The FA sensibly arranged for Terry Venables to be there too, giving full backing to his successor. They both said the right things but Hoddle won't get the same honeymoon period that Venables had – his first match will be a competitive World Cup qualifier.

England are not the only ones planning for next season. I was invited to a 'think tank' lunch today by David Welch, the sports editor of the *Daily Telegraph*.

Quite apart from producing their comprehensive sports pages and weekly supplement, the *Telegraph* boys are always looking to improve and tone up their coverage.

Niall Sloane, my editor at the BBC, was also among the guests, and the deliberations really centred around whether the Monday sports supplement should have three football pages rather than two.

David's two chief assistants, Keith Perry and Brian Oliver, were anxious for new ideas, and the only one I came up with was a weekly diary from one of the overseas players now earning his living in the Premiership.

They felt the likes of Ruud Gullit or even the now departed Jurgen Klinsmann might prove too expensive, so I suggested that one of the Croatians like Slaven Bilic, of West Ham (who is a qualified lawyer), might be able to put an interesting new perspective on our football.

But before we get on to *next* season, there is still the little matter of *this* season's Championship to be sorted out. Newcastle again lost a winning position at Nottingham Forest tonight, Woan's equaliser robbing them of the two points that would have sent them into the last day of the season level with Manchester United.

This time, Kevin Keegan did not appear in front of the cameras after the match. Frankly, I don't blame him. He now has to hope that Middlesbrough will beat Manchester United on Sunday.

I don't think there will be any old pals act between Bryan Robson and Alex Ferguson. After all, Robson was left out of United's Cup Final thirteen on his last day at the club!

Friday 3rd
The papers were full of the Glenn Hoddle press conference, but he gave no individual interviews and will not do so in the near future.

I was charged with helping to follow up the story for *Football Focus*, and we decided the angle would have moved on tomorrow as to who might be the next Chelsea manager.

So while I was at Barnet at lunchtime interviewing Ray Clemence for our 1977 Cup Final revisited feature, the office arranged for me to interview Ken Bates later in the afternoon.

While I was commiserating with Clemence on the fact that Barnet had almost certainly narrowly missed out on the play-offs, Matthew Harding rang and left him a message to ring back. I joked that Ray was about to be offered the Chelsea job, and on second thoughts it was not to be laughed at, the way Barnet stormed up the table in the second half of the season.

However, the newspaper writers were plumping for either George Graham or Ruud Gullit, so I put those names directly to Ken Bates in the interview. He knocked down the first theory, denying reports that he had said he wanted Graham, and suggested it might be too early for Gullit.

Bates rarely agrees to recorded interviews, because he is suspicious of the way they might be edited. But he obliged today without demur, and then ushered me out of a secret door near his office into the main stand.

Football grounds have an aura of their own even when they are empty, and Stamford Bridge looked serene if not stately in the stillness of the Friday afternoon sunshine. It held a lot of memories for me, having been there so often with my late father, but Ken Bates was now in full flow, explaining his plans for a hotel, new stands, and an apartment block which have been at the centre of his widely reported debate with Matthew Harding over the direction Chelsea should take in the future.

At that moment it was almost as though nobody else, from the Royal Family to Glenn Hoddle, Matthew Harding and down in descending order of importance to John Motson, really existed.

Dear old irascible Ken, he of the pungent programme notes, was in a mood so sensitive that I swear he became almost sentimental. One man lost in a dream which he believed he could fulfil.

We all have them, Ken. We all have them.

Saturday 4th

I am sure the final of the Pilkington Cup matters immensely to rugby union followers, and today's match between Bath and Leicester ended in controversy, but Saturday afternoon without football really doesn't stack up. It just doesn't feel like Saturday.

We all know the reasons why the FA Carling Premiership and the First Division of the Endsleigh League switched their programme to Sunday. On the last day of the season, with the most significant matches set aside for live television, everybody has to play at the same time.

Having said that, why do *both* leagues need to switch? Why not play the Endsleigh games on Saturday, since the old rule about live television affecting attendances elsewhere seems to have been conveniently ignored at other times during the season – especially on Wednesday nights.

I say this because having timed my journey to North York-shire to coincide with *Sport on Five*, I wanted something more gripping on the radio than the relegation battle at the bottom of Endsleigh Division Two.

Having decided to break my journey to Middlesbrough by staying the night in Harrogate, I was further reminded that this was no normal Saturday when I discovered the hotel was hosting a lorry drivers' convention. Truckers on a weekend away can be at least as boisterous as football fans, and they seemed to have come from all over Europe.

Quite apart from standing three abreast at the bar so that nobody else could buy a drink, they also appeared to have bugged the hotel's telephone system.

Every time I dialled '9' for an outside line, a voice came on in four or five different languages with a recorded announcement.

What it was probably trying to tell me was that it was long odds against getting any dinner tonight. Every hotel in Harro-gate seemed to be staging some conference or other, and the delegates were flooding into the town to pack any restaurant they could find.

In the end I found a spare table in the upstairs section of a nice little Italian. And an added bonus was that the guys at the next table were remarkably quiet.

Not surprising really. It later transpired they were Newcastle supporters.

Sunday 5th

This *was* the day to be sitting by the radio. Just about everybody in the ground had one, apart from me, in Middles-brough's Cellnet Riverside Stadium, which I had not visited before and which, even with careful directions from two Boro supporters, I managed to find at the third attempt having got lost first in a railway siding and then in an industrial estate.

There were quite a few managers who would have willingly swapped places with me and spent the afternoon in one of those. If you are playing your last match of a season, the outcome of which also depends on other teams' results, it must be sheer agony.

And for the supporters too. But those Manchester United fans with their transistors clamped against their ears needed to worry only for about fifteen minutes once the game at Middlesbrough started.

Once their team scored, they were never going to lose, so what was happening at Newcastle became academic. For a commentator, it made for a more satisfying if less dramatic afternoon than a year earlier, when Blackburn had won the title.

If you are going to see the trophy presented, you want it to be because the champions secured it by their own efforts on the final day, and not because of what may have happened elsewhere. Manchester United's 3-0 win was suitably emphatic.

Once the ceremonials were over, the interviews completed and the celebrations underway, it occurred to me that this was the last domestic commentary I would do until August.

Maybe it was because I started in October this season that it seems to have ended so quickly. Even before I have had time to answer another question commentators regularly get asked: 'Can you go back and change your words afterwards?'

In a word, no. Even in recorded matches, the commentator has to assume he is 'live'. There are little editing points you try to observe, such as by not talking over goal kicks, so that by the time the ball lands, the viewer can remain unaware that he has just missed twenty minutes of the match!

A horrendous howler could be removed with some difficulty by the video-tape editors, but it is not something I want them to have to consider. They have quite enough to do back at the studio, what with editing the matches and interviews and setting up the evening programme.

I always try to get home to watch *Match of the Day* as it happens, but when you are driving back from Middlesbrough and you don't get away from the ground until seven o'clock, it is a tall order.

In the end I got as far as Luton and stopped to have a beer and a sandwich in front of a television in a convenient hotel.

The BBC had to do in an hour what Sky had spent five hours doing – telling the story of the last day at the top and bottom of the Premiership.

And tomorrow I have got to tell the story of the whole

season in just under two hours. The script for BBC Video's *Race for the Title* needs writing and dubbing by Wednesday.

Perhaps I should get my neighbour Bruce Rioch to do it. He certainly wrote a good script today. With Arsenal a goal down to relegated Bolton, and a European place slipping away, he took off Ian Wright and then saw his only two signings since taking over, David Platt and Dennis Bergkamp, score the late goals that ensured there will be European football in London next season.

Now that really is putting your reputation on the line.

Monday 6th

Less than twelve hours after driving back from Middlesbrough, the last thing I really felt like doing was running in the East Barnet 10k road race. And it looked like it.

One of these days I will enter a run that takes place when I have had a nice quiet day off, when the course is flat, and when I don't need to stop to catch my breath at one of the water stations.

But there were compensations today. Barnet and District Athletic Club know how to organise an event, and afterwards there was a warm shower, hot cups of tea and delicious cake.

This is the nearest I ever get to athletes. It has never been one of my sports, and unlike some of my versatile colleagues I won't be turning my hand to anything outside football in order to earn a ticket for the Olympics in Atlanta this summer.

Mind you, those with long memories have a habit of reminding me what happened when I *did* try my luck at Olympic sports in my early years with BBC Television.

In the 1972 Olympics (remembered for the Israeli massacre), I was sent out of Munich to cover the wild-water canoe slalom at a place called Augsburg.

The British team welcomed me warmly (they had never had any coverage before) and supplied me with bags of information about the course and the technicalities involved.

Unfortunately, things did not go too well for them, and on the second day the last British competitor found himself upside down in the water.

It was my first overseas broadcast so I decided not to go too strong. 'I don't want to sound pessimistic, but I think Britain's chances of a medal are receding a bit here,' was, however, a little understated.

They obviously decided that was enough where Motson and canoeing were concerned, because when I went to Montreal four years later, I spent the first ten days of the 1976 Olympics covering Greco-Roman wrestling.

For over a week not one foot of what I covered made the air, but suddenly one morning there was a delay at the equestrian centre and they came to me 'live' for a bout between a Russian and a Bulgarian.

I launched into the commentary, keen to expound all the knowledge about the rules and history of the sport that I had mugged up from a book that David Vine had lent me.

When the fight was finished, I suddenly realised to my horror that far from educating the British public about the hidden truths of Greco-Roman wrestling, I had actually managed to get the two fighters the wrong way round! I had assumed the Soviet wrestler was the one in the red leotard (well, you would, wouldn't you?) but it turned out he was wearing blue.

John Goodbody, an expert in combat sports who writes for *The Times* these days, was standing behind me. 'I've really cocked that up,' I said. 'I've got those two guys the wrong way round.'

'I shouldn't worry if I were you,' said Goodbody consolingly. 'Only four people in Britain know anything at all about Greco-Roman wrestling. And they'll all be out training.'

Tuesday 7th
Not being a very willing or talented after-dinner speaker, I was apprehensive about joining Jimmy Hill on the platform to co-host the Fantasy Football League dinner held by the *Daily Telegraph* in aid of Jimmy's favourite charity SPARKS (Sport Aiding Medical Research for Kids).

In the end, I need not have worried. They had quite a formidable line-up including Tim Brooke-Taylor, Ron Atkinson, Tommy Docherty and a professional toastmaster all doing their bit, and yours truly only had to say a few words of appreciation over the video clips of the top Fantasy League players.

Somehow my team, Killigrew Juniors, had finished in the top five of the Celebrity League run by the *Telegraph*, although the winner, Mick Mills, proved a worthy champion by a wide margin.

It was the first dinner of its kind and the SPARKS people

were worried about how it would go. To their great credit, they avoided the trap that seems to blight all sporting dinners – too many speakers and the evening dragging on too long.

This was due in no small measure to the professionalism of Tommy Docherty, who timed his speech to perfection and brought the formal proceedings to a close at five minutes to eleven.

When you have been to as many dinners as I have, and sat there shifting in your seat while the third speaker drones on at about half-past twelve, you come to appreciate the opportunity to chat to some of the other guests before everybody falls asleep.

Docherty has a fund of stories that never suffer from retelling. Like the one about the provocative journalist who had the temerity to suggest to the late Bill Shankly that a certain current England international was probably as good a player as Tom Finney.

Now everybody knows that Finney was, in Shankly's opinion, the greatest player of all time. 'I'd play him in his overcoat,' the Liverpool manager had once said.

Anyway, on this occasion Shankly fixed the reporter with a withering look for about five seconds and replied: 'Aye, he might be nearly as good as Finney. But then again, Tom Finney *is* sixty-five.'

Wednesday 8th

In the broadcasting game, 'dubbing' is not something you do to your football boots. It is the term used for laying words of commentary on to an item that has already been shot and edited.

Those who work in daily outlets like the national news become practised at the art of adding their voice-over under fierce time restraints. More considered, longer pieces require a more measured technique.

Race for the Title is an annual production by BBC Video. It tells the story of the Championship race from day one to its climax, with most of the action taken from *Match of the Day* and *Sportsnight* footage over the season.

Brian Barwick, the producer, spent many hours in the Ace Editing production house in West London making the tape, which lasts just under two hours.

In the gaps he has between matches, I had to find some

words to link from the previous piece of action to the next. That meant fiddling around on my video at home until the script made some sort of sense.

Having worked with the cassette for a couple of days, I spent this morning dubbing the words on to the master copy, which is then sent to BBC Video to be duplicated and released within a few days.

Sales of football videos are not what they were. *Race for the Title* will do well to hit the 20,000 mark.

Thursday 9th
I must have done all right at the SPARKS dinner, because today I was invited to Jimmy Hill's pre-Cup Final lunch which he and an old Fulham colleague, Tom Wilson, set up with a few friends including Bob Abrahams, the former BBC editor who looked after me when I first joined the sports department.

It had a nice relaxed ring about it. The one o'clock call was obviously flexible, and by the time everybody had arrived and the conversation got going, it was nearer half-past three by the time we did justice to the menu.

The time seemed to fly by in such convivial company, and when Jimmy left to go to the recording of Frank Skinner and David Baddiel's *Fantasy Football League*, I repaired to the Cafe Royal to meet some friends who were celebrating the end of a particularly tough week.

Steve Hamer, who used to run the commentators' football team, and Jane Morgan, who used to organise my day-to-day activities when she worked for John Hockey Associates, had both been unceremoniously arrested and taken for police questioning the week before, over a Euro 96 ticket investigation. As it turned out, they were completely in the clear. Their company, the National Sporting Club, had bought the tickets in good faith from an approved source, but there had clearly been some confusion at the Football Association. It led to the resignation of their Commercial Director, Trevor Phillips. As this row rumbled on, it rather knocked the FA Cup Final off the back pages for a day or two.

Friday 10th
Not that I was giving this year's final quite the undivided attention that it has demanded from me when I have been the commentator.

For the first time in nearly twenty years, I was able to take

Annie out to dinner on Cup Final eve. Our friends and neighbours Bob and Lesley Sims entertained us in style at a restaurant at nearby Ivinghoe.

And nobody mentioned the Cup Final.

Saturday 11th

Manchester United made history, and proved me wrong for the second time this season. I honestly doubted whether they could make up a twelve-point deficit on Newcastle in the Premiership race, but having done that I believed mental tiredness might set in, and that a fresher, fitter Liverpool would win the FA Cup.

The early indications from Cup Final *Grandstand*, which I was able to enjoy before leaving for Wembley, suggested that the Liverpool lads were indeed more chirpy. The United players seemed quiet by comparison, but later we realised it masked a grim determination to put themselves beyond the reach of any other club in history.

As a spectator, I shared the general view that it was a bitterly disappointing match. Sitting in the stand, which I rarely have the chance to do these days, I was also surprised by the amount of time certain sections of the crowd spent baiting each other and ignoring the match in the process. It reflected the bitter rivalry between the supporters of Liverpool and Manchester United, but it's a pretty expensive way of brooking an argument.

I wasn't doing a commentary under my breath, but it did occur to me that we were four minutes away from the first goalless final in Wembley history when Cantona wrote every-body's story for them.

He also spared Terry Venables from some embarrassment. I met him in the Wembley restaurant afterwards. Had the final gone to a replay, the England coach would have lost a crop of players from the squad for the friendly against Hungary next Saturday.

Also passing through the Wembley entrance hall were the young players of Manchester United. Looking at the fresh faces of the Neville brothers, David Beckham and Nicky Butt, you had to convince yourself that they were not still at school, and you wondered how long it would take *them* to convince themselves just what they had achieved.

How do you follow the double? Quite simply, as Manchester United have proved, by going out and doing it again.

Sunday 12th

Having said what I feel about Eric Cantona earlier, where then would the FA Cup Final have stood without his intervention? Surely the dullest Wembley final in many years, save perhaps for the turgid affair between Arsenal and Sheffield Wednesday three years ago.

Come to that, when did we last have a final to savour? Even the 3-3 draw between Crystal Palace and Manchester United was labelled too rugged and robust; you have to go back to the Coventry v. Tottenham match in 1987 for anything approaching a football classic.

Other finals stick in the memory for different reasons. Wimbledon's victory over Liverpool, because it was such a startling result; Spurs replay against Manchester City, because of Ricky Villa's goal; Arsenal v. Manchester United back in 1979, but only because of the last five minutes; the triumph of Second Division clubs Southampton (over Manchester United in 1976), Sunderland (against Leeds in 1973) and West Ham (over Arsenal in 1980).

Each and every one had their moments, but in the end the 1996 final will be remembered for the fact that it sealed the 'double double'.

Ten years earlier, Liverpool had completed *their* League and Cup double on the same pitch. When their beaten players looked up on the final whistle this year, they saw that half their supporters had walked out in utter dejection.

One female supporter I have met at many Liverpool matches down the years was quick to make a comparison. 'Old Liverpool teams would never have capitulated like that. The players aren't hungry enough any more – they earn so much, defeat doesn't hurt their pride like it used to.'

All in all, it was a bad weekend for Liverpool. *The Sunday Times* television critic, A. A. Gill, savaged the city and its people in his waspish review of *The Liver Birds*.

Gill said the first episode 'pointed up a great truth about the Liverpool in your living room. It's a place that worships, adores and yearns for failure. It's whole *raison d'être* is coping with a brave face and a smart one-liner as you stand with ripped tights as life drives off, splashing you with muddy water.

'You couldn't have a Liverpool drama about success and wealth and elegance and sophistication with a wine list and clean hair. It wouldn't be Liverpool. Liverpool wouldn't know what to do with full employment or a win on the lottery. The sentimentalising of ignorance and poverty is one of the most nauseating things to be made party to. Liverpool has turned into a municipal culture, a way of life, and a lorra, lorra television. If Beryl and Sandra had come from Hove or Stoke or Aberdeen, they might have had a life, but coming from Liverpool they didn't stand a chance.'

Wow. Come on, Mr Gill, they only lost one-nil; and *Karaoke* wasn't that good on the telly tonight, either.

Monday 13th
There was a big press launch in Kensington today for the BBC's forthcoming *Summer of Sport*.

We all knew about Euro 96 and the Olympics, but even those of us who work there are sometimes taken aback by the amount of output generated by the sports department.

Wimbledon, the Open Golf, two Test series, not to mention a series of special programmes looking at the background and history of certain events.

I have got involved in one of those. Michael Jackson, the Controller of BBC2, wants to put the whole of the 1966 World Cup Final out again on his channel, and Geoff Hurst and myself have been asked to take part at the start and finish of the programme.

I always remember what Ron Greenwood said about the 1966 World Cup Final. 'Every time I watch it, I keep expecting West Germany to win.'

After the press launch, at which the BBC's summer signing Ruud Gullit was in big demand having just been appointed manager of Chelsea, I popped round the corner to Scribes to see the proprietor, a certain Mr Venables.

The 1966 theme was still prevalent because Terry has commissioned an artist to produce a series of drawings of football legends to adorn the walls of one of his club's lounges.

Gordon Banks would be the goalkeeper, and they would roll back the years to include the great pre-war goalscorer, Dixie Dean. There were obviously places for Stanley Matthews and Tom Finney, while Terry insisted on Duncan Edwards.

There was a bit of a hiatus while the assembled company threw a few more names around but there would only be space on the wall for one more.

Somebody mentioned Dave Mackay, and there was no point in discussing it any further.

Tuesday 14th

While Venables gave Fowler and McManaman a week off, and wondered whether certain other players were *short* of games after injuries, his opposite numbers in Holland, Spain, Italy and Germany announced their list of 22 players for Euro 96 nearly three weeks ahead of schedule.

Already, it is quite clear that some famous names will be missing. Roberto Baggio and Giuseppe Signori, two central figures in US 94, have been left out of the Italian squad; Lothar Matthaus will not be leading the German challenge; and the Spanish coach, Javier Clemente, has decided this Championship has come too early for two 'wonder boys' – eighteen-year-old Raul of Real Madrid and nineteen-year-old Ivo De La Pena of Barcelona. Brian Roy of Nottingham Forest and Glenn Helder of Arsenal are omitted from the Netherlands party, while two of Venables' more difficult decisions have been made for him – Rob Jones of Liverpool and his colleague Stan Collymore are both ruled out with injury.

Meanwhile, England's coach at the *last* European Championship was busy addressing an audience of 300 supporters and businessmen at Watford Football Club's annual dinner.

Graham Taylor cut a slightly incongruous figure in his lounge suit, since the rest of the assembled company had turned up in their dinner jackets, but he quickly explained that his wife had rushed off to be near their daughter at the birth of their second grandchild, and taken his evening suit and his wallet with her by mistake.

'Did he not like that,' muttered the guy sitting next to me.

Taylor spoke with a lot of passion about how the current trend in football's finances had left the likes of Watford needing the support of the local community and backing from business houses in the area more than ever. He believed Watford could one day regain Premiership status but doubted whether a club of their size could ever repeat his team's performance when they were runners-up to Liverpool in 1983.

The same might be said by Queens Park Rangers (second to Liverpool in 1976), Ipswich Town (runners-up in successive seasons in 1981 and 1982) and Southampton (second in 1984).

The fat cats with the financial muscle are getting fatter, and the rest are feeding on the scraps. But as the Cup Final proved, the game cannot necessarily justify the hype it is getting right now.

Wednesday 15th

Stand by your beds, Ferguson, Keegan and Venables. A new managerial brain is about to break your ranks.

When they added up the points at the end of the *Daily Telegraph* Fantasy League season, the leader among the celebrity managers' 'public eye' section was yours truly with 293 points. Des Lynam was third, Kenneth Wolstenholme seventh, and 'real' managers Dave Bassett (5th), David Pleat (6th) and Brian Horton (9th) can only bow in my direction and admit they are not worthy.

So where did this leave me in the *Telegraph*'s Fantasy League overall? Well, 35,202nd actually. So I don't think I'll be getting a Premiership job just yet.

Thursday 16th

Watching kids play sport because they simply enjoy it still gives me the best feeling in the world. Quite apart from being a reminder of a long-lost youth, it fosters a sense of healthy innocence to offset the shrieking commercialisation that now surrounds the games we grew up with.

Frederick has joined a group of ten to twelve year olds in a weekly tennis course at our local sports centre. Watching them try to improve under gentle tuition is a scene common to most parents – you would like them to be good at sport, but above all you want them to *enjoy* hitting or kicking the ball.

The last game of tennis I played was against Ricky George in Guernsey about twenty years ago. I seem to remember I beat him, which is something I shall remind him about when we mark his 50th birthday next week.

He will doubtless remind *me* of the time he came to sit in the commentary box at Wimbledon when I was doing radio commentary.

He was in good company. The other guy I smuggled through the security cordon so that he could get a better view on one of the outside courts was called Jack Nicholson.

The star of *Five Easy Pieces* and *Terms of Endearment*, among countless other movies, was on a brief visit to London during the Wimbledon fortnight in the early eighties. He had a particular interest in an American competitor and, despite the protestations of a worried BBC radio producer, asked me if he could sit in our eyrie above the court to watch the concluding set.

I managed to get a message to the editor, Bob Burrows, telling him that we had a world-famous figure sitting a couple of feet away from an open microphone.

Nicholson was soon enthusiastically joining in the broadcast, telling us at the change of ends about his interest in tennis, and what had brought him to the strawberries and cream counter in south-west London.

In fact, he became so wrapped up in the subject that the match below us went on for about five minutes without my getting a word in. Back in the control room, Bob Burrows decided it was great radio, but it would still be a good idea to keep the listeners abreast of what was happening in the match.

'Don't forget the score, John,' he whispered across the studio talkback, not realising that Nicholson by now was wearing the headphones usually reserved for the co-commentator.

What a pro. As the umpire called the next point he turned to me with a laconic smile and growled: 'Give 'em the score, Johnny.'

Desmond Lynam, who was also part of the Wimbledon radio team at that time, was listening on an adjacent court. It appealed to his sense of humour and he also happens to be an impressionist in the same category as Rory Bremner and his cohorts. I know, because he imitates me.

Nicholson's slow American drawl presented no problem to Desmond, nor does it to this day. Whenever we leave the production meeting to go our separate ways before a big match – Lynam to the studio, me to the camera gantry – he always gives me the parting shot: 'Don't forget to give 'em the score, Johnny.'

Friday 17th
Stood on the pitch at Wembley with Geoff Hurst this morning. In fact, I got rather nearer to him than those German defenders did 30 years ago, when Geoff ran through to complete his hat-trick and seal the proudest moment in the history of English football.

Hurst and I were recording an interview to follow the reshowing of the 1966 World Cup Final on BBC2 early next month. At the age of 54, Geoff has those enduring features that make you think he could still go out there and be first at the near post.

It wasn't the first time I had gone down memory lane with

Hurst. Ten years ago, to mark the twentieth anniversary, the BBC filmed a series called *The Summer of '66*, in which we dedicated a separate programme to each member of the successful England team.

I went to Ray Wilson's funeral parlour, Roger Hunt's haulage company, Alan Ball's favourite racing stables and Nobby Stiles' old school. It was a wonderful experience meeting them all, and the fact I have kept the tapes of the series, while dispensing with most of my old matches, marks it down as the most satisfying assignment of my television career.

The only disappointment was that we could not persuade Sir Alf Ramsey to take part. I even knocked on his front door in Ipswich in a vain bid to get him to change his mind, but to no avail.

Today's reports that Alex Ferguson has agreed a new four-year contract with Manchester United worth £2.6 million made me wonder what Alf would command today. His salary when we won the World Cup was something like £7,000.

The lovely thing about the 1966 troupe was that almost to a man, they expressed no bitterness about the gulf in earning power between themselves and the players of today.

Gordon Banks certainly felt they should have capitalised a lot better commercially, but Ray Wilson said: 'The opportunities were just not around then like they are now. The only thing I earned outside my one thousand pounds bonus for winning the World Cup was ten pounds for signing a ball.'

And that was *not* the ball with which Hurst scored his hat-trick, and for which the *Daily Mirror* are believed to have paid £80,000 when it was found to be in the possession of the family of Helmut Haller.

As Hurst explained to me this morning: 'When the final whistle went and we were celebrating, Haller picked up the ball and carried it under his arm to the Royal Box while he collected his loser's medal. When I told him it was traditional for English players to keep the match ball when they scored a hat-trick, he said in Germany it was the man who got the first goal who kept the ball.'

Hurst hoped to finally lay his hands on the ball for keeps after the *Daily Mirror* and Richard Branson, who partially funded its return, have used it for publicity purposes during Euro 96.

'You won't mind though, Geoff, if England win the final and

somebody scores a hat-trick,' I suggested at the end of our interview today.

'Yes, I would mind very much,' countered Hurst. 'Ideally, I would like England to win 4-2, but for two of our players to score two each.'

Saturday 18th

The injury jinx that always strikes England on the eve of a major tournament surfaced again today. Mark Wright, who pulled out of the last European Championship finals at the last minute, damaged knee ligaments against Hungary at Wembley and seems certain to miss Euro 96.

So Terry Venables, who planned to play a system with only one recognised centre back, takes his squad to the Far East on Monday without Pallister and Wright, and with Tony Adams and Steve Howey still doubtful.

But as Venables told me last week, injuries sustained earlier in the season could work to England's advantage. Today's goalscorers, the rejuvenated Darren Anderton and captain David Platt, missed a large chunk of the season, and Jason Wilcox, who slotted in perfectly on his debut, did not play at all until February. So freshness, not fatigue, could be the order of the day. Added to which, Alan Shearer has just returned after a groin operation, and Paul Gascoigne came unscathed through the Scottish Cup Final.

A couple of defensive positions apart, it is starting to look as though Venables will have a full squad to choose from in three weeks' time.

As long as nobody gets injured in China or Hong Kong, that is.

Sunday 19th

There was something strange about today. I mean, it started quite normally. I got up early, made a cup of tea, took one to my wife in bed, and then got ready to run the Cople 10-mile organised by Bedford and County Athletic Club.

This time, my excuse was not the hilly course, the driving I had done the day before, or being up late watching *Match of the Day*. No, today my excuse was the wind.

It was blowing a gale when we set off, had become a monsoon by the three-mile mark, and by seven miles was nothing short of a hurricane. A pity really, because otherwise it would have been a nice run.

But the strange feeling that came over me at teatime had nothing to do with my recovery rate. It had everything to do with the fact that this was Sunday, and I had almost finished reading the papers.

I may have already alluded to the fact that the Sunday newspapers should, in my opinion, be delivered by a furniture van rather than a boy on a bicycle.

We only take four, but there are a total of 21 sections, supplements or magazines. I know, because I have counted them.

And today, by five o'clock, I had read them. Not word for word, you understand, but flipped through every one, taking in a feature here, a review there, even scanning the advertisements.

By six o'clock I was suited and booted, ready for evening service at the Methodist Church – a visit that was long overdue on my part.

And why did all this normality seem so unnerving? Simply because the reason for it hit me like that bitter south-westerly in Bedfordshire this morning.

For the first, and maybe only, Sunday in this year of 1996, there was no major football on television this afternoon.

Monday 20th

They sure made up for that in the evening though. BBC2 devoted three hours and more to a 'Best Night', to celebrate George Best's 50th birthday this week.

I was particularly keen to see some of the old action, because my commentating career started just as George Best's glittering football career was on the wane.

As we are the same age, and I thought I was a baby starting with *Match of the Day* at the age of 26, goodness knows what he was doing announcing his retirement in that 1971–72 season.

Our paths crossed only in that I had the privilege of commentating on a couple of Manchester United games in which he played, but I never met him or interviewed him then.

In the 1973–74 season, George attempted a comeback under Tommy Docherty, and United were drawn at home to Plymouth Argyle in the third round of the FA Cup.

I got to Old Trafford early that morning, and was surprised to see Docherty and Best come hurrying round a corner together and disappear into a private room.

It transpired a couple of hours later that Best would not be playing that day. He had failed to report for training the previous Thursday, and Docherty had decided to leave him out. George never played for Manchester United again.

Hence this writer is not equipped to compare him with Pele, Cruyff, Maradona or even Cantona. But the action we saw last night – a lot of it inevitably black and white – suggested that from the age of nineteen, when he destroyed Benfica in Lisbon, to the age of 25, when he first became disillusioned with life at Old Trafford, George Best was certainly among the three best players in the world.

Yet he never played in the finals of either the World Cup or the European Championship. And he never even played in an FA Cup Final – something that Ryan Giggs, for example, has done in each of the last three seasons.

In more ways than one, it was a contradictory career. But George lives to tell the tale, and there are a lot of people around who are mighty relieved about that.

And, contrary to what I felt after the first episode, a few of us are also relieved that *Karaoke* is finished. It went downhill fast, and in the end I have to agree with A. A. Gill about needing an acquired taste to appreciate Dennis Potter.

Tuesday 21st
Two of my first three matches in Euro 96 are in Group C – Germany versus the Czech Republic at Old Trafford, and Italy against Russia at Anfield.

On the day before my first game, I want to be at Wembley as a spectator to enjoy the experience of the opening match between England and Switzerland.

And on the day in between my first two 'live' games, I shall be at Villa Park commentating on Scotland v. Holland for the BBC's recorded highlights show.

This tight schedule means that most of my work on the four teams in the north-west must be done well in advance – and today was dedicated to that particular target.

The Russians are going to be based at Wigan, the Czechs at nearby Preston; further south, the Germans are doing their training partly at Macclesfield and partly on a pitch specially built in the grounds of their hotel, while the Italians are using the Manchester Metropolitan University campus at Alsager, near Stoke.

Security will be strict around the team hotels, so I have spoken personally to all the hotel managers in an attempt to smooth a path.

The purpose of all this is to try to ensure that I can recognise every one of the 22 players at first sight. Come the opening matches, identification will be a top priority from kick-off, and there will be little margin for error.

Pronunciations are a different problem again. The BBC pronunciation unit issues a guide as to the phonetic way of saying difficult names, but I always find one or two players whose family name is a variation on the theme.

Basically, there are no short cuts here. Commentators shut themselves away in their hotel rooms and practise the names over and over again; alternatively, if you ever pull up alongside me at a set of traffic lights and wonder why I am talking to myself, I am probably rehearsing the Czech Republic squad in numerical order!

Memorising the names, and putting them to the correct faces, is all I shall be doing in the week leading up to the tournament. It is a meticulous and sometimes tedious process, but when all is said and done, it forms the backbone of the job I am paid to do.

Wednesday 22nd
It was only a small paragraph, but had it appeared when I started as a commentator rather than now, we might all have been spared the ugly years of football hooliganism.

'Football hooligans arrested on foreign soil should face prosecution in that country rather than being put on the first boat home, Euro MPs decided yesterday,' reported the *Daily Mail*.

Well, fancy that. The Strasbourg parliament has finally faced up to the problem that has been confounding governments across Europe – notably ours – for something like twenty years.

I have lost count of the number of England matches I attended where the arrests ran into three figures, only for the offenders to be detained for a few hours and then shipped back to this country with no further action to be taken against them.

It was, in my view, the crux of the whole issue. Anybody could choose to misbehave when an English team travelled overseas, in the comfortable knowledge that somebody else would be left to clear up the carnage while they escaped scot-free.

238

Poignantly, this news item appeared on the day Juventus played in their first European Cup Final since 30 and more of their supporters perished in the Heysel Stadium.

So their victory tonight, albeit on penalties, was the first Champions Cup triumph the club known as the 'Old Lady' had really been able to celebrate.

What interested me was the performance of the Spanish referee, Manuel Diaz Vega, who is scheduled to take charge of England's opening match against Switzerland in just over two weeks. Although he handed out several yellow cards, he allowed to go unpunished a lot of untidy tackling that would have brought earlier retribution from most of our Premiership referees.

Are we going to see a more lenient approach from their continental counterparts in Euro 96, or will UEFA instruct the referees to apply the FIFA mandates strictly? I suspect the latter.

As always, the prime requirement must be consistency. When did you last see a non-English referee pull up a goalkeeper for taking more than four steps?

Thursday 23rd
Today was settle your bets time. I am not a big gambler – a few pounds here or there is about my limit – but at various points during the season you find yourself striking fun bets with friends, testing your judgement as to who is going to win what, who will go up and who will go down.

Four old friends of mine from the business world assembled in Kavanagh's Bar in Kensington today to collect the residue of my poor FA Cup forecasts at Christmas time.

Colin Rillstone, who acts as the group bookmaker, made a killing this year because none of us had heavily backed Manchester United. Had Liverpool won the final, I would have been in the money.

The other members – John d'Arcy, Mike Hall and Brian Leonard – each had to pay me for forecasting that Huddersfield Town would get further in the competition than any other Endsleigh League side.

But by the time we had sorted out who owed what to who, we were swapping small change and the kitty was going towards lunch anyway. It's all a bit of harmless fun and an excuse for us to get together twice a year.

Later, I was joined by some friends from the legal firm Lloyd Associates, based just across the road, with whom I had wagered on the Premiership relegation battle.

This time it was my turn to collect a few pennies. When I met Karl Daly and Marc Watson in March, I had nominated Bolton, Queens Park Rangers and Manchester City to be relegated.

I like all three clubs so it wasn't a bet I especially enjoyed winning. But Lloyd Associates were marking their first year's trading, so it made for a convivial evening.

Friday 24th

Very soon now events like England's match in China yesterday will be reported not just in our traditional media outlets but in greater depth in *Sport First* – the first national daily sports paper to be published in Britain.

Last night they nominated the start of next season as their launch date, and having talked to the editor, Bob Harris, I have reconsidered the views I expressed earlier in the year when the publisher, Keith Young, made his intentions clear.

At that time, I could not see quite what a sports paper could do that our existing national dailies can't or don't, but Harris has set his sights on rivalling *L'Equipe*, the French daily that is regarded as the best sports paper in the world.

Sport First will be published every day except Sunday, and in addition to in-depth reporting, will carry an abundance of statistics including a 24-page tabloid supplement on Mondays.

A lot of the papers already do something along these lines, but that only underlines that there is a demand for detail from sports fans. It will be fascinating to see whether Harris and his staff of 31 can mount a challenge to the quality newspapers, who pride themselves on their accuracy and comprehensive coverage.

Bob Harris spent twenty years as chief sports writer for Thomson Newspapers, followed by three years as a correspondent for *Today* and six years as a sports editor at the *Sunday Mirror*. If anybody can make a sports paper work in this country, it is probably him. One thing he was never short of when I saw him operating round the world on football trips was self-confidence.

Saturday 25th

Talking of newspapers, I spent much of today typing sixteen pages of copy for the *Daily Telegraph*. They asked me to provide the editorial for their Euro 96 pull-out supplement, and making the transition from the spoken to the written word is something that readers of this diary will know by now does not come easy.

All writers need a good sub-editor and in this respect I am lucky to have two friends with a reliable literary streak about them. Robin Russell is the Football Association's assistant director of coaching and education, while Steve Walford (not to be confused with the footballer of that name) is an English master at St George's College, Weybridge.

Robin's girlfriend Nicola Denham is personal assistant to Rick Parry at the Premier League, but when Anne and I met them at Steve's dinner party tonight she was giving nothing away about the new television contract.

The other guests were Alan Cork and his wife Emma. A fully paid-up member of Wimbledon's Crazy Gang, Corky is one of the game's great characters and has recently been appointed first team coach at Fulham.

Besides serving up an excellent meal, Steve had organised a pop music quiz which kept us there until very late. That, and some of Alan's stories.

He and Emma had been guests at George Best's wedding recently. The one where he turned up on time.

Sunday 26th
Thanks to the wonders of modern broadcasting technology, ITV presenter Jim Rosenthal will be commenting on the Olympic Games from the comfort of his own house.

The EMAP Radio Network, who have some 30 commercial stations across the country, have asked him to present an early morning bulletin with the up-to-date overnight news from Atlanta.

Instead of flying to Georgia, or even having to drive to a studio in London, Rosenthal can have his breakfast in his pyjamas and then switch on the portable studio and sound line that they are installing in the front room of his house at Cookham Dean in Berkshire.

I know we are in the era of virtual reality, but how much further can we go? Sooner or later, perhaps they will play the FA Cup Final in my back garden.

And I won't allow the fence to obstruct the view of the ticket holders on the front row!

Monday 27th

The play-offs. When they started I was dead against them. Why should a team finishing sixth, in some cases many points behind the side in third place, have the right to enter an end-of-season lottery that often means promotion to a division for which they are not equipped?

I still hold that view, believing that the hard work done over the League programme should dictate who succeeds and fails, but the excitement that the play-offs have created, not just in themselves but in what used to be called 'middle of the table matches' towards the end of the season, has heightened interest among supporters whose team's season might otherwise have just tailed away.

And financially, of course, there is no argument. A crowd of 43,000 saw Plymouth beat Darlington at Wembley on Saturday; yesterday, there were nearly as many to see Bradford (yes, they finished sixth, nine points behind Blackpool) defeat Notts County; and today 73,500 were inside the stadium to see Steve Claridge regain Premiership status for Leicester with virtually the last kick of the game.

Leicester were taking part in a play-off final for the fourth time in five years. Indeed, only two of the last eight clubs to be promoted to the top division by this method have survived their first season among the elite.

Not that Leicester's players or supporters were worried about that as they celebrated an astonishing end to the English domestic season.

Just a few weeks earlier, when Leicester were in mid-table, Martin O'Neill met with disgruntled supporters after they had staged a demonstration of discontent at Filbert Street.

O'Neill, whose sudden departure from Norwich has since been vindicated, will become one of the hottest properties in the managerial market if he can keep Leicester in the Premiership.

Having just substituted his goalkeeper in anticipation of a penalty shoot-out, he then experienced seconds later what he later described as 'one of the greatest moments of my life'.

From a man moving speedily on the managerial merry-go-round to one who, temporarily, has been forced to step off.

Tonight I met with Peter Shreeves, a good friend of mine from his days at Tottenham and latterly Chelsea. He is lecturing some American coaches during Euro 96, and wanted some background about teams like Croatia and Turkey.

Peter is a mine of information when it comes to football matters, and when he left I was certain he would be back in the game within a few weeks. Probably in the Premiership.

Tuesday 28th
The headlines made by the England team's return flight from Hong Kong are destined to dominate the next few days. This was one of the few England tours in recent years that I have missed – Clive Tyldesley was making his BBC 'debut' in that respect – but in any event, the press and media party did not travel in the accustomed manner with the England squad.

Had there been a newspaper presence on the plane, either the incident would have been reported in far more detail, or else it might not even have happened.

As it is, the last thing Terry Venables wanted on the eve of the tournament, and the last thing the host nation needed more to the point, was an alleged outbreak of bad behaviour that does nothing for the image of the country.

Nobody from the FA is saying much today, which suggests – like a lot more football indiscretions – they hope the matter will be dealt with 'internally'. Some chance. The papers are not going to let this one go.

As it so happens, I was in the air at roughly the same time, flying to Edinburgh for the launch of the Great Caledonian Run. But I didn't smash any television monitors and the nearest I got to tearing off my shirt was when Yvonne Murray and I had to pose for a photograph in running tops and tracksuit trousers.

Wednesday 29th
It was on the flight from Edinburgh to Belfast that I began to feel edgy. Not about being a passenger on a plane with propellors, nor because I had a broadcast ahead of me. In fact, I was going to watch the Northern Ireland v. Germany friendly purely as an observer.

No, it suddenly hit me that the start of Euro 96 was merely ten days away, and the serious business of preparing my first three commentaries was about to begin.

I had arranged to stay at the same hotel as the Northern Ireland squad, and the managerial team of Bryan Hamilton and Gerry Armstrong made life a lot easier by allowing me to travel on the team coach to Windsor Park. I found myself sitting next to Iain Dowie, the West Ham striker who qualifies for Ireland because both his parents come from Belfast. Iain himself was born in Hertfordshire – he has a master's degree in mechanical engineering from the university once known as Hatfield Polytechnic – and was aware that I lived in the area. I told him the road where we had settled had recently been disrupted by a lot of building contractors' vehicles, because some unknown purchaser of a nearby house had had the whole place gutted out and rebuilt.

'Yes, I know about that,' said Dowie. 'We are moving in to that house in the first week in July.'

Having unexpectedly met a new neighbour, I was greeted like an old friend when I arrived at the ground by none other than Jurgen Klinsmann. Ever the European gentleman, he had fond memories of working briefly for the BBC in his time at Tottenham, and our recent meeting in Munich had reminded him of the way English commentators go about their business.

So when the Germans strolled out on to the pitch in their tracksuits an hour before kick-off, Klinsmann took time out to stand with me and point out the members of the squad I did not know. He was so patient that by the time he finished, I felt any one of the 22 Germans could walk past me and be instantly recognisable.

After the match ended in a 1-1 draw, we repaired to the Irish hotel, and an ebullient Martin O'Neill, 48 hours after taking Leicester into the Premiership, joined us after his radio stint with Jon Champion.

If I had to be holed up by terrorists for a few weeks and was allowed one companion from the football world, O'Neill would be high on my list. He is engaging company, a charming companion and a brilliant raconteur. How did he finish up as a football manager?

Thursday 30th

I tried to cram in too much today, what with all the commitments and requests that I want to get out of the way so that I can concentrate on what promises to be the most exciting three weeks of my career.

The driver who picked up a tired-looking commentator from Heathrow, after a late night in Belfast, had to whisk him straight to the Methodist Church in Marlborough Road, St Albans, where I was due to address the lunchtime service.

Bearing in mind the television screens of the nation are about to be awash with football, I chose Euro 96 as my subject and tried to explain to the congregation how the tournament worked and what to look out for. By the time I had finished, and the minister announced the closing hymn, there were a few eyes glazing over already. Mine included.

In the afternoon, *Runners World* sent a reporter and photographer to do a feature, a sharp reminder that in the week leading up to the St Albans half-marathon on Sunday I have done no preparatory running whatsoever.

Any prospect of putting that right disappeared when Brian Viner of the *Mail on Sunday* arrived on time for an interview for their magazine. The subject? Yes, you've guessed it. Euro 96.

Friday 31st
Ray Stubbs was delighted with his tracksuit, Barry Davies was happy to relieve me of a box of video-tapes, and Gerald Sinstadt produced a tome of statistics on each team straight off his computer.

The BBC football office this morning was like a car boot sale. There were carrier bags here, box files there, books, magazines and bound volumes of information lying across the room as though somebody had decided that the English language was about to go out of fashion and we had better keep something back for the next generation.

This was what they called the 'Briefing Meeting' for Euro 96. Only now have I remembered just how complex the arrangements for these big television operations are, and it remains a matter of some relief that all I have to worry about is the commentary and leave the organisation in the good hands of the girls in our office.

The editor Niall Sloane gave a succinct outline of what we hoped to achieve with our coverage and how. He then asked for any questions, but was somewhat taken aback when one commentator (not me by the way) put his hand up and asked: 'Where is the party afterwards?'

JUNE
1996

Saturday 1st

The last thing the commentators' secretary, Julie Priest, thrust into my hand as I left the office heavy laden yesterday, was the official list of players with squad numbers.

For a commentator on a big event such as Euro 96, this is as sweet a moment as slaking the thirst of a man in the desert.

Until you get those names with the relevant numbers alongside, you are still unable to build up a picture of the teams you are about to cover. Now the pieces of the jigsaw are starting to fall into place. This weekend, apart from watching yet more tapes, I shall draw up on a piece of white cardboard my own squad list for each country, using different colour pens to enter the name, age, position and club of every participating player.

This is an on-going process which will take me several days. For one thing, some countries are still playing friendlies (five of the finalists are in action today) so the total of caps and goals will have to be updated as we go along.

As somebody said at the office yesterday: 'It will be a great relief when they start kicking the ball.'

Sunday 2nd

Well, there are still six days to go before that first ball is kicked, and the country has already gone Euro 96 crazy. At least, the Sunday newspapers have.

Just about everywhere you looked today there was a special supplement, many of them saying much the same things. How many ways are there of predicting that Germany are as dangerous as ever and that France could be dark horses?

Understandably, the television line-up is under the microscope already. Presenters, studio experts and commentators are being compared before they utter a word – in my case probably a good thing!

Norman Giller in the *Sunday Express* has given my style a six out of ten, but Dennis Wise in the *Sunday People* magazine has me down for nine. One thing is for certain – BBC and ITV are definitely centre stage again. Sky have no access to the European Championship.

Neither, I learned today, has our friend Mr Shishkovsky, the gentleman to whom I had to send the fax about Russian training.

Poor Mr Shishkovsky has suffered a stroke, and is lying in a Moscow hospital with no prospect of returning in time for Euro 96.

But the Russians need not worry. When they check into their base at a hotel and country club near Wigan on Tuesday, they will be put swiftly into the hands of his replacement, who is, believe it or not ... another Mr Shishkovsky.

The younger version, the sick man's son George, has been transferred swiftly from being a musical journalist for Russian radio to rescue the situation.

Having just watched a tape of Italy's latest friendly against Belgium, I rather think the Russians might pull off the first big surprise of the tournament.

What was no surprise was my moderate performance in the St Albans half-marathon this morning, sponsored by the local *Review* newspaper. A time of one hour 52 minutes reflected the fact that I had not done any training beyond ten miles.

As I tumbled untidily across the finishing line, a man with a microphone announced that J. Motson of Sky Television has just completed the course.

Either he knows more than me, or else I've got to be a sight more accurate with those Russians next week.

Monday 3rd
The teams started to arrive today. Romania were the first to register, at their base in County Durham. But tomorrow the Russians arrive, and then on Wednesday the Czechs and the Italians. It's going to be a busy week.

There was one consolation for me, as I drove north to watch some training, in not being the commentator at England's opening match against Switzerland.

The whole country is waiting to see what the Football Association and Terry Venables decide to do about the incident on the flight back from Hong Kong. I have a hunch that feelings will be running high at England's training camp at Bisham Abbey over the next few days. They have set up a tented village for the media and a few tomahawks might come out between now and next Saturday.

The FA's diplomatic statement today, in which they named no names responsible for the Hong Kong episode, reminded me of the time Bobby Moore and a few of his colleagues broke curfew when Alf Ramsey was manager. When they returned to their hotel, they found their passports on their beds.

Ramsey never carried out his threat to send them home, and the story only came out some time later. Either those England players were more careful when they broke ranks, or else the gaze of the media was not as intense.

The thought of George Cohen or Roger Hunt having their shirts torn in a nightclub, or Bobby Charlton having tequilas poured down his neck, must have brought a wry smile to those who enjoyed the re-run of the 1966 World Cup Final tonight.

We thought we had seen it all before, but 30 years on there were still moments in the match that raised the eyebrows as well as stirring the soul.

Jack Charlton was always self-deprecating when he referred to himself as a centre half who 'couldn't play, but just gave the ball to someone who could'.

Yet there was Jack bringing the ball out of defence deep into the German half early in the game, and later making an inspired overlap on the left wing to get in a telling cross.

As for Wolfgang Weber, the villain at the far post who forced the match into extra time, did any of us realise that just five minutes earlier he made a mess of a great heading opportunity?

Then again, England should have wrapped the match up before Weber's last-minute equaliser. Four minutes earlier, with the score 2-1, Hunt, Charlton and Hurst broke clear against two German defenders, but failed to score.

Bearing in mind the game was supposed to be a lot slower in those days, it seemed to crack along at quite a pace to me. There was very little square passing, not much time wasting, and the only thing you heard the crowd sing until the end was: 'Oh my, what a referee.'

As for Ken Wolstenholme's commentary, it was controlled and informative in an almost understated way. No hysterics or spurious facts in those days!

Quite apart from his famous last words, I liked the way he reacted when Helmut Haller gave Germany the lead.

'This is the fourth World Cup Final I have seen,' remarked Ken, 'and in the previous three, the team that scored first eventually lost.'

Tuesday 4th

When England and West Germany met in the World Cup again four years later – the Germans coming from 2-0 behind in Leon to end England's reign as world champions – this erstwhile radio reporter made his international 'debut' as a commentator in the bowels of Broadcasting House.

It was early in my time with BBC Radio Sport. Senior commentators Peter Jones and Maurice Edelston – sadly both have passed away since – were in Mexico covering the games live, and suddenly the sound line went down. This was 1970, after all.

The junior Motson was shut away in a cubicle watching the television pictures, prepared for such a contingency but hoping it would never happen.

In the event, my stint lasted only five or six minutes before normal service from Mexico was resumed. However, I still have a memo from Robert Hudson, then the Head of Radio Outside Broadcasts, thanking me for coping well in an emergency!

This came to mind today when I received a letter from a woman in Coventry, Pat Holdsworth, who knew me in my newspaper days. Her daughter is keen to pursue a media career and wanted some advice on how to start. It struck me again that the biggest break I ever had was joining the *Morning Telegraph* in Sheffield, after completing my apprenticeship with the *Barnet Press*. Although at the time it was intended to be a straightforward move from a local weekly paper to a respected provincial daily, and an opportunity to cover sport full-time, it proved an unexpected avenue into broadcasting.

David Jones, the *Telegraph* sports editor at the time, was asked to put together a sports programme for the fledgling Radio Sheffield, one of the first BBC local stations to take to the air. Jones had no staff and no budget, so for a couple of guineas a time the lads reporting football for his *Telegraph* pages would wander nervously into the radio studio, and deliver their thoughts even more nervously into the microphone.

This limited experience stood me in good stead when I faced the formidable figure of Angus Mackay at my BBC network radio 'board' a year or so later.

The first piece of advice David Jones gave me in Sheffield is one I sometimes pass on to the students and graduates who write asking for guidance.

'It's the sort of business in which, if you are keen enough and determined enough, you will do what you really want to do.'

Wednesday 5th
Enough of all that reminiscing. Today it was back to reality and the tedious business of memorising and learning how to pronounce the first batch of 350 names of players who will figure in the European Championship.

I started with the Russians, and on arriving at their hotel base near Wigan, was met by a very harassed Mr Shishkovsky junior, who quite apart from handling any number of problems in the wake of the team's arrival, was wondering how on earth he was going to find time to record his music programme for Radio Moscow this week.

He seemed pessimistic about my chances of watching the training. The coach Mr Romantsev, he said solemnly, was displeased when he saw some regional television cameras waiting for the Russians when they arrived, and was not in a media-friendly mood.

Fortunately, I had taken along a copy of *4-4-2* magazine, which included an up-to-date interview in English with all sixteen coaches involved in Euro 96. I know the black market is supposed to be a thing of the past in Russia, but Mr Romantsev shook my hand warmly when I handed over the magazine with his picture on the front cover. After that, getting into the training was a doddle.

The session lasted a good two hours, which surprised me since the Russians had only flown in from Moscow that afternoon. Romantsev walked off the pitch after an hour and a half, leaving the players to do their own thing. He retired to the touchline and casually lit a cigarette.

As the players walked off, a voice behind me boomed out, 'John Motson – the best.' Not an accolade that has come my way too often, so you can imagine my surprise when I turned round to face Russia's moustachioed goalkeeper, Stanislav Cherchesov.

It transpired his wife was an English teacher in Russia before they started a family, and that, together with his spells as a footballer in Germany and Austria, has made him quite a cosmopolitan figure. He has played over here for club and country, and takes a special interest in English football on television.

In fact, he speaks better English than either of his teammates, Dmitri Kharine and Andrei Kanchelskis, who have earned their living in the Premier League for the last few years.

Thursday 6th
Having memorised the names and faces of 22 Russians, I motored five junctions up the M6 to face the next hurdle – the Czech Republic.

At the Preston Marriott Hotel, the manager Paul Le Roi was having palpitations about which way to place the Czech flag to welcome them on their arrival. Was it the blue or the red strip that went on the left?

Somebody had placed a lifelike, model figure of a Czech footballer in the foyer, and the usual intimidating team of Euro 96 security men had taken up their positions in and around the hotel. It was clear that nothing was being left to chance.

Not that the Czech party, if you will forgive the pun, needed to check on anything. They strolled in from the airport immaculately dressed, like a group of businessmen going to a seminar. They politely refused a welcoming drink of champagne and orange juice, had their lunch, and set off for their first training session at the nearby rugby ground of Preston Grasshoppers.

This was followed by an exercise in public relations which got the local populace firmly on their side. The full Czech squad travelled down the motorway to Bamber Bridge to play a friendly against the Unibond League champions whose tight little ground with its 3,000 capacity was packed to the limit. There were people standing on the roofs of nearby houses and garages to glimpse this unique occasion.

A brass band played the national anthems, the Czechs wore their full Euro 96 strip with their names on their shirts, and then purposefully set about toning up for their encounter with the Germans.

The fact that Bamber Bridge lost 9-1 was of no importance. What they did was enhance the spirit of Euro 96 – or how we hope it will be – by making their visitors welcome and proving again that football, at whatever level and in whatever language, is exactly that – a *bridge*, which given its due respect, can span the most unlikely opposites.

In the evening, a few of the Czech players went out into Preston. But they wore blazers and ties, and for that reason only, they were noticeably different from the other young people out for a quiet drink.

Friday 7th
'It will happen, it will happen. But how and when, who knows? We're Italian, you understand?'

Giacomo Malverni, liaison officer to the Italian team, was assuring our group of anxious media types that yes, there would be training; yes, we would be allowed to stand at a distance and watch; and yes, there would be a press conference to which the coach Sacchi and some of his players were definitely coming.

It was nine o'clock in the morning at the Manchester Metropolitan University campus in Alsager, near Stoke. After the rigorous routine of the Russians and the cheerful company of the Czechs, joining up with the 1994 beaten World Cup finalists was a different experience entirely.

For a start, you had to be pretty fit to get around the campus. There was a press hut here, a canteen there, a football pitch in the distance, and any number of wide-eyed students hoping to catch a glimpse of Paulo Maldini, or better still snatch an autograph.

What they probably got was a reminder of what they should have been doing that morning. Arrigo Sacchi walked on to the training pitch as though he was about to give a dissertation. There was paper everywhere as he studied his clipboard. You couldn't really see his face under his baseball cap, but then they say Sacchi never gives much away anyway.

They also said nobody had any idea of what team he would field in the first match against Russia. The daily Italian sports papers all had different ideas.

And you could see why. In the first hour of training, he must have stopped his practice match three or four times, called the players into the centre and made them change the colour of their bibs.

I was standing with Olivia Blair, chief football writer for

4-4-2 magazine, but we still couldn't work out who was playing where when the rain came down in buckets and everybody rushed for cover.

After an interminable delay and several changes of plan, a media lunch organised by sponsors Nike was suddenly called, and Sacchi, Zola and Donadoni appeared for interviews.

Even in Italian terms, this was a frantic exercise. Newspaper writers, radio reporters and television cameramen almost fell over themselves to hear the latest thoughts on Italy's opening match against Russia.

As far as I could ascertain with my limited Italian, nobody said very much of any consequence. But the players were very patient and Giacomo Malverni, who lives in England, played a blinder as the interpreter.

Among the questioners was Graeme Le Saux, ruled out of the England squad through injury and turning his hand to journalism during the tournament – one of the few footballers who can manage without a ghost writer.

When the Italians left for their hotel and life on the campus returned to normal for a few hours, we packed our bags and headed south for the Scotland camp, calling in at the German headquarters on the way to collect a media guide containing all their facts and figures.

Driving down to see Craig Brown and the Scots at Stratford, I was able to absorb the news that *Match of the Day* would be safe and sound until the next century.

Brian Barwick had left a message at my hotel the night before to say a deal had been struck, and the papers were full of the financial bonanza that was coming football's way over the next five years from Sky and the BBC.

Quite apart from my own involvement over 25 years, I was pleased for the lads and girls who work on the programme. There has been a lot of hidden concern about what would happen under the new contract, and now everybody can concentrate on Euro 96 knowing the BBC's football portfolio is safe.

A lot safer, it seemed, than being around the Scotland training camp at the National Farmers Union Mutual ground at Stratford. Here, there was plenty of practical joking – as you might expect from a squad that included the likes of Ally McCoist and Andy Goram.

It made for a pleasant evening, because they were serving

Pimms in a members' tent on the far side of the ground. After a couple of those, trying to identify Scott Booth, Eoin Jess and Tosh McKinlay in the fading light was proving a tiny bit difficult.

Still, it brought to a satisfactory end a long week of watching training, and now – like everybody else – I am full up with preparation and just want the action to start. As Giacomo said: 'It will happen. I promise you it will happen.'

Saturday 8th
I walked out of Wembley during the opening match. Not in protest, you understand, because when I left England were leading Switzerland 1-0 and that was how I expected it to stay.

My early departure was purely in professional interest. I had to get to Manchester in time to see the Germans and Czech Republic train at Old Trafford in advance of the first 'live' game I'm to cover for the BBC tomorrow.

When I got to the car, the radio commentators Alan Green, Steve Coppell and Ian Wright were very edgy about England's position. The game was slipping away from them, they said, and moments later they were proved 'spot on' by the penalty awarded against Stuart Pearce.

The first person I bumped into when I got to Manchester was the last man to score for England against Switzerland in the European Championship, before Alan Shearer did so today.

Mike Summerbee, whose goal in 1971 also gave England the lead only for the Swiss to equalise and force a 1-1 draw, was optimistic about England's chances 25 years later.

'They will go on from here and get better. I can see them coming close to winning the tournament.'

Before Mike and his wife Tina left for the cinema, he introduced me to Nicholas Parker, head chef at the Copthorne Hotel, who is to oversee my dietary requirements over the next two or three days. Commentators need to work in their rooms for long hours between matches, keeping up a detailed record of everything that happens in the tournament and preparing for the next game.

It didn't take Nicholas long to establish my tastes. Steak sandwiches with a side plate of chips in the evening; a large English fry-up for breakfast in the morning.

Washed down by the odd shandy here and there to calm the nerves. Even after 25 years, I still get apprehensive while waiting for a big competition to start. You hope you don't have to handle an awkward moment or two in your first match.

Sunday 9th
As it turned out, the Germans made my first assignment pretty straightforward. Two goals in the first half, both shots from a distance that seemed to catch the Czech goalkeeper, Kouba, by surprise, more or less settled the match.

At major Championships, all the commentators from different countries are banked close together at a block of desks in the centre of the stand. Wearing headphones means you don't really get distracted by the guy next to you speaking in a different language, and sometimes we can help each other out.

Today Peter Brackley, who was working for ITV, had heard a rumour that the Germans were going to make a late change to their team. Who better to sort that one out than Gunther Netzer, who sorted *England* out good and proper when West Germany knocked Alf Ramsey's team out of these Championships in 1972.

Netzer went on one of those lazy runs of his, down a few flights of stairs and back, returning to assure us that the German team would be as we expected.

As, indeed, was their performance.

Monday 10th
What did I say about travel being a lot easier when you are working in your own country? The hideous stretch of the M6 between Stoke and Birmingham was blocked solid this morning, so I arrived later than intended at the Hyatt Hotel in readiness for the Holland v. Scotland match this afternoon.

Ever since watching my first American movie, I have wanted to toss my car keys to the concierge and let him have the hassle of manoeuvring it into a space in the underground car park. With a suitcase, two briefcases, a raincoat and various other bits and pieces, I was more than grateful for this luxury today.

The receptionist gave me a strange look and proceeded to ask my name three times over before giving me the keys to the room. Somehow I don't think she'll make a commentator.

My companion Bob Abrahams and I got a taxi to the ground, where there was all hell let loose in the commentary area. The computer that prints the team sheets had broken down, and nobody had a clue what line-up canny Craig Brown of Scotland had been keeping up his sleeve.

Fortunately for me, this match was only going to take the form of recorded highlights on BBC, but for the 'live' commentators the delay was very stressful. In this age of advanced technology, you would think they could come up with a faster and better system. Maybe it will improve as the tournament goes on.

As for *Scotland*'s system, a flat back four, with Kevin Gallacher the surprise selection further forward, worked well against a Dutch side lacking the imagination of some of their predecessors.

A lot was made about John Collins handling the ball on the line. I was far from adamant about that in my commentary. The word 'intentional' still applies in the laws when it comes to handball offences, and I thought (wrongly, as the replay showed) the ball just bounced up and happened to hit his arm.

All right, it prevented a goal, but does that mean that if the referee had given the penalty, he would have had to send Collins off as well?

It all goes to prove that red and yellow cards are making more news than goals in these early games. The referees are handing them out like smarties and at this rate, some players will be suspended for important matches.

Tuesday 11th

In fact, the referees have shown 47 yellow cards and two reds in the first eight games. The FIFA mandate that preceded the 1994 World Cup is beginning to bite again, but you have to say that in principle, it is designed to protect forwards and encourage attacking play.

Our English-speaking friend Stanislav Cherchesov, the Russian goalkeeper, made *his* contribution to that cause with an awful clearance early in the match at Anfield. He kicked the ball straight to Di Livio, who the Italians call 'the little soldier'. He dutifully put his marching foot to the ball and before you could say Casiraghi it was in the back of the net.

This happened inside four minutes, but there was still some chaos in the comentary area. This time, the team sheets were distributed on time, but having spoken to the Russian press liaison man by sneaking into the dressing room area, I remained convinced that the printed line-up contained a mistake.

That proved to be the case, and an amended sheet was then issued. Another reminder of how important it is for commentators to know players' faces.

At half-time today, Ruud Gullit predicted the Italians would take off their young star Del Piero and replace him with the experienced Donadoni. When the teams came out again, that is exactly what had happened.

Quite apart from keeping abreast of the yellow cards, substitutions are now a bigger test of the commentator's concentration than ever. Most teams are using three per game, which means twelve names to change over in the memory bank – six coming on for six going off.

Until recently, each country had to name five substitutes to sit on the bench, as is the case with European club football. But as from the last World Cup, all the members of the squad not selected in the starting line-up were allowed to strip and be ready for action. So in this Championship, any one of eleven players could suddenly join the action.

Just to show how fluid the whole situation can be, both today's goalscorers, Casiraghi (who got both for Italy) and Tsymbalar (the equaliser for Russia) were substituted before the end of the match.

We almost needed a substitute in the commentary box. Just as I asked David Pleat a tongue-in-cheek question about the Italian coach's salary, he managed to pull the cord out of the bottom of his microphone, thus rendering himself speechless and making the viewers think he was refusing to talk to me.

Mind you, I didn't want anyone to talk to me at the end of the match. Having done three games in three days, I was ready for a break, and that little argument between England and Scotland is already looming large.

Wednesday 12th
Every nation having played their opening game, there is now a free day for everybody to reflect on the opening phase of Euro 96.

It is too early to tempt fate, but so far there have been no crowd disturbances either inside or outside the stadiums. The attendances at some matches have been surprisingly small, but largely because tickets obliged to go overseas have not all been taken up. Added to which, there appears to be some confusion as to when and where English supporters can buy tickets.

What has been a rare treat has been walking around outside the venues, and in the surrounding streets, enjoying the camaraderie of the supporters without, as yet, any sense of threat or aggravation.

Even at Wembley on Saturday, there was a great contrast between the mood in the crowd as compared to the FA Cup Final. The hostility was missing and was replaced by genuine enthusiasm and expectancy.

What, with England winning a test match while all this football is going on, I am starting to think it could be a good summer after all.

But there was a sad side to the events of the last two days. The death of our colleague and friend Alan Weeks, about whom I wrote on his retirement a few weeks ago, cast a shadow over the BBC's operation at the start of Euro 96.

It wasn't just in the English commentary boxes and studios that Alan's passing was mourned. He was a great friend to many of our European counterparts and he will be missed in many places, across many sports.

Thursday 13th

Geoff Hurst can sleep easy in his bed tonight. Any doubts about whether his shot was over the line were clearly dispelled by what happened in the match between Bulgaria and Romania at Newcastle.

Dorinel Munteanu, who I had picked out as my Romanian player to watch in the *Daily Telegraph* preview, struck a perfect shot against the underside of the bar and the ball came out after bouncing down just as it did in 1966.

Now, of course, we have cameras to prove whether it crossed the line or not. And in Munteanu's case, it clearly did. Concrete evidence that the back spin on the ball can make that happen.

This was of no consolation to the Romanians, or my friend the chef who had told me they would be the surprise package of Euro 96. The Danish referee, Peter Mikkelsen, waved play on without even consulting his linesman.

Bulgaria held on to the lead given them early in the game by Stoichkov, and Romania were out of the tournament after two matches.

Mind you, both the goals scored against them were down to their shaky goalkeeper, Bogdan Stelea. So far, the major disappointments of Euro 96 have been the corners, the free kicks, and the goalkeepers.

Friday 14th

It was when I heard Colin Hendry say it was the biggest match of his life that I started to feel nervous. England v. Scotland, the one everybody has been looking forward to since the draw six months ago, is now just 24 hours away.

After a week of antagonism between the England players and the media, the mood at the Bisham Abbey training camp this morning seemed almost benign.

Once you could find your way through the photographers, who now seem to make up 90 per cent of the entourage surrounding England (where do all those pictures finish up?), the press and television were allowed to watch the last few minutes of training – by which time the players were enjoying some lighthearted shooting practice.

Paul Gascoigne was the first to leave the training pitch – he slipped away behind a shed to avoid the cameras. The other players walked off in groups – McManaman and Fowler stopping for a chat with their former teammate, Jan Molby, who was working for Danish television.

Most of the others made straight for the coach. I had a brief chat with Alan Shearer to establish that tomorrow's referee – Pairetto of Italy – was the man who sent off Hendry when Blackburn played Spartak in Moscow.

As for Terry Venables, he sauntered jauntily through the daily routine established by the FA's Head of External Affairs, David Davies. First, he faced a battery of television cameras and interviewers. Then, the daily press. After that, into another room for radio. Separate interviews across the way for BBC and ITV. Finally, back across the grass to meet the Sunday paper writers.

I had arranged to meet Venables privately at the Compleat Angler Hotel, just down the road at Marlow. It was the biggest game of the tournament as far as the BBC was concerned – unless England got to the final – and with no sign of any commentators from ITV or Sky, I had the man to myself for a couple of hours.

Quite apart from discovering that the England team would be unchanged – a confidence I was put on trust by Venables to keep even from my own television colleagues – I established once and for all that it was the FA's reluctance to extend his contract that led to the England coach announcing his resignation to take effect after Euro 96.

The court cases, in my view, were something of a red herring. A couple of members of the International Committee wanted to see how Euro 96 went before inviting Venables to carry on until the 1998 World Cup. He wanted a decision earlier than that.

The irony of the whole episode lies in the fact that one of his doubters reputedly said later that had Venables held his decision over until Easter, he would probably have been asked unanimously to stay on.

It may seem like a lack of coherent policy within the Football Association, but what I don't subscribe to is that they have ever appointed the wrong man at the time.

Who questioned the appointment of Don Revie when it was made in 1974? How many of us offered a better alternative to Bobby Robson in 1982? And come on, who came out in public and challenged the choice of Graham Taylor after the 1990 World Cup? It is easy to be a second guesser in hindsight.

Venables was the right man in 1994 – 'we needed each other' he said to me today – and given that he is now going, his successor Glenn Hoddle's credentials put him just ahead of his contemporaries. But there is still something about the international job that makes me think it comes a little easier to the older man.

Saturday 15th

Breaking the Wembley security cordon was always going to be difficult this weekend. Neither my media accreditation, nor 25 years of working at the stadium, cuts ice with the stewards who have been drilled into a routine that allows no favours on a nod and a wink to the likes of commentators.

Last night, thanks to a premeditated agreement with Craig Brown, I was the only person inside the stadium at Scotland's last, private training session.

He still wouldn't give me his starting line-up, and neither did I breathe a word of what I knew about England.

By half-past one today, we still had no idea of the Scotland team. It is my normal practice on these occasions – even on Cup Final day – to gain access to the players' tunnel to check the teamsheet.

When you are toying with your opening words of a commentary, and trying to build up in your mind a picture of the way a team are going to play, a few minutes' notice of the official announcement can be the difference between a confident broadcast and a diffident one.

Especially on a match as big as this.

The BBC had given me a numbered 'bib' with which I was supposed to clear all barriers, but I still needed some Kissinger-style diplomacy to get into the tunnel just before two o'clock.

For once in his life, Terry Venables looked anxious. UEFA had designated Scotland as the 'home team', and as such they were apparently supposed to submit their teamsheet fifteen minutes before England. They had not done so.

It was two o'clock before the completed form came out of the Scotland dressing room. I read it over Venables' shoulder, established that they had made a couple of changes, and then got myself escorted by a couple of helpful security men through the crowd in the main Wembley concourse, and back to the television gantry in the Olympic Gallery.

After all that hassle, the commentary came and went in a flash. The first half I could make no sense of – there was hardly an incident to get your teeth into – but the two minutes that effectively settled the match in the second half made up for all that. Seaman's penalty save and Gascoigne's goal were moments that any commentator would want in his library.

The only time I ever see our studio panel on occasions like this is when we have a drink after the game. Lynam, Hill, Hansen and Gullit looked a bit flushed after three hours in the hot Wembley studio, but nothing like as dishevelled as I did.

It was only when our production secretary, Claire Donohoe, thrust a glass of wine in my hand, that I realised I was still wearing the security 'bib' under my jacket. As Tosh McKinlay had said earlier when the teams were inspecting the pitch: 'It doesn't really go with the suit.'

Just as I was starting to think that I was the only one behaving in an eccentric manner, the door of our tiny hospitality box opened and Will Carling was framed in the doorway wearing a motorcycle helmet.

The former England rugby captain had apparently decided that the quickest way to get to Wembley through the traffic was to ditch his car and settle for two wheels instead.

Sunday 16th
This was supposed to be a day off for me, but it didn't work out that way. The BBC production 'bus' – which our producer

Vivien Kent has organised to carry the team around – was on its way to Sheffield for the Denmark v. Croatia match. I was not involved, but there was a lot of paperwork to catch up on.

I find the most convenient way of keeping up with the information such as goalscorers, bookings and substitutions is to keep a running record of the tournament as it goes along. But my little book needs constant updating.

Also, days in between matches are valuable for planning the next assignment. Our production assistant in charge of travel, Karen Williamson, has a towering job in arranging and monitoring the movements of a BBC team that numbers somewhere near a hundred. Karen phoned today to tell me a hire car has been organised for me to get from my next match in Newcastle to the one the following day in Nottingham. Two venues I have yet to work at.

Life in the Motson household returned to normality when Frederick came home from his first school trip – five days in the Peak District where his class were based in a youth hostel and set out each day on educational trips.

He even remembered it was Father's Day, which I must admit I had forgotten. So I have got two new leisure shirts to wear in Newcastle and Nottingham.

Monday 17th
Our old friend Billy with his taxi Noda 30 got into the Euro 96 act today. The scene switched to Newcastle, where the BBC have got live coverage of tomorrow's match between France and Bulgaria, but Billy and a lot of his friends have been put off from going to St James's Park by the ticket prices.

The only seats left are priced at £35 and £45, and there are no concessions for children. Bearing in mind the crowd is likely to be 10,000 below capacity, it seems a shame that provision could not have been made for kids to come out of school and watch Stoichkov, Djorkaeff and company.

Even so, try telling the people of Newcastle that Bulgaria against France is top of the agenda where football is concerned. The *Evening Chronicle* has the fixtures for the new English season plastered across the back page – they are more interested in when Newcastle will be renewing their rivalry with Sunderland.

Having gatecrashed Bulgaria's closed training session on the pretext of checking out my commentary position, I couldn't work the same trick twice when the French arrived. Their training too was 'closed' to the media and the UEFA officials at St James's Park were sticking to the letter of the law.

Fortunately Patrick Corcoran, the French team's liaison officer, appreciated my predicament and drove down to the ground ahead of the team coach. Then, as the players got off one by one, he identified each and every one of them for me. It was the first time I had covered the French, and this was the only glimpse of them I was going to get.

I guess all the other BBC and ITV commentators are going about their business in the same way, but I have not met any of my colleagues once in the last two weeks.

Barry Davies, Clive Tyldesley and Tony Gubba, with their respective producers, have been following their own match schedules, and operating as we do in our own separate 'cells' we probably won't meet up until the last day of the Championship.

On that subject, Kay Satterley, our production assistant, asked my advice today on a venue for the BBC party on the night of the final. There's little doubt where they feel my expertise lies.

Tuesday 18th
One of the frustrations of working for the BBC in tournaments like this – yes, there are a few – is that the split of matches between ourselves and ITV means you are not always where you would ideally like to be.

When England sent most of the country into raptures tonight with their demolition of the Dutch – described by Jack Charlton as the best English performance since 1966 – I was down in the basement of a Newcastle hotel watching the match on television.

The agreement between the two host broadcasters meant that the BBC had exclusive rights to the England v. Scotland match and to England's quarter-final, while ITV majored on the group matches against Switzerland and Holland.

For our terrestrial rivals, tonight's result was just as good as England's; A huge audience would have thrilled to the manner of Venables' team's display, but in our group of about twelve viewers there was one with a very long face indeed.

Ruud Gullit, who had been part of our broadcast at St James's Park earlier in the evening, seemed to take every English goal personally.

When Kluivert came on and scored for Holland, he leapt to his feet with a cry of '*Si! Si!*' as his fellow countrymen squeezed into the quarter-finals at the expense of Scotland.

Personally, I was glad this round of matches was over. Trying to work out the different criteria for qualification when teams finish level on points, especially when you are trying to do a commentary at the same time, has proved a strenuous test of my mental agility. At one point in today's match I got confused and had to hurriedly correct myself.

Wednesday 19th
Volunteering to drive myself around in this Championship is now proving something of a mixed blessing. While Desmond Lynam and company boarded their coach for the trip to Manchester – they were off to the Italy v. Germany match – Bob Abrahams and I motored from Newcastle to Nottingham to get our first glimpse of Portugal and Croatia.

It wasn't the Croatia we expected. They decided to rest several of their star players with qualification already assured, and it wasn't until they were two goals down that they brought on Suker, Boban and company in the second half.

The atmosphere between the two sets of supporters was cordial, underlining that at the halfway stage, Euro 96 has been the festival of football we all wanted – without serious outbreaks of bad behaviour.

The only vandalism I have heard about occurred in one of the media car parks near Villa Park, where Liam Brady's Mercedes was apparently badly smashed up.

Thursday 20th
A day for taking stock and getting my record books up to date now that we have reached the quarter-final stage. My pretournament predictions have come out quite well, although I thought it would be the Russians, and not the Czech Republic, who would shorten Italy's stay in Euro 96.

It was only when I read the papers today that I realised just how out of touch I was with the feeling back home during Italia 90. Those of us working in Italy were never aware of how utterly obsessed the nation became with England's presence in the semi-final – even though they got there after trailing 2-1 to Cameroon.

Now, following the flamboyant destruction of the Dutch, the

headlines are as extreme as they have been all too often when things have not gone well for the England team.

Suddenly, all our lads are heroes. How can we possibly let Terry Venables go? And wasn't Teddy Sheringham right on the button when he said last year that we are just as good as Brazil?

Steady on, everybody. We have to play Spain on Saturday.

Friday 21st

The last fortnight seems to have flown by, but it was two weeks ago today that I stood on the side of the pitch at Manchester Metropolitan University's campus at Alsager and watched Arrigo Sacchi conduct an Italian training session.

Sacchi and his team have just returned home to a mixture of sympathy and criticism, the latter mostly aimed in his direction for the way he chopped and changed his team before their second match against the Czech Republic.

I saw the Italians' first match against Russia, which they won narrowly, and found so many changes perplexing and unnecessary, as did the Italian press.

But I also clearly remember that training session, with Sacchi stopping the practice match every three or four minutes, referring to the wad of paper he had in his hand, and changing the players over time and again.

Was this a man who, for all his success at AC Milan, did not know his own mind when it came to the acid test of international competition? Having left out the likes of Vialli, Signori and Roberto Baggio in the first place, you would have thought he would have arrived in England with his mind made up about his best line-up – and then stuck with it.

By and large, it is the teams who have been most settled that have reached the quarter-finals. Terry Venables picked the same starting line-up in all three group matches, and was rewarded with that beguiling display against Holland.

Quite how much of the euphoria now surrounding England is down to Venables himself we may find out tomorrow. He pits his wits against Spain's Javier Clemente, an old rival from their days as adversaries in Barcelona, where Clemente was coach to Espagnol. They know each other's mentality well.

With Royal Ascot finishing and Wimbledon about to start, this is developing into a sporting summer beyond recent comparison. And Jack Russell got England's cause off to a flying start this weekend with a glorious century against the Indians at Lords.

The nation expects something just as uplifting from our footballers again tomorrow.

Saturday 22nd

Joining the throng of 75,000 at Wembley, it stirred something deep in the memory from 30 years ago. Was it not at this stage of the World Cup that I went with my late father to see England play Argentina, the day Rattin was sent off and Ramsey's men scraped through against a team technically better than we were?

The quarter-final against Spain had its similarities. They played to their full potential, Clemente's tactics worked for him just as cleverly as did Venables' for England, and what we got was the closest and the most gripping match of the tournament so far.

Both teams missed chances, both had penalty claims turned down, and Spain had a goal dubiously disallowed for offside – the French linesman standing on precisely the spot where his Russian counterpart had helped Geoff Hurst make history in 1966.

You couldn't help making those sort of comparisons. David Seaman with Gordon Banks was one I had alluded to in the Scotland game a week earlier. Now, with his penalty save that put England through, players and scribes alike are calling him the best in the world.

Asked before Euro 96 got underway what my expectations were for England, I said the semi-finals. And as we have progressed to that stage, so has the nation's thirst for success. Never mind the atmosphere inside Wembley, people are going to work humming Skinner and Baddiel's song 'Three Lions', with its chorus 'Football's Coming Home'.

Seeing Graeme Le Saux on ITV's panel of experts *brought* home the realisation that he alone of those who could reasonably have expected to play has missed out through injury. Maybe Gary Pallister and Mark Wright as well, but could either have conceivably done better up to now than Gareth Southgate? And who would begrudge Stuart Pearce his chance to put the horror of Turin behind him in today's penalty shoot-out?

All of which makes me think England can now go all the way. I wrote earlier about how in previous Championships we have been blighted by injuries, absentees and end-of-season fatigue.

Venables, by accident or design, seems to have obviated this. Sitting near to Steve Coppell today, I was reminded of his remarks a few years ago about our best recent performance – the World Cup of 1990 – occurring in a season when the top players had a programme of only 38 League matches and not 42.

Is it just a coincidence that the reduced Premiership programme this season has pre-empted an England team that look as fresh as the Wembley surface on which they are playing?

Sunday 23rd
So the Dutch are out after the second penalty competition of the quarter-finals. Dissent in the camp is nothing new to them, and the French brought back memories of shoot-outs past by scoring all their penalties – just like England.

We still haven't seen a 'golden goal', which was a topic of conversation on the BBC team bus transporting us to the Midlands for the semi-final between Portugal and the Czech Republic.

Jiri Dudl, the Czech administration officer who helped me out at Bamber Bridge before the competition started, was brimming with confidence when I rang his mobile phone for the starting line-up at lunchtime. He said the Czechs were happy to be the underdogs and told me to keep an eye on Poborsky – this time he would operate just behind the two main strikers.

From that position, the Bjorn Borg lookalike scored what most pundits felt was the goal of the tournament so far. It put paid to the powder-puff Portuguese in a quarter-final spoiled by the punctilious German referee, Helmut Krug, who booked nine players and sent one off.

This meant that four Czech players would miss the semi-final against France, but that hardly mattered to the more jingoistic English newspapers. Far more important to them was the fact that Jurgen Klinsmann's calf injury, sustained against Croatia, rules him out of the other semi-final against England at Wembley.

In a Championship patently devoid of authentic match-winners, it seems as though Terry Venables has put an Indian sign on opposing strikers. No Adrian Knup for Switzerland, no Duncan Ferguson for Scotland, and only a late introduction for Patrick Kluivert for Holland, who never looked the same team without Marc Overmars.

For once, the tide is turning in England's direction. Not only does the nation expect us to win the European Championship, but the word is we could be staging the World Cup in 2006.

It cannot go wrong now, can it?

Monday 24th
Having been invited to Lords by the *Daily Telegraph* for the final day of the second test, I relished the idea of a day off from Euro 96 and football.

That lasted about ten minutes into our lunch, when Sir Tim Rice lured me into a silly bet about where his team Sunderland would finish in the Premiership next season. I don't pretend to know anything about spread betting, but if they come anywhere between tenth and fifteenth he wins, and lower than that I win.

It was an unnerving dining table at which we were sitting. Opposite me was Rory Bremner, and it's not easy having lunch with yourself. The fact that he has just finished his latest television series and is about to take a three-month break before deciding what to do next, did not deter him from indulging in Motson-speak for most of the main course.

Also present was E. W. 'Jim' Swanton, doyen of cricket writers, who celebrates his 90th birthday next year. He makes Peter O'Sullevan seem a youngster, and as for Michael Parkinson, who insistently quizzed Swanton about the year ball-by-ball commentary started on radio, he gave his age away when he said, 'I wasn't even born then.'

Christopher Martin-Jenkins, the *Telegraph* cricket correspondent and an old colleague of mine in radio days, brought a bit of order to the proceedings when he came in with a huge diary to discuss his newspaper's plans for the winter ahead.

With so much football and cricket on the agenda, the first day of Wimbledon could almost have gone unnoticed. Except that Agassi, Chang and Courier all went out in the first round.

It's a full fifteen years since I ended my radio stint at the All-England Championships, although people often remind me of my limited experience as a tennis commentator.

The truth of the matter is, I never felt really comfortable at the microphone covering a sport which required more knowledge and research than my eleven-month a year football schedule allowed.

That was also why I curtailed my brief attempt at boxing commentary on radio and television. It's a purely personal view

– I know certain television producers and other commentators feel differently – but I just feel happier sticking to one sport and giving it my undivided attention.

And that, at the moment, is focused firmly on the semi-finals of Euro 96. I won't pretend I wouldn't love to be covering England's momentous meeting with Germany, but it was decided months ago that Barry would have first call on the semi-final and I wish him well.

So it's off on the shuttle to Manchester to see France play the Czech Republic. And I have a sneaking feeling that the boys from Bamber Bridge may reach the final.

Tuesday 25th
We were warned that there would be a lot of transfer activity towards the end of Euro 96, but I hadn't expected it to lead to a pivotal move in the sports broadcasting game.

On Sunday, Ruud Gullit confirmed to me that Chelsea had definitely signed Frank Leboeuf from Strasbourg, and when I arrived in Manchester this afternoon, David Pleat was on his mobile phone trying to tie up the sale of Marc Degryse to PSV Eindhoven.

Pleat and I are working together on the semi-final at Old Trafford, when we will be 'head to head' with ITV's live commentary team of Alan Parry and Ron Atkinson.

I have known Alan for over twenty years – he took one of the vacant jobs in BBC Radio Sport when I left to join *Match of the Day*, and later spent four years with our programme before leaving to join ITV as their senior athletics commentator in 1984.

But football has always been his first love, and just as I was telling him I had never heard him in better form, he told me he had just accepted an offer to join Sky Sports as from the end of Euro 96.

You can count the number of jobs for television football commentators on the fingers of two hands, so the occupants tend to stay in them for quite a long time. Cross-channel moves are something of a rarity.

The prospect of regular Premiership football obviously tempted Alan, who for the last four years has been spending his Sundays covering the Endsleigh League for Central Television.

Our little group in the hotel in Manchester seemed strangely removed from all the excitement in London. There were apparently no fewer than 29 film crews at Bisham Abbey today, covering Terry Venables' press conference prior to the England v. Germany game.

How quickly things change in football. Three years ago, Venables was out of work after his fall-out with Alan Sugar. In a few days' time, he could find himself on the same pedestal as Sir Alf Ramsey.

Wednesday 26th

My heart almost stopped and my nerves froze when he stepped up to take that penalty. It is bad enough for a commentator having to concentrate while each side takes the five prescribed kicks in the shoot-out, but when they all go in and you are into 'sudden death', the tension becomes almost unbearable.

The goalkeepers had done their best, but in truth the penalties were so well placed – mostly right in the corner – that they never had a hope in hell of stopping them.

You then start to remind yourself of the rules. The first man to miss now will put his side out, unless of course they have taken one more penalty and the other side fail to score from their next kick. Then the lottery continues.

So there we were. Standing at five-all. A place in the final of Euro 96 hanging precariously on the next kick. When they started the shoot-out, they gave the names of the first five kickers to the referee. Now, they had to find fresh volunteers.

As he walked somewhat reluctantly out of the centre circle and towards the penalty area, I was jolted by the sudden realisation that my professional reputation, as well as his, was on the line.

And you think I'm talking about Gareth Southgate.

In fact, I was nowhere near Wembley. As traffic built up in north-west London, we were at Old Trafford, where the Czech Republic and France had been on the pitch for nearly three hours with no sign of a result.

There was no score in 90 minutes, and the 'Golden Goal' rule, designed to produce an instant finish in extra time, seemed to have passed them by completely.

As zero hour at Wembley approached, and the penalty shoot-out at Old Trafford dragged on, the BBC had to hurriedly reschedule today's edition of *Neighbours* for tomorrow.

It was then that Lubos Kubik, who was once a transfer target for Robert Maxwell, came close to rewriting the rules and leaving the Euro 96 organisers with a headache of gigantic proportions.

The Czech No. 12 had already taken their first penalty – and scored. Now, he emerged from a huddle of players, picked up the ball, and prepared to take their sixth kick. Pedros having just had his shot saved, the next penalty could win a place in the final for the Czechs.

Just for a moment, I wondered whether they had changed the Laws of the Game. The section on penalty shoot-outs makes it clear that every member of the team must take one before they start going round again.

Having put my neck in the noose, I watched the referee and linesman save *their* faces – and the status of the tournament – by realising what Kubik was about to do and stopping him just in time.

Miroslav Kadlec took over, and scored to put the Czech Republic into Sunday's final. But as David Pleat said to me afterwards, how would UEFA have resolved the situation if Kubik had been allowed to take that penalty?

Thursday 27th
There was a numbness all over the country today. When I got back to London from Manchester, the agony of England's defeat in *their* semi-final penalty shoot-out was still sinking in.

Taxi drivers, telephonists, everybody from trick cyclists to trappist monks probably, seemed utterly drained and devasatated by what happened last night at Wembley.

The most sanguine person around seemed to be Terry Venables. He spoke lucidly and in lively fashion about how far his team had come, and about how much he had enjoyed the challenge of the tournament.

On reflection, Euro 96 seemed ready made for Venables. Towards the end of his career in club management, I got the impression he was bored with day-to-day coaching and had his sights set on more ambitious projects. That may explain his involvement in so many widely publicised business affairs.

But give the man a one-off match situation, the opportunity to measure his knowledge and appreciation of tactics against that of any other coach in the world, and you seem to open a cannister of enthusiasm in the compartmentalised mentality of Terry Venables.

He has the capacity to switch seamlessly from one subject to another – 'a butterfly brain', one of his critics once called it – but I have borne witness to his prodigious memory, and there is nobody more focused than Venables when it comes to studying the habits of his opponents – on or off the field.

As he has said himself, speculation as to what could have happened had he carried on in the job is now idle talk. The Venables chapter is closed, and the Glenn Hoddle era opens tomorrow morning, with a press conference on the very spot that Venables vacated today.

In football, things never stand still. But neither, thankfully, did England's development in those two and a half years under the tutelage of Terry Venables. There *was* a point and a purpose in all those friendlies after all, and nobody is questioning today why he took the players to China and Hong Kong.

Friday 28th
Having soothed our disappointment with the satisfaction of knowing that England met and exceeded our expectations, what of Euro 96 as a football tournament in isolation?

Not dissimilar, I have to say, to Italia 90. England reaching the semi-final shoot-out is the coincidental arm of the comparison, but the fact is that not enough of the teams who we thought would be a class act actually measured up to their advance publicity.

Italy were irrational where we thought they might be irrefutable; Holland were squabbling when they should have been scoring; the Russians retreated when they could have rampaged; the Danes disappointed where four years ago they delighted; the Portuguese danced but never delivered; and, in the end, the Croat temperament got the better of their talent.

Neither did any individual write his name across the competition. With the honourable exception of our own Alan Shearer, match-winners were in short supply. The Championship was short of genuine stars.

But on second thoughts, perhaps it wasn't. Maybe there were thousands of them. Sitting in the stand of our renovated stadiums.

The violence on Wednesday night apart, Euro 96 met its responsibilities when it came to safety and security. Inside the grounds the mood was upbeat and infectious. When the Wembley crowd adopted the 'Three Lions' song as their theme tune, men and women of all ages could be seen joining in the 'Football's Coming Home' chorus.

Contrast that with the ugly, hostile atmosphere that polluted our grounds in the eighties. Compare the joyful backing that England had at Wembley in Euro 96, with the mindless thuggery that brought a premature end to their friendly in Dublin just sixteen months ago.

The real heroes when football came home were the welcoming committee on the doorstep. If the England team planted a seed or two which might grow in the 1998 World Cup, then our football public showed their enthusiasm for an event which might just be the forerunner of another World Cup . . . here, in England, in 2006.

Sunday 30th

Football evolves but the Germans remain constant. Not my words, but those of my colleague John Rowlinson as we travelled back on the coach from Wembley tonight to the BBC party at the end of Euro 96.

John had come up with a statistic that had completely eluded the commentator during the final. From 1966 onwards, the Germans have figured in no fewer than ten of the sixteen major international finals – five in the World Cup and five in the European Championship.

Their durability was plain for all to see at Wembley tonight. Without six of their original squad through injury or suspension, they came from behind to beat the Czech Republic and secure their third European title – the only team to win a match in Euro 96 after going a goal down.

For me, the competition and the season ended on a scary note. While the Germans were celebrating their 'Golden Goal' – the scorer Bierhoff had pulled his shirt off and the substitutes were cavorting on the pitch – I noticed the Italian referee, Pierluigi Pairetto, hold a belated consultation with his linesman on the far touchline.

'A pregnant pause' I called it in the commentary, while silently praying that he wasn't going to cancel out the goal because another German player was in an offside position. That would have meant clearing the pitch, cutting short the celebrations and leaving the ecstatic Germans – not to mention an already committed commentator – with egg on their faces.

As our coach made its way through west London, we passed the Royal Lancaster Hotel where, by coincidence, the late Sam Leitch offered me my job with *Match of the Day* exactly 25 years ago today. Which put me in a reflective mood rather than a celebratory one.

Of course it's a job a lot of people would love to do, and it is nothing short of a privilege to be well paid for something you would gladly do for nothing. Don't ever label me ungrateful.

But unless you're Jurgen Klinsmann, nothing is perfect. The realisation hit me tonight that for nine months I have hardly seen the inside of a cinema, theatre or good book. Next season and beyond, that has to change. And the stress factor where football commentators are concerned is summed up by what might have happened tonight. One bad moment, as racing's Peter O'Sullevan maintains, is all you might find yourself remembered for.

To be honest, it was because I was weary of living on the knife edge that I sought that longer break last summer. Matches can come and go without a word being said – certainly not in praise – but in the end the commentator is in the same sort of firing line as a goalkeeper or referee. The possibility of one mistake in what might be two hours of live, unscripted broadcasting shouldn't induce a fear factor – but it does.

Having said that, it's the challenge that *makes* the job in many ways. The day that I don't look forward to preparing for the next game is the day I put down the microphone for good. I hope that day is still some way off, but this is an everchanging business, and who knows what will happen in the future?

Play it again, Sam. It's been a quarter of a century and I'm pleased to say I'm still enjoying it. But as Pat Jennings said, only when the game is over.

It is now. Until next season.